The roots of the recent financi
changes which have affected E
last three decades. In economic
a predominantly industrial natio...   ...ative
industries, while society has als   ...ustrial with new
class 'networks' emerging. Post-w   ...ocial democracy in its original
form – as advocated by Tony Crosland – relied heavily on an industrial economy and society. A central statist, ideal-oriented version of social democracy can only go so far in the post-crash economy and society, hence the ease with which many of New Labour's reforms and resource allocation have since been reversed by the Conservative–Liberal Democrat coalition. The centre-left has always been at its strongest when building new long-term institutions such as the NHS, expanding higher education, establishing the national minimum wage and increasing access to national parks. Anthony Painter here argues that this institution-building tradition is the one to which the left should return. He advocates new economic, social and cultural policies which provide a manifesto for the future development of social democracy – and centre-left institutions – in Britain.

Anthony Painter

left without a future?

Social Justice in Anxious Times

I.B. TAURIS

LONDON · NEW YORK

Published in 2013 by I.B.Tauris & Co. Ltd
6 Salem Road, London W2 4BU
175 Fifth Avenue, New York NY 10010
www.ibtauris.com

Distributed in the United States and Canada Exclusively by Palgrave Macmillan
175 Fifth Avenue, New York NY 10010

ISBN: 978 1 78076 660 7 (HB)
ISBN: 978 1 78076 661 4 (PB)

A full CIP record for this book is available from the British Library
A full CIP record is available from the Library of Congress

Library of Congress Catalog Card Number: available

Typeset in Minion by 4word Ltd, Bristol
Printed and bound in Great Britain by T.J. International, Padstow, Cornwall

MIX
Paper from
responsible sources
FSC® C013056

About Policy Network

Policy Network is a leading thinktank and international political network based in London. It promotes strategic thinking on progressive solutions to the challenges of the twenty-first century and the future of social democracy, impacting upon policy debates in the UK, the rest of Europe and the wider world.

Through a distinctly collaborative and cross-national approach to research, events and publications, the thinktank has acquired a reputation as a highly valued platform for perceptive and challenging political analysis, debate and exchange. Building from our origins in the late 1990s, the network has become an unrivalled international point-of-contact between political thinkers and opinion formers, serving as a bridge between the worlds of politics, academia, public policy-making, business, civil society and the media.

www.policy-network.net

Contents

Acknowledgements

It is usual to leave the personal acknowledgements to last. On this occasion, though, there is an exception. Jessica Studdert has had an enormous hand in not only supporting me in writing this book, but also in ensuring that the book even happened in the first place. She insisted that I write it, talked it through with me, and edited it. As a simple matter of fact, this book would not have been written or completed without her. The final text is entirely my responsibility, of course, but it is many times better for Jessica's work, love and support. I got lucky.

The book was also edited by others. One of these editors – let's call the person 'H' – wishes not to be mentioned. Needless to say 'H's' input was incredibly valuable on every level – adding greater style and solidity to the text. Michael McTernan and Olaf Cramme at Policy Network have been instrumental and generous in ensuring this book was published. Joanna Godfrey at I.B.Tauris was an astute and intelligent editor who improved the final copy considerably. Thank you to Angeline Rothermundt, who helped edit it at an early stage. Jennifer Painter also helped me to sense-check and edit the text. Thank you to all of those who helped me to make the work significantly better than it would otherwise have been.

Much of this book's analysis is built on articles, blogs and reports. Special mention should be made of Alex Smith and Mark Ferguson, the former and current editors of LabourList, who have regularly allowed me to air my ideas. Sion Simon, David Reilly and Atul Hatwal at Labour Uncut have published my fortnightly book review, and the ideas explored in these reviews can be found throughout this book. Will Straw, Shamik Das and Daniel Elton of Left Foot Forward have also published a number of my pieces which went on to inform this book. Daniel gets a special mention as it was he who insisted that I read the H. M. Drucker book, which became an important foundation for the chapter on organisation. He also contributed other ideas. Sunder Katwala, when he was at the Next Left blog run by the Fabian Society, encouraged me to think and write about both co-operatism and conservatism and the left. The process of writing and engaging actively with readers of these blogs and elsewhere was an extremely valuable one. It has helped me to develop my ideas significantly.

Policy Network has been particularly encouraging over the last couple of years. Lord Liddle, Olaf Cramme, Patrick Diamond and Michael McTernan have provided me with the opportunity and space to write on fiscal policy and co-operatism. *In the Black Labour* and 'Co-operatism as a means to a bigger society' were the result. The first of these was co-authored with Adam Lent, Hopi Sen and Graeme Cooke, who all combine sound political judgement with ferocious intellect. Along with James Purnell, Graeme Cooke also commissioned me to write 'The politics of perpetual renewal' for the Demos Open Left project. My co-writer on that project was Ali Moussavi. He continues to respond imaginatively to my ideas – both good and not so good. While working with Demos I was involved with the Oxford–London seminars organised by Jonathan Rutherford, Maurice Glasman, Marc Stears and Stuart White. *The Labour Tradition and the Politics of Paradox* came out of that process. 'Keeping the family together' was my contribution to that publication – I am very grateful to have been involved in the process and included in the final publication. Jonathan Rutherford also persuaded me to explore the politics of Englishness for *Soundings* journal. That became 'Time for an optimistic Englishness', which appears in this book in Chapter 5.

Nick Lowles of 'HOPE not hate' asked me to co-write the *Fear and Hope* report with him. Ruth Smeeth and Cormac Hollingsworth of 'HOPE not hate' should also be acknowledged. Jon Cruddas, MP, and David Miliband, former MP for South Shields, both responded generously and enthusiastically to that report, which helped to give it a high profile in debates about identity and politics. Matt Browne and Ruy Teixeira, from the Center for American Progress, asked me to join the Global Progress Council, and commissioned *The New Pluralist Imperative in Britain*. The Foundation and Bondy Consulting published *This Human Business – The New Bottom Line Is Social*.

Some ideas from this found their way into the chapter in this book on institutions, as did ideas from 'Business as if it really matters', which appeared in *Labour's Business*, edited by Alex Smith.

Marcus Roberts of the Fabian Society is a constant source of drive and determination, and has helped considerably by responding to many of the ideas included in this book. Rob Philpot of Progress continues to enable me to contribute to the debates on the left, both at Progress events and in *Progress* magazine. Duncan Weldon of the TUC helped with a number of sources on wages and the economy. Much of the considerable work of others has helped to make a book such as this a much less onerous exercise than it would otherwise have been. I found myself referring constantly to publications from the Resolution Foundation and the IPPR.

Practical insights gained by working with others has informed much of this book. The political nous and experience of Caroline Badley in Birmingham Edgbaston, Ian Reilly in the West Midlands regional Labour Party, and colleagues I worked with in Rugby Labour Party – Jim Shera, Ish Mistry, Tom Mahoney, Claire Edwards and many others – helped me to explore some of the themes of party organisation. It never fails to amaze me how the staff at Hackney Community College are able to pursue their public purpose despite being buffeted constantly by waves of others' making. Ian Ashman, the College's principal, is a genuine public-sector leader and entrepreneur, and I have learned an immense amount from working with him. And now, Hackney University Technical College is an example of the type of new networked institution that we will need for the future. Building the school with Annie Blackmore and her team is an inspirational journey.

Considerable friendship and support has been given to me during the course of this book by Stephen Adshead, Hamza Elahi, Richard Hurley, Ed Williams and many others. My family – Chris, Norah, Jennifer, Joe and George – of course warrant a special mention. And finally, as always, a special memory for Claire, not here but always near.

Thank you all.

Anthony Painter

Introduction

Advanced economies and societies have been through a period of major upheaval. Socially, economically and culturally, fundamental changes have taken place; Western economies have crashed. This turmoil alone would be expected to challenge conventional politics, but alongside this people have a far less rigid and more contingent association with social structures such as class, traditional institutions such as trade unions or churches, and identities – race, ethnicity, nation and community. People exercise greater choice and control over these commitments. Yet, despite these enormous economic, social and cultural changes, politics has barely shifted. Twenty-first-century society is more fluid and plural, and the economies of the developed world have transformed radically, but politics is little different from the way it was in the middle of the twentieth century – at least in the UK.

It is little wonder that people are becoming less likely to vote and more likely to seek new forms of political expression – whether through the populist right, the idealist left or in tents outside St Paul's Cathedral. The financial crash was meant to challenge old assumptions, but what has been striking is the resilience of familiar ideologies on both the left and the right. A British politician from the 1950s could be taken through time and, with one or two exceptions such as foreign policy, could instantly start participating in debates in today's Parliament without much difficulty at all. As we shall see, this creates a particular challenge for the left. Those who seek sustainable change through collective action need to understand the context in which they operate. They have to build enduring coalitions of support. Should the left – the centre-left in particular – fail to adapt to the economy, society and cultural identities of today, irrelevance beckons. It will be left without a future.

If the left exists for a singular purpose it is to advance social justice. Should the centre-left not adapt to this changing environment – not only to win elections but, even more important, to govern effectively – then the futures of many will be threatened. Many millions of philosopher hours have been expended on defining 'social justice'. For some it is outright social and economic equality through the means of state intervention, while for others it is 'fairness' – either through helping the least well-off or rewarding those who contribute in proportion to their income. Social justice in the argument of the book is something more practical: it is simply a rebalancing of power – whenever it becomes concentrated through markets, the state or within society – to ensure that people all have the capability to pursue a life of their making to the extent that it doesn't harm the ability of others to do the same. This is not a utopian idea. It is about making practical interventions through building new institutions, intervening where necessary, and connecting people to the services and institutions – including democratic ones – that impact their lives.

The first chapter looks at the political context in the US and UK as contrasting fortunes for the centre-left. The next four chapters look at the social, economic, cultural and national changes that have been so significant. Some routes forward – on the economy, on the politics of culture and immigration, and changes to the way the British state is arranged constitutionally – are suggested in these chapters. Chapter 6 – Imagining the Future – analyses the major ideas that contend for primacy in modern British politics, such as the Big Society (Red Toryism), Blue Labour, free-market liberalism, and Croslandite traditional egalitarian social democracy. It concludes that none of these quite fits the bill despite the contributions that all have to make to varying degrees. The final two chapters then suggest further institutional changes based on the approach to social justice described above: first, changes to public and private institutions including the corporate and financial worlds; and, second, for a fundamental change to the way that parties on the left are organised so they are more open to the plural and shifting world in which they operate.

The argument is a radical one. What is not required is merely a re-positioning exercise. Instead, a major reappraisal of the economic, social and cultural world in which social justice is to be pursued

– in anxious times – is necessary. The alternative is an ever more unequal, unstable, chaotic world in which only the strong can thrive. Only deep reform and institutional change will endure, but without such depth there will be false dawns and rapid reversals. It would be of greater worth to craft a new set of enduring institutions that can meet people's needs and help them shape their lives. To do that requires knowledge of where we are and to where we might head. I hope that *Left Without a Future?* is a contribution in that regard.

Riding on Hope Road

Hope is the intrinsic resource of the left. It can also be its downfall. Without hope, the left cannot succeed. But because of the optimism that defines hope, unless it combines with a heavy dose of humility – a foot on the brake pedal – it cannot be sustained. When hope and humility combine, then greater social justice is within reach.

We have but one life and it is short. The American theologian Reinhold Niebuhr identifies the potential tragedy in this. In his commentary on American power entitled *The Irony of American History*, he writes: 'The whole drama of history is enacted in a frame of meaning too large for human comprehension or management.' Yet managing history not only on their own terms but also in their own lifetimes is what political movements seek – and that, most definitely, applies to the left. Niebuhr's answer is to seek the salvation of hope. For Niebuhr: 'Nothing which is true or beautiful or good makes complete sense in any immediate context of history.' Nonetheless, we consider ourselves to be all-powerful, and therein lies our ironic failure.

This over-confidence which is followed inevitably by despondency is one of the tragedies of the modern left. In many ways, it has been triumphant. It seems unlikely that we shall return to pre-social democratic times; that is a historic achievement. There will always be a welfare state of sorts in every developed society. While poverty is real and corrosive it seems unimaginable that the disease, squalor, starvation and denial of basic education common in even the most advanced societies less than a century ago could return. In that sense, the left has succeeded. Yet we live in societies where social mobility is freezing, the middle-class is stagnating, the wealthy secure unimaginable rewards, and millions of people languish with little if any toehold in security or opportunities for themselves, their families and their community.

The waste is grotesque – and avoidable. Perhaps the defining distinction between right and left is in their analysis of this failure. The right leans towards laying the blame at the individual's door, while the left sees individual failure as a consequence of societal weaknesses. It is easy to overstate these distinctions, and easy for each to question the motivation of the other. For the right, those on the left suffer from utopianism and tolerate irresponsibility. Meanwhile, the left considers those on the right to be morally myopic when it comes to suffering, and deceitful in their espousal of self-interest clad in public policy. Perhaps each should recognise its faults in the eyes of the other and adjust their responses accordingly.

What is certain is that both the left and the right spend rather too much time indulging themselves in the perceived faults of the other and rather too little engaged in self-reflection. The adversary's weaknesses are to some extent exposed while their own remain unaddressed. In a sense this is a definition of a politics without humility. Of course, self-reflection is mainly an internal process, but the public need to gain a sense that it is going on. Instead, they are treated to a spectacle of false partisan divides, dishonest posture, lessons missed and opportunities wasted. Is it any wonder that our politicians are held in such low regard?

Left Without a Future? is such an exercise in political self-reflection. The basic question it investigates is: 'Despite the failure of neoliberalism, why has the left failed to provide a convincing alternative?' By the term 'left', the focus is on mainstream views of how we can act collectively and democratically to advance greater social justice – the centre-left in other words. Within the party political sphere in the UK, this view is embodied most particularly, though not exclusively, by the Labour Party. It is in parallel with Labour's political successes in recent decades that this outlook has been most advanced. The 'left' more widely is considered as a set of ideas, a movement, a set of organisations and parties, the most important of which, in the UK context, is the Labour Party. Given that the concern is winning power and governing over time, then it is the mainstream centre-left that draws most of the attention in this analysis. The central argument of this book is that the electoral and political difficulties – not only winning elections but also ensuring a governing coalition of change for a long period of time – faced by the left and its parties across Europe have at their core many of the same factors. Class solidarity has been replaced by pluralism in society, and the industrial economy, which was the wellspring of the modern left, has evolved beyond recognition. The parties, ideas and movements of the left have largely failed to adapt. The left depends on building sustainable coalitions behind change, and it is finding this increasingly difficult.

Traditional social democracy is a philosophy of an industrial era that has been superseded – in Europe and the US at least. Nonetheless, too many people still lack the political, economic and social power to be authors of their own life stories: the freedom at the heart of the left's purpose. Social democratic utopianism – the belief in the creation of a perfectly egalitarian society which then feeds into state-centric policies – will no longer address this injustice. Instead, a more measured and institution-cultivating left, focused on the long term and on fundamental change rather than short-lived tactical wins, is better suited to this changing world.

While there has been a degree of political misfortune leading to the left's travails – not least incumbency when financial crises hit – there is also something much deeper at play. That many of these changes also afflict the centre-right can be of little consolation. Without a profound reappraisal of what it means to be 'left' in a post-financial-crisis world, an enduring governing agenda will be more difficult to sustain even when there are election victories to savour. In other words, the left is in a crisis moment that calls for fundamental change. It is not simply a crisis of electoral politics – in fact, there are occasional signs of electoral success, as François Hollande's victory in France indicates. Notwithstanding this success, however, the left still faces profound challenges that run deeper than the flow of one election or another.

The Fast Lane to Social Justice

The pre-financial crash world now seems like a distant haze. It was a time of 'things can only get better', 'no more boom and bust', record investment in and spending on public services, and the longest consecutive quarters of positive growth for centuries. The abolition of child poverty within a generation did not seem an impossible aim. However, underneath all that optimism, something was corroding the foundations, and this corrosion came into view spectacularly from 2007 onwards.

Britain went on a spending spree in the 2000s. As individuals, boosted by unprecedented access to cheap credit, too many indulged in excessive consumption backed by new-found housing asset wealth. Labour in office bought into the spirit of unlimited wealth and income growth. But there was another aspect to this story that was more hidden at the time: incomes in the middle were beginning to stagnate. People were slipping into debt in the face of rising living costs and lifestyle expectations; and incomes were failing to rise to match spending. The consumer boom was a seemingly easy course to take, but as soon as the flowing credit lines froze a hectic reverse would take hold or the government would have to step in. That point was not properly addressed at the time.

What was happening in the private economy had a corollary in public expenditure. In the USA under the Bush administration, fiscal expansion went unfunded as an enlarging state – mainly for defence purposes – went alongside tax cuts, mainly for the wealthy. In the UK, on the other hand, expansionism was prudent and funded until around 2005. A small structural current deficit opened up in the UK from 2005 as a slowdown in City growth started to filter through into lower tax revenues. Much has been made of this, but it could certainly have been remedied. Unfortunately, the financial crisis hit before it was put right, so that became part of the political attack on Labour's so-called 'profligacy'.

Much that was profoundly necessary in terms of public investment occurred in the 2000s. The NHS was secured as a public-financed service providing comprehensive health care to all citizens – a different destiny could have awaited it had there been another term of Conservative government in 1997. Waiting lists declined, while survival rates and life expectancy increased. Sure Start, a government initiative providing facilities for early education and family support, was established as a lifeline to many families – an institutional innovation that will offer social returns over many years if it survives the period of austerity. New schools were built across the land – especially in the most deprived communities, where educational opportunities were often transformed. Tax credits took the edge off market-driven inequality and helped hundreds of thousands of pensioners out of poverty. Child poverty was set on a downward trend.

Alongside these successes, health-service inflation through salary increases and other costs consumed too much of the extra investment. Educational progress for too many – especially in basic skills – was inadequate. Repairs to the state machinery in terms of reform slowed over time. While the extent of rising inequality was mitigated and steadied, it was not reversed. Most critically, the UK's economic imbalances were not only neglected but were exacerbated – the economy remained too weighted towards global financial services, too consumption-heavy and under-institutionalised to promote sustained long-term growth.

In both the private and public economies, too much was consumed, too little was invested and in too few of the right activities. Too much was consumed now, not enough was built to last and ever greater risks were taken in the process. As a nation, Britain was driving in the fast lane; a quicker but more risky way to pursue social justice. It is easy but politically dishonest to lay the blame solely at Labour's door. This was the logic of the post-Thatcher world. Everyone was along for the ride. Then the car left the road.

The Crash

The private economy was travelling in the fast lane to higher consumption. Meanwhile, we were also consuming public goods – most notably tax credits, health care, defence and education – in a similar way. Just as private outlays rely on steady incomes, the ambition to expand public provision continuously was reliant on an increasing national income or an expanding tax base as a proportion of the national economy. It is not the government's ambition to secure a more socially just nation that is being called into question; it is the sustainability of the means that is problematic.

Increasing collective provision requires a certain degree of solidarity to survive the bad times as well as enjoy the good. Labour supposed itself to be riding a new progressive spirit, but the engine turned out to be less sound than the party had assumed. From the 1970s onwards, social theorists and others had identified a disintegration of old class loyalties. Eric Hobsbawm discussed this in his famous article on the future of the labour movement, 'The forward march of Labour halted'. As work fragmented – people worked in smaller groups in ever more specialised fields – so class started to separate into sections and groups.

Where class as a political phenomenon once stood, there is now a multiplicity of interests, identities, ethical outlooks, values, needs, lifestyles and associations. In the aftermath of universal suffrage, political life was dominated by blocks of class interest. While class today remains real and has an enormous impact on the life outcomes of all – particularly in a divided society – in political terms it is much less potent. This is the class paradox. Political outlooks now tend to cluster around 'tribes' or 'bubbles' of interest, identity, culture, lifestyle and value-driven need. This process has in part been prompted by changes to culture, media and civic life, as explored in Chapter 2. Where the community and civic institutions of church, union, club, pub and neighbourliness once thrived, we now live increasingly private lives sustained by our families and private networks.

This makes the formation of enduring political coalitions far more fraught – a phenomenon that matters across the political spectrum. The left requires a collective commitment to action and change in order to succeed. Without that, it is neither able to defend its position nor advance its notions of social justice; such solidarity is in decline across advanced societies.

There is a commonplace analysis of why Labour 'lost' 5 million votes between 1997 and 2010. It is mainly a charge made by those on the left of Labour or to the left of the party. It blames New Labour for failing to retain the commitment of Labour's 'core' vote (on the basis that it was disproportionately voters from social grades C2, D and E – roughly, the working and skilled working classes – who deserted the party throughout the 2000s). Essentially, the argument is that the party failed to be left-wing enough – more redistributive, higher-spending and anti-market. It is a claim that is not backed by evidence. Polling has shown that the voters Labour lost tended in the main to be more hostile to immigration and welfare dependency than the voters it retained. They also thought too much of the party's spending was wasteful, and that the state had become too intrusive.

On these issues, public support in general has tended to drift away from the left since the late 1990s. Of course, New Labour frequently gets the blame here too – charged that its rhetoric provoked these right-ward shifts. The left wing of Labour ends up arguing that Labour lost support both by encouraging people to be more right-wing and by not being left-wing enough. This does not make any sense – it can only be one or the other. It also fails to take the long view. These social changes – fragmentation and pluralisation – were well established as a process before Labour was in office. In fact, New Labour was, in part, a response to these changes. The changes have continued. Variety is replacing soli-darity. The old politics no longer works. Something else is required if the left's purpose of advancing social justice is to be achieved.

Regardless of whether or not there had been an economic crash, the social engine on which the fast-lane model of social justice was based was suffering wear and tear. There might well have been a breakdown with or without the crash. In every respect, the 2008 financial melt-down can be seen as an utter failure of neo-liberalism. There are many debates about the nature of 'neo-liberalism'. The basic meaning of the term employed here is a set of ideas that sought to reduce the state's involvement in the economy, and to contain the market and democ-racy in separate spaces other than through using the tools of basic monetary policy. This serves as a typology – of course, the reality was far more complex, contextual and contingent.

The optimistic bias of the neo-liberal assessment of the free-market economy's efficiency was exposed. The nations that sustained the greatest hits were those that had adopted a neo-liberal framework to the largest extent and were the most exposed. They lacked the intellectual, financial and regulatory resilience to prevent collapse. Luckily, in the case of the UK, the government was able to respond rapidly with bailouts, bank nationalisations, quantitative easing and fiscal stimulus to avert an even greater calamity. The car had crashed but its passengers escaped with their lives – had the response of Gordon Brown and his chancellor, Alistair Darling, not been so decisive, in nationalising and capitalising the banks, driving international co-ordination and stepping in with an immediate economic stimulus, it would have been a disaster of an even greater magnitude.

The causes of the crash matter. In three main respects this crash was a failure of neo-liberalism. First, stagnating incomes lay at its foundation. As Raghuram Rajan argued in his analysis of the crash, *Fault Lines*: 'Cynical as it may seem, easy credit has been used as a palliative throughout history by governments that are unable to address the deeper anxieties of the middle class directly.' When this easy money is allowed to flow and comes into contact with 'a sophisticated, competitive and amoral' financial sector, a deep fault line develops. Rajan identifies inequality and stagnating median incomes as structural economic weaknesses. Status anxiety added to faulty political motivation, wage stagnation and hazardous financial risk-taking proved to be an explosive mix.

After a prolonged boom, the worst excesses of financial risk-taking emerge. Instead of the indulgent efficient-market hypothesis so loved by neo-liberal theology, it is to the financial instability hypothesis that we should turn. Hyman Minsky argued that, over time, financial markets move from the relatively safe mode of 'hedge' (where both principal and interest are covered) to 'speculative' (where only the interest is covered) to 'Ponzi' (where neither is covered). An asset price crash soon follows. That this was not properly factored into the financial markets' own calculations, the assessments of the credit ratings agencies, or the considerations of the regulators, constituted neo-liberalism's second great failure.

Finally, the globalising nature of neo-liberalism meant that the contagion spread. 'Too big to fail' was one particular concern, but 'too connected to fail' was as great a challenge. The networked nature of international finance meant that risk spread from bank to bank like wildfire, and a similar situation arose in 2011 in the context of sovereign debt. The European financial system and credit markets are being slowly nationalised as a result.

Yet, while the neo-liberal approach to markets cracked, it was often social democracy that suffered. There were two reasons for this – one financial and the other political. Neither financial markets nor other nations seem willing to continue funding unsustainable structural deficits. Hence some form of austerity or withdrawal from the international financial system became inevitable. Only Iceland has so far chosen the latter course.

There was also a shift in public opinion as people became more anxious about large-scale debt. This is a nuanced point: yes, people reject austerity, but that doesn't mean that they aren't concerned about large deficits and debt. There are opposite anxieties that are both felt intensely. Parties of the left do have some room for manoeuvre but they have too often given the impression that they are not constrained. This can mean some short-term popularity. However, as the rapid fall in support for French President Hollande – who promised to end austerity and did no such thing – has shown, this is quickly reversed as reality bites.

Across Europe, the left has failed electorally in the aftermath of the global financial crisis – while this book is focused on the UK, its analysis and conclusions also have application for the left more widely. In the UK, the left had its second-worst defeat in the era of universal suffrage in 2010. In Sweden, the Social Democrats had their worst result since 1911. In Germany, support for the SPD fell to 23 per cent. In Denmark, the left returned to power but the Social Democrats subsequently lost support. In Spain, PSOE lost 15 per cent of their vote in 2011, falling below 30 per cent in the process. Even Barack Obama's stunning 2008 success was reversed two years later, with the Democrats losing control of the House of Representatives. Incumbency was a major factor in some of these cases, but just to take the Dutch, German and Swedish social democrats as examples, they were not the leading parties of government when the crisis hit (though the first two were in coalition as the junior partners) and yet they still suffered stinging defeats.

Traditional social democratic parties have been failing almost everywhere amid social change and economic collapse. Their support has been picked away at by young liberalism and nationalism; populism and anti-populism; Occupy and apathy; green politics and materialist concerns; a desire to see the welfare state expanded and an equal desire to see it constrained; despair at austerity and resignation to it; pro- and anti-immigration; internet activism and old communitarian concerns; power to the people and the desire for new leadership. In the good times, these divides can be glossed over, but they are cruelly exposed when economic times are tougher. Neo-liberalism has failed, but the mainstream left is in crisis.

Salvage or Replace the Wreck?

The test for the left is not whether it can win elections – that is essential, of course. Many roguish political parties have won elections. Indeed, by promising the earth and faced with a discredited opponent, electoral success can be won cheaply. The question is whether a governing agenda can survive, succeed and introduce irreversible change. In education, transport, welfare and local finance, the UK Coalition will have largely reversed Labour's spending increases of the 2000s by 2015. Ambitious left-wing programmes have collapsed from time to time despite electoral success: Labour in 1976 and François Mitterrand's 'tournant de la rigeur' in 1983 are two such cases, where victory was followed by impotence. It is against a measure of sustained change that any future agenda must be judged.

It is critical to ask, therefore, where the political energy for sustained change might come from. In the search for it, the obvious first ports of call are what is articulated most passionately in the present and what has worked in the past. In the face of austerity there is clearly a political energy within the populist left. This populism has a number of features: it is active, it rejects the entire analysis of the necessity of fiscal consolidation, it decries the growth of inequality as an outcome of a corrupt system, and it is angry at the excesses of the wealthy

– particularly those who extract economic rents in the financial sector. Many of these anxieties are entirely justified, but as a package there is little prospect for a leftist populism to be sustained even if it secures short-term success.

This populism is gathered around many components of the trade union movement, new political action groups such as UK Uncut, and the 'We are the 99 per cent' sit-in movement, Occupy. Its unity should not be overstated; it is diffuse and plural. Chosen modes of populist expression are direct action, marches, protests, petitions, media stunts and social media for both message dissemination and organisation. Activists tend to be young but far from exclusively so. There is little doubt that such popular action has helped to drive a media interest in high executive pay in the UK, austerity in Spain, and inequality in the case of Occupy Wall Street in the US.

No matter how great a level of energy individuals possess, it will be insufficient without mass support to secure long-lasting change, as opposed to simply a wave of media interest and rare but vociferously celebrated tactical victories. This populism has swelled at exactly the moment that the left has faced its current decline. Cause and effect are complex, yet each feeds off the other. Orthodox leftist parties have to face real decisions about the economic future and political context. The purity of expectation of left populism cannot face these choices and so totally rejects their existence. The bar has been raised to a level that no serious challenger to the right can clear. Yet, as this energy force gathers, it also pulls away: reality is a bar that this populism will not clear. States cannot go on borrowing ever more each year at the sorts of levels we have seen. Reducing inequality is more complex than simply getting a handful of bankers to hand back their bonuses. The public's appetite for massive fiscal transfers is exhausted (other than from the very wealthy to the rest). So populism has nowhere to go. By pursuing populism the left will ultimately allow the right to ride freely.

It is difficult not to glance across the Atlantic at the fate of the Tea Party in the US when looking at the likely destiny of the populists of the left. Much-hyped Tea Party-backed candidates lost winnable contests in the 2010 US Senate elections in Colorado, Delaware and Nevada.

While the movement gave significant energy to other candidates and the Republicans in 2010, it is incapable of having enough political energy, as things stand, to build a national majority. In the process, it is dragging the Republican Party to the right and decreasing its legitimacy in the eyes of mainstream America – particularly in the eyes of independent voters. US politics is, as a consequence, more polarised now than at any point since the Civil War. It is the Republicans who have vacated the pragmatic centre. What applies to the US right also applies to the European left. If they allow themselves to fly towards the intense political light, they will get burnt. The problem is that, by not doing so, they may be equally exposed. An ascendant 'Tea Party left' could only lead to disaster as, like its US right-wing counterpart, it would promise more than could ever be delivered.

Some, like the late Tony Judt, have argued that a restorationist and ebullient left, as opposed to a populist left, will be able to provide a way forward. Judt, in an eloquent extended essay on the future of social democracy – and hence our Western societies – entitled 'Ill Fares the Land', pleads with us to recognise the virtue of what was built largely in the period after World War II. He accepted that the social democratic left has lost its way. Despite the collapse of neo-liberalism, social democracy has not taken its chance. Judt starts off with a plea for modesty, bemoaning the 'overweening confidence' of the 1960s that provoked a reactionary backlash. This confidence manifested itself in an argument for a liberal culture that became threatening to many who felt the need for more security and stability.

For Judt, post-war social democracy was a monumental human achievement. He quotes Ralf Dahrendorf: '[i]n many respects the social democratic consensus signifies the greatest progress which history has seen so far. Never before have so many people had so many life chances.' In this he is absolutely right. Judt then implores us to respond to neo-liberalism's failure by seeking to restore social democracy. This will not happen by chance. Social democrats must cast off their reticence and the mind-set of surrender. They must defend fiercely what remains of social democracy. This 'defensive' social democracy is founded, in Judt's words, on 'a transformation whose scale and impact was unprecedented. There is much to defend.'

Judt's chosen method of defence is clarity. He implores the left to adopt a language of 'ends' rather than 'means'. What are the ends to which he refers? Expressed in a 'moral language', the left must argue for justice, the good society, freedom and equality. These are collective purposes that transcend our actions and give them meaning. In so doing, the left will connect with a deeply ingrained desire for virtue that we all possess innately. It is a powerful argument, and one that has deep resonance with the commentators, thinkers and political leaders on today's left. There is a major flaw in playing defensively, however: once your defences are breached, then defeat soon looms. Harold Wilson once said 'the Labour Party is a moral crusade or it is nothing'. For much of Labour's history, that sentiment has defined its self-image. There has been a moralist revival on the left in recent times. The risk, though, is that moral certainty and Maginot-line-style defence will coincide: the defence will not simply be breached but will be circumnavigated completely.

We have seen the limits to social justice of driving in the fast lane, and the moral road to justice is equally fraught. The present-day economy, society and politics are vastly different from the world in which post-war social democracy took root. In the present time of anxiety, fragmentation, scepticism, division and caution, this overtly morally expressive approach seems discordant – particularly once the degree to which politicians are held in contempt and Labour is blamed for the problems the British people face is factored in. The left applauds its own morals rather consistently. And that grates.

To return to the opening of Judt's argument, this seems more a time for humility and modesty than moral fervour and grand claims. There is room within this for a moral conversation, but it should not be a case of replacing moral blindness with a judgemental discourse. Moral conversation is an important part of civic and democratic life; it needs to be done in a careful rather than a didactic fashion. This goes for both the left and the right. For the left, the question becomes one of whether a more humble politics can secure lasting change. The argument of this book is that such an approach is not only politically necessary, but it has a greater chance of enduring success. Beyond energetic but self-defeating populism and morally self-assured but off-key restorationism, there is another path. It is not a return or a repair. It is a new model, with a new engine.

The New Engine of Social Justice

A social democracy that pursues its ends through ever-increasing transfers within the tax system is always going to be vulnerable to economic meltdown and slowdown. With tax and spending as a tool of social justice blunted, social democrats went straight for an alternative means – a political economy based on the economic writings of John Maynard Keynes. This was essential in the aftermath of the global financial crisis. If there had not been the stimulus response in 2008–10, the drop in economic output and rise in unemployment could have been even more catastrophic and socially destabilising than they were.

Keynesianism has become the new means of the left avoiding the very real constraints it faces. Those constraints are financial, fiscal and political. Large-scale deficits can only be sustained realistically for a certain period of time – especially if they sit on top of large structural current deficits (i.e. deficits in spending instead of capital investment that would remain even after recovery). Four years into this economic crisis, with Eurozone sovereign-debt interest rates soaring, there were still some who were arguing for vastly increased borrowing. The social and legal theorist Roberto Unger called this 'vulgar Keynesianism'.

In a co-authored essay 'Crisis, slump, superstition and recovery', Unger and Tamara Lothian argue: 'The truth is that, under the conditions of contemporary democracies and markets, no fiscal and monetary stimulus is ever likely to be large enough to help ensure a broad-based and vigorous recovery from a major slump.'

To go back to the 1980s game show *Play Your Cards Right*, the 'vulgar Keynesian' answer is always 'higher' and never 'lower'. It is a hungry beast that, no matter how much it is fed, still wants more. So while the social democratic baton has passed from growth-financed welfare and public services expansion to Keynesianism, it is not a convincing replacement as it can only work for a limited period of

time. For the rest of the present decade, politics will be defined by a
large deficit and sluggish growth. The next decade will be defined by
shifting demographics: almost half of all state spending will go on
age-related provision such as the NHS, social care and pensions by
the end of the 2020s. The easy times are not coming back, so other
means are needed to pursue the end of greater social justice.

Unger and Lothian go on to argue that the advancement of social
justice should instead be focused on institutional reform. Institutions
are ways of changing the way people interact. They are governed by
rules and norms; and are designed to rig a game so that more desirable outcomes are achieved rather than simply leaving things to chance
or the market. They sit between the state and the market or between
different actors – such as workers and owners – within the market-
place or around public services. If they are adaptable and make sense
to those who rely on them, they can safeguard both opportunity and
security. If done correctly, they are a public good. Daron Acemoglu
and James Robinson make a powerful, if to some extent an overstated, case for the role of institutions in leading to the differential
development of nations in their work *Why Nations Fail: The Origins
of Power, Prosperity, and Poverty.* Nations with inclusive political and
economic institutions and the right degree of security provided by the
state are more likely to succeed economically.

This book will take that argument forward – it is through forming
inclusive institutions that the left will be in a position to advance social
justice. These institutions will not be utopian. They will be practical,
and will address the concentrations and skews of power that prevent
more people from having the realisable opportunity to secure a
better life.

The market should be reformed and so should the state. The market
is not a force of nature; it operates in accordance with a deliberate
institutional design. It is to thinking about the institutional design of
the future that the left's energy should now be directed rather than
seeking to achieve an impossible social democratic utopia. New institutions and wider institutional change are ways of ensuring that the
populace get more out of both the state and the market. Unger and
Lothian argued that the Keynesian stimulus bought us some time:

this should have been used more deliberately to create a better market economy through institutional reform. We have some catching up to do – though there is still some time left.

A new political economy would require finance to be democratised and decentralised. It should be adapted to the needs of those small- and medium-sized firms (SMEs) that are the engines of future growth. They need skilled workers, marketing advice, finance and access to knowledge assets. A radically engaged government should adapt to the needs of local economies in such ways. It is not a question of more state or more market: we need more of both. But both market and state must be radically and institutionally reformed.

In the golden age of social democracy, local and civic institutions – trade unions, local firms or local banks and building societies – would have served many of these needs, but these sources have now been closed, weakened or centralised. The state should tread carefully, but must at the same time realise that there is institutional thinning-out that needs to be reversed. There is much that the state can offer – as long as it goes with the grain of local opportunity and market forces rather than seeking to replace them or work against them. The education system – at all three levels of higher, further and schools – is too dissociated from local economic, cultural and civic life. State institutions stand too far away from the communities they are intended to serve. The 'Big Society' initiative seeks to address this. However, the Coalition government's rhetoric undercuts the state rather than supporting it in rejuvenating life opportunities in the communities to which people feel attached. Prime Minister David Cameron believes in a 'big society, not a big state'. While he would protest differently, it has felt to many as though the big society and the state are opposed to one another, given the government's wider rhetoric on austerity when they should be working in tandem.

While the 'Big Society' will fall short through an absence of disruptive energy, leaving power pretty much where it currently resides, the alternative can't simply rest on defending the state as it is. Neither can it be solely about technocratic reform. The left needs its own 'language of ends', to channel Tony Judt. This new institutional architecture is there to equip us all with the power to thrive in accordance with our talents and character. These new means of acquiring a greater stake in society are in essence about enhancing humanity. With a greater stake and a greater say, people would be able to mutually explore the possibilities of co-operation. Rather than being provided for, they can provide for themselves. Instead of dependence, they will be in a position to share. New possibilities to achieve for oneself and one's family become apparent in co-operation rather than antagonism.

These new institutions, or old institutions reformed, will harness the energy and democratic spirit of the rising power of networks in society. The old models of bureaucratic presumption and 'get what you are given' are no longer good enough. State resources and power must be shared, devolved, made flexible and chase the ends rather than simply administratively managing the means. The best sort of service is one that is produced collectively: people for one another. Britain is a pluralistic nation; if it is to have a democracy worth having it must also be pluralistic. New institutions, creating new ways of ensuring people have a decent wage or getting credit to the right businesses at the right time, must work with the market, not against it. There is no need to replace what works. Instead, it is a case of building smart institutions that can adapt yet build long-term value in which all can share. This approach to political economy will emphasise both the democratic *and* the social in a way that traditional social democracy never quite did. It will be more effective as a result.

This spirit of democratic liberation has a history, but one that has too often been the exception rather than the rule. David Marquand describes this spirit as 'democratic republicanism' in his monumental history of modern Britain, *Britain Since 1918*. For Marquand, democratic republicans are the 'awkward squad' or the 'outsiders' of British democracy. So be it. This school of thought emphasises not only freedom from domination but true democracy backed by a stake in society. It is not enough in itself and tends to drift into the vague and the potentially problematic language of the 'common good' (whose good is that in an imperfect democracy?). It is, though, a good starting point, as explored in Chapter 6. If social justice is to be advanced, new economic, political and social institutions are also needed. These would, as Amartya Sen would describe it, enhance 'capabilities' – health, financial assets, skills, social networks and individuals' ability to have greater control over their economic life. Of Marquand's four democracies, 'democratic republicanism' is the consistent loser in British history. It has no sense of inevitability; every democratic battle has to be hard fought. That is the left's fight to wage.

The task is to enable a greater space for individuals to write their own life stories. A humble yet imaginative and determined left is the means by which to accomplish this. There are many false '1945 moments'. It is not going to be that easy, unfortunately, no matter what the populist or restorationist left might claim. They will promise many more glorious victories than are ever secured. Instead, the left must produce a different argument. The context is this society with these economic challenges, fragments and contradictions, national and civic identities, hopes and anxieties, distractions and obsessions, disappointments and dreams. A constructive spirit that neither despairs nor hoodwinks – an honest mode of leadership that crafts and builds consent for an alternative – is what is called for during these difficult times.

In the Sophocles play *Philoctetes*, Neoptolemus first tries mendacity before being rewarded for honesty in persuading Philoctetes to accompany him to Troy. The left can try the dishonest path or the more trying yet humble path. It is on this road – as Seamus Heaney's poem expresses – that hope and history may rhyme. That path may deny us glory in our own lifetime – that is the purpose of hope, as Reinhold Niebuhr reassures us. Just as American power is greatest when exercised with care and compassion, so the left's power is greatest when it knows its limits. The left can't create a new utopia but it can work to cultivate a different future; one that may not be immediate. If we understand the real economic, social and institutional constraints that face us, greater social justice will become attainable. The journey can then resume.

CHAPTER 1

Witnessing the Left's Decline

I t was not meant to be this way. The global financial crash, the election of a new type of movement-driven inspirational leader in Barack Obama and the collapse of an age of deregulation ushered in from the 1970s onwards by a broadly neo-liberal worldview were supposed to ignite a revival of the left. As it happened, however, Obama's success was an exception that has proved the rule of the left's decline. Rather than providing European or global leadership, the left is instead locked in to the rhythms of opposition-first and populism. There is a political uncertainty to these times reminiscent of the 1930s and 1970s. What has been noticeable, in observation, is the way in which the left has aimed to project a remarkable, if not entirely convincing, self-confidence in an uncertain political environment. It has proposed risk, whereas people, unsure about which way to go, have preferred security.

A witness always sees things from a particular angle. He or she will inevitably have his or her own perceptions and preconceptions to wrestle with. What such an observer might find striking about this moment of political history is the doubt of the majority and a desire for a different course – a different leadership – yet an uncertainty about what exactly is wanted. Our political leaders, on the other hand, exude certainty and confidence. And yet – and this is not a partisan point – their failure to track a way out of the thicket has been near universal.

The front cover of the David Marquand book *Britain Since 1918*, mentioned in the Introduction, is decorated with portraits of all the post-1918 British prime ministers. With a handful of notable exceptions, these were great men, and one woman. Whatever their politics, they had ambition for Britain, believed the country to be a player on the world stage and saw politics as being capable of purposeful change. Now, at this very moment of necessity – when we are crying out for statecraft and leadership – such leadership is sorely needed. As one YouGov poll in February 2012 showed, 42 per cent of respondents said 'neither of them' when asked which of the two main parties was led by 'people of real ability'. There is a leadership opportunity; one for which people are thirsting.

For all his difficulties, and for all his tendency to seek compromise when confrontation may actually be what is needed, Barack Obama stands alone in finding a language and meaning to articulate a different future for his nation. It is a constructive future: one that invests in science, new energy sources, industry, jobs and skills. He has been blocked pretty much every step of the way since the Republicans took control of the House of Representatives in 2010, such is the current state of American democracy. Where his first term showed the promise, his second term will be focusing on the institutional changes that will provide the spark for America's next upward curve.

There were moments when others on the left demonstrated a practical and poetic vision – Gordon Brown at Methodist Central Hall a few days before the 2010 General Election springs to mind. But this has largely been a time in which the left failed to anticipate and respond to the social, economic and political change around it. What follows are dispatches from the front line of that decline. The purpose is not to wallow but to reflect. The hope is that, after a pause, the need for a more reasoned and reflective path might be agreed. In the UK and beyond, the left has met every setback with a forward march. These reflections and dispatches provide the foundation for a more fundamental rethink in later chapters.

After Change

On the morning of Barack Obama's inaugural presidential address, 20 January 2009, I was picked up by a cab at 6.15 a.m. The driver, who was Afro-Caribbean, told me that his two daughters, aged four and five, were excited about the inauguration. His five-year-old had got up at 5.30 a.m. that morning. She told him that she just wanted to share a moment with her father on what was, for her, an important day in her very young life. This was a global moment, touching the lives of small children in London as much as in Los Angeles.

Racial inequality does not evaporate with the election of a single man. Nor can four or eight years reverse the legacy of 250 years of injustice. But the election of Barack Obama was not only a story of racial division and injustice. It was not about looking back in a regressive sense, but rather reaching into America's history to define a new future. If America could change, then we all could.

When five-year-old children feel a sense of history, when they feel a connection to the prevailing political wind, then there is promise anew. What more jolting a message could there be for us in Britain, who far too often slouch in cynicism and scepticism? It was a moment that not only resonated with the very young, but also with those rather longer in the tooth. While I was discussing the election of Barack Obama during a meeting in Nottinghamshire back in 2009, the conversation drifted towards UK politics, as the MP expenses scandal had started to take hold. It is probably fair to assume that a good many of those attending were naturally conservative – with both a small and a big 'c'. In the local County Council elections of that year the Conservatives beat Labour overwhelmingly, with 3,333 votes to Labour's 879.

Even addressing this conservative sensibility, there was a strong sentiment that political change was not something that should be reserved for the other side of the Atlantic; change was demanded here too. It was not just a change of government these people were interested in – it was a change in the whole of politics. The general consensus was that an intolerable chasm had opened up between the people and their representatives. They felt more connected to a man across the Atlantic than to their own political representatives – even those with whom they agreed politically.

The impact of the Obama 'effect' is worth considering more closely. With the inevitable downgrading of his fortunes since the Democrats lost the House of Representatives in 2010, it is easy to forget the enormous legislative victories won in the first year or so of his presidency – especially in the first 100 days. The change was more than symbolic.

Barack Obama's election campaign was a lesson in how to accumulate political capital, and the first 100 days of his presidency were a lesson in how to use it. Political capital is a perishable good to be consumed rapidly after purchase. A spirit of urgency – the fierce urgency of *now* – defined the new President's early period in office. The economy was the priority. He outlined his approach with lawyerly clarity in a speech at Georgetown University in April 2009, where he invoked the parable at the end of the Sermon on the Mount: 'the rain descended, and the floods came, and the winds blew, and beat upon that house … it fell not: for it was founded upon a rock'. George W. Bush's America was built on sand instead of rock. Obama went on to argue that it was not sustainable to have an economy where 40 per cent of all corporate profits come from a financial sector, based on, 'inflated home prices, maxed out credit cards, overleveraged banks and overvalued assets'.

As Representative Henry Steagall once said during the Great Depression,

> We cannot stand by when a house is on fire to engage in lengthy debates over the methods to be employed in extinguishing the fire. In such a situation we instinctively seize upon and utilize whatever method is most available and offers assurance of speediest success.

This has been the approach of the Obama administration, when Congress has allowed. It included: a $787 billion stimulus plan which kept the US out of depression and mass unemployment; the Dodd–Frank Act to regulate Wall Street; a G20 agreement; a toxic bank asset plan; the $80 billion auto-industry bailout – opposed by many Republicans, including Mitt Romney – which saved around 1.5 million jobs; a budget for long-term investment in education; health care reform – greeted as 'socialism' by hysterical Republicans despite its resemblance to a plan proposed by Richard Nixon and one introduced by Mitt Romney when he was Governor of Massachusetts; and investment in the green economy of the future. The stimulus legislation was called the American Recovery and Reinvestment Act. And that is precisely what it was.

Congress has played ball on a less and less frequent basis since 2010 as Obama has struggled to pass his American Jobs Act, aiming to stimulate the US economy. This places Congress in the same 'do nothing' position that enabled Harry Truman to pull off an unlikely presidential victory in 1948.

There are still those who struggle to reconcile the transformative candidate and inspirational global voice with the instinctive pragmatist who resides in the Oval Office. Many even question whether he is of the left at all. His domestic policy approach suggests that he is centrist and pragmatic, but certainly pursues the policy goals of the centre-left – namely, greater social justice. Pressing questions remain: what does Barack Obama want to achieve in office? Why remain reasonable when faced with Tea Party lunacy every which way he turns? Is his presidency about more than helping America adapt to relative decline? Does he have the right approach but in the wrong times?

Some of the criticism of Obama's presidency has failed to acknowledge the reality of the political system in which he found himself. The American constitution is a wonderful construct for a nation of reasonable men and women. The problem is that the political representatives who currently populate the nation's capital are not, in the main, reasonable people. How can a reasonable man lead in a political system stacked with checks and balances that allow unreasonable people to obstruct reasonable endeavour?

Reasonable men reach for consensus first. Time and again, Obama has sought to demonstrate the virtues of restraint and compromise: choosing his primary opponent Hillary Clinton as his Secretary of State; seeking a bi-partisan deal on health care; or pursuing consensus and balance on reducing the federal deficit. It has often worked to his advantage – but frequently it has not. A system designed for the likes of Obama has been hijacked by such Republican representatives as Paul Ryan, Eric Cantor and Tom Coburn. In a battle between a dove and a hawk, it is the hawk that wins.

Obama's domestic style extends also to the international arena as he works to define a more restrained and collegiate model of American leadership. He reached out to Iran; found a co-operative way of dealing with Dmitry Medvedev of Russia; and allowed France and Britain to make the running in confronting Colonel Gaddafi in Libya. The record is ultimately mixed, but there have been successes. Obama oversaw the capture and elimination of Osama bin Laden and much of the senior Al Qaeda leadership. He has ended US engagement in Iraq and at the time of writing is drawing down troops from Afghanistan.

In terms of objectives, foreign policy has been defined by a degree of continuity with the Bush administration – and this creates strategic, political and moral dilemmas, such as the increased usage of predator drone strikes. Yet the means by which these objectives are pursued and secured are very different. He has sought to lead in partnership rather than alone; isolated leadership has been abandoned. He exercises Niebuhrian restraint by temperament; he knows that the more America uses its hard power, the more it demonstrates its limits.

The critical moment – when it was clear that we had a break with the past – came in the post-G20 Summit press conference in London in 2009, when Obama declared:

> What I've tried to do … is communicate the notion that America is a critical actor and leader on the world stage, and that we shouldn't be embarrassed about that, but that we exercise our leadership best when we are listening.

In a single off-the-cuff statement, the world encountered a new American leadership: one that listens, engages, negotiates and will find itself better able to achieve its goals. Most clearly and critically, Obama's approach placed a new notion of leadership at its core. From that point onwards, leadership was to be primarily a collective endeavour. Power would be sought from distributed authority and alliance-building, not through demonstrations of military might and assertive international relations.

His style, both at home and abroad, was to seek strength through consensus – the success of a second term will depend on finding reasonable allies at home and abroad, combined with a harder edge when they do not emerge. As Andrew Sullivan described in *Newsweek*: 'What liberals have never understood about Obama is that he practices a show-don't-tell, long-game form of domestic politics. What matters to him is what he can get done, not what he can immediately take credit for.'

The election of Barack Obama was, from the perspective of the global left, a false dawn. However, in its careful alliance- and institution-building focus it provides some important lessons: ruthless pragmatism over utopianism. His achievements in office

– especially in the domestic sphere – have been significant, given the context. His re-election gives him a fresh opportunity to take this approach further. Elsewhere, though, the mainstream left has found it more difficult to obtain, retain and use power – not least in the UK.

The Sun Setting on the Progressive Consensus

In 1933, the midst of a global recession, world leaders came together in London, but they failed to respond to their collective challenge – the repayment of war debt, competitive devaluation and the rising tide of protectionism – and so the world continued on a catastrophic course. The new administration of Franklin D. Roosevelt was largely uninterested in the international dimension of its domestic economic difficulties. From a yacht in New England, Roosevelt effectively torpedoed any deal.

At Bretton Woods in 1944, a system of pegged exchange rates was created, alongside the IMF and the International Bank for Reconstruction and Development (IBRD) (now incorporated into the World Bank), ushering in a new international system that had more flexibility and security. The new system catalysed – along with post-war reconstruction – 30 years of prosperity for liberal democratic nations. It enabled a massive expansion of trade, investment and the creation of the European welfare states with which we are familiar. From London 1933 to Bretton Woods in 1944 there was a wide gulf in what was achieved.

The G20 Summit of April 2009, held at the Excel Centre in London's Docklands, lay somewhere between the two in terms of success. The deal was meaningful: beefing up the IMF, greater emergency support for emerging economies, and the beginnings of a new system of international regulation that would better manage risk in global capital markets (though still not fully). The centrepiece was a deal to co-ordinate global fiscal expansion. It was also a personal triumph for Gordon Brown, as he demonstrated an ability to shift global decision-making in the context of crisis.

At every stage of the crisis from 2007, the Conservatives had underestimated its nature and its severity. In its immediate aftermath, they had fallen short on providing meaningful solutions and looked dangerously out of their depth. Had they been in power when the crash occurred, it could have been a case of blind panic. Economic storm could well have turned into economic catastrophe. Ideological preconceptions would have meant that a Conservative government would have been extremely slow off the mark in bailing out the banks and stimulus would only have been pursued reluctantly and inadequately.

David Cameron would have been a million miles away from the Obama presidency line of regulate and stimulate. Nor would he have had influence with the European leaders – as has been shown since with his 'veto' of the Fiscal Union treaty. Ever since he took his party out of the European People's Party, David Cameron's posturing politics has not gone down well in the EU. He is now isolated in Europe – and, consequently, so is the UK.

Yet none of the achievements of the Labour government and Gordon Brown percolated into the national political conversation back in 2009. They remained in the transnational ether and were mocked in the domestic media-political chatter: a fact that was clear in the European elections that followed the Summit in June 2009. Labour gained just 15.7 per cent of the vote, finishing behind the UK Independence Party (UKIP).

The distance between the global economic debate and doorstep concerns seemed very clear. The dominating issues were immigration and MPs' expenses. One May morning I had a long chat with a British National Party (BNP) voter in Birmingham. The political reality of that conversation could not have been further away from the global summitry of the Excel centre a month or so previously (from where I had been reporting).

The man was a roofer by trade but had recently lost his job and was claiming Jobseeker's Allowance. He had voted BNP for the previous five years. His job had become ever more pressured as overtime was decreasingly available and he was expected, nonetheless, to do evening and weekend work without higher pay to compensate. He asked why he should have to sacrifice his family life for no extra benefit?

Unfortunately, with conditions as they were in the construction industry, his firm had since laid him off. He said that he had been experiencing increasing competition from Eastern European and East African workers. They were willing to work longer hours and be more flexible, without demanding the type of wage he required. He had applied for mortgage relief to no avail, though he did have another four months of mortgage holiday left.

I asked him whether any of his colleagues were black or Asian, and whether they faced similar challenges to him? He said they did, and that a lot of them felt the same way as him. He felt solidarity with them as working people facing similar challenges. So why did he begin voting BNP – a party that wanted to repatriate his colleagues? He told me that one of his colleagues was a BNP activist and had told him about the party. This colleague had said it wasn't racist at all, as the *Daily Mirror* and the *Sun* claimed. It was just concerned about a fair deal for British people. He worked hard, paid his taxes and national insurance, and for what? Immigrants were coming in and getting housing, pushing him back in the queue for health services, and now they had a job and he was on the dole. It just wasn't right, to his mind. What is more, with the rights culture as it is, all the wrong people were protected while honest people like himself suffered. He seemed more confused than angry about his predicament.

We talked about his black and Asian colleagues: I asked him whether he felt it was right that they be denied citizenship and told that they weren't really British, as this is what the BNP's politics amounted to. He thought about it and then acknowledged that, no, he didn't think that was right, though he did think that whenever Nick Griffin (the leader of the BNP) says something 'out of order, people come down on him like a ton of bricks'. I asked, 'Given we are in tough times, surely the last thing we want is people turning on each other? Besides, isn't picking on people just because of the colour of their skin actually anti-British?'

We shook hands at the end of the conversation, smiled, and he promised that he would give it some more thought. Did he go on to vote BNP? I would be surprised if he hadn't. He had genuine griev-ances – mainly at his harsh treatment by his employers – and an articulated position as a result of having been reached out to by the BNP in a one-to-one situation by one of his former colleagues. Nearly a million people voted for the BNP nationally in the June 2009 elections, and they won two seats in the European Parliament.

A number of underlying features of support for the BNP became clear: a sense of wage competition and stagnation; feelings of loss; cultural anxiety, amplified through difficult economic times; and the community/workplace activity of the BNP, albeit being highly misleading about their motives. One person can make a case against the BNP, but it takes some time. It needs thousands more in local communities making the case in similar ways if far right politics is to be properly beaten back. But that sort of community/workplace presence needs organisation. Whole communities can fight back once they realise that more unites than divides them. But that sort of community awareness and trust building is a long process.

More broadly, it is clear that the politics of material angst and identity anxiety are interacting in deeply fraught ways. Winning intellectual or technocratic battles was never going to be enough. The left has found no convincing answer to this rise of identity anxiety. It is symptomatic of wage stagnation, the destruction of class solidarity and the scarcity of public resources. But to see it in purely economic terms would be a mistake; attachment and loss have just as much resonance. Just how far Labour had drifted from this cultural shift became apparent during the General Election of 2010. Many of its sister parties across Europe – in the Netherlands, Sweden, Norway and elsewhere – faced exactly the same challenge.

Power Slipping Away

On the May Day bank holiday of 2010 – the last Monday before the election – the community-organising group, Citizens UK, invited the three main party leaders to address its annual meeting. The event took place in the Methodist Central Hall in Westminster, the birthplace of the UN General Assembly. Gordon Brown found his authentic voice; not only did he enjoy himself, but the room went along with him completely.

Multi-faith choirs, community organiser testimony, Chinese dragons, Bible readings, cheering, foot-stamping, hand-shaking politics, campaigning and celebratory affirmation – such is the church of civil society that is Citizens UK. And it was to a Labour beat that they danced that day.

Gordon Brown soared in that environment. He was received enthusiastically from the start. The audience sensed an authenticity and passion in his speech. There was real conviction. Community organising is about testimony and the Prime Minister gave his testimony as a 'son of the manse'. His flourishing rhetoric read the mood of exaltation in the room to perfection. His peroration was powerful, and the speech had some truly inspirational moments: 'If you fight for fairness, you have a friend, a partner and a brother in me,' Brown said. He finished with the imperative: 'Let's march!', before leaving to thunderous applause.

Very few people saw this performance. Eight million people had seen his performance in the televised leadership debates a few days earlier. Even more were aware of the 'Gillian Duffy' moment where he was challenged about immigration by a Rochdale pensioner: with a broadcasting microphone still live, he referred to her as a 'bigoted woman'.

A chronic misunderstanding has developed; voters' needs and impulses have been met with cold rationalism and technocratic jargon. It is as if Labour and the voters had woken up one morning to find that they have become different people. The contrast between the emotional connection with Citizens UK in the Methodist Central Hall and the ability to connect emotionally with the nation was stark. Almost all UK politicians are suffering in a similar way. But Labour as a self-styled people's party relies on an emotional connection for its existence. Unless 'the people' *feel* it is capable of improving their lives, then it is nowhere. That's where Labour found itself in 2010 – perhaps only saved from annihilation by voters' residual fear of the Conservatives.

On the morning of the election, Thursday 6 May, I drove from Birmingham to London and stopped off at various places to campaign. I began my day in the constituency of Meriden, which had a Conservative majority of 7,767 in 2005. By that evening it was 16,253. This was the Conservative bookend. My journey ended in London – in Hackney South and Shoreditch, which had a Labour majority of 9,911: the Labour bookend. Labour increased its vote there by 3 per cent. Labour's core inner-city vote held up and even strengthened as memories of the Iraq War faded and the Conservatives failed to connect with urban Britain. But beyond Scotland, Wales, the northern heartlands and large city seats, the country turned its back on Labour.

My journey from Birmingham to Hackney took me through or near to a number of key swing seats that were critical to the outcome of the election. With the exception of Luton, whose demographic mix and very strong local campaigns favoured Labour, it was a clean sweep for the Conservatives:

- Warwickshire North: the Conservatives won by just 54 votes on a swing of 7.7 per cent.
- Nuneaton: a Conservative win, with a 2,069 majority on a 7.2 per cent swing.
- Rugby: a seat I knew well, having lived there for a few years – a bellwether middle England seat if there was one. The Conservatives won with a majority of 6,000 and a swing of 8.9 per cent.
- Warwick and Leamington: a Conservative majority of 3,513 on a swing of 8.8 per cent.
- Northampton North and South: North became a Conservative gain, with a majority of 1,936 on a swing of 6.9 per cent; and South a Conservative gain on a 7.4 per cent swing with a 1,772 majority.
- Milton Keynes North and South: North was won by the Conservatives on an 8,961 majority with a 9.2 per cent swing; and South was won by them on a 6.2 per cent swing with a 5,201 majority.
- Luton North and South were the exceptions, behaving like urban constituencies, and there was actually a swing to Labour in Luton North.
- Watford: the Conservatives won a 1,425 majority on a 6.1 per cent swing.

The journey down the M6 and M1 motorways, following the route of the West Coast Mainline for some of the way, takes you through 'swing England', where the outcomes of general elections are largely decided. The towns you pass through are a mix of the industrial, new and market towns that make up much of English life. It is city and rural life that preoccupies much of our cultural awareness – this is the area where soaps and dramas are set, the media and business elites live, and our iconic art and literature is based. It is the England of towns that are ignored but actually represent typical English life in all its variety. The demographic mix is more typical of the nation than are the areas where Labour did well.

These towns, based around major transport corridors, went blue en masse. They are the emotional heartbeat of the nation. On that journey from Meriden to Hackney, support was swinging to the Conservatives by up to 9.2 per cent against a national average of 5 per cent. With anything up to two-fifths of the population living in towns (depending on how you interpret the Office for National Statistics (ONS) data), these places are a major component of English civic and cultural life. Too often, Labour seems like an outsider in these towns.

Labour's disorientation following its 2010 defeat is clear. It is still struggling to make itself relevant to the very different mood and spirit of 'austerity' politics, but it seems neither to be plugging in to the emotional or the rational needs of modern England or, more widely, Britain. That journey from Meriden to Hackney is a harder political journey for Labour than it could ever imagine.

In Opposition

Labour's reaction to its electoral predicament was immediately to graft a language of moral economy on to the default mode of social democracy, becoming an Opposition in the purest sense of the word. The party wanted to be once again, in the words of former prime minister Harold Wilson, a 'moral crusade'. Yes, there is public anger at bankers' bonuses and the lack of punishment for those who placed the country's entire economic system at risk. So when The Royal Bank of Scotland's (RBS's) chief executive, Stephen Hester, handed back his 'performance-related' bonus in February 2012, in the same week that Fred Goodwin, former boss of the same bank, was stripped of his knighthood, there was a degree of satisfaction. Nonetheless, the left has a bad habit of over-interpreting popular impulses. Left-leaning newspaper columns are filled with predictions of 'seismic moments', 'inflection points' and new political realities.

Politics and society has changed in some quite fundamental ways, as we shall see. Unfortunately, it is much more complex and challenging than the left is assuming. It's not a simple case of triangulating between left and right either. Electoral strategy is not enough. People crave leadership but they are suspicious of leaders who do not seem to make any tough choices.

The notion of 'centre-ground' as the magical 'sweet spot' of politics is outmoded in the pluralistic politics of the present time: there are a number of available 'centres'. The question for Labour, and this applies across all of Europe's social democratic parties and some beyond, is how to read the economic, political and social changes that are appearing around them. For Labour leaders such as Ed Miliband, it means choosing between leading an increasingly failing governing ideology or ushering in a genuinely new political argument. And his early period of leadership strongly suggests that he is – rightly – reaching for the latter. As we shall see, his 'one nation' theme has abundant potential as a means of Labour emotionally reconnecting and rebuilding its severed relationship with voters. It must, however, be accompanied by new and more sustainable routes to social justice.

Witnessing the struggles faced by the Obama administration, the collapse of Labour in office, and the challenges it has faced in re-establishing itself in opposition, instantly draws attention to the social, economic and cultural changes that underpin these political and personal phenomena. These difficulties weren't simply contextual; they are related to the modern social and economic condition. Without understanding these forces it is impossible to build a viable political future, as the changes are deeper than simply a change in mood or attitude. There are fundamental social forces at work underneath political change. They are changing the nature of political leadership and the means by which political arguments take hold.

CHAPTER 2

Society's 'Bubbles', 'Networks' and 'Tribes'

Not long ago, three teenagers – two boys and a girl – sat near me on a train one morning. They boarded at Gatwick Airport and were heading to Clapham Junction, but they hadn't just returned from a holiday. They were just 'cruising' the train – presumably jumping barriers at each end. The eldest of the three was 15 or so at a guess and he was bullying his 'bitch', tormenting and humiliating her. His phone would go off from time to time and a short, aggressive, affected 'gangsta' two-way conversation would ensue. It was all about deals and whereabouts. But then his tone changed.

He turned to the younger boy, who had been much quieter and more introspective, and asked how things were with him. He replied, not so bad, but still tough. He was staying with his grandmother that night and had been for a while, since he moved out of his brother's flat. His brother was about to have a child with his girlfriend and he didn't know where that left him. The oldest boy asked whether his Dad's new girlfriend was nice to him. 'She was to begin with. Now not so much.'

As they were getting off at Clapham, the pattern of verbal and physical bullying of the girl continued as the oldest boy quickly put away the empathy, but actually, underneath it all, there was some real love and support for his friend. At least that was something.

A few weeks later riots erupted across London. Clapham Junction was one of the hotspots. The question of whether these teenagers had become embroiled in the mayhem did cross my mind. Their futures are bleak as they give each other support of sorts and are left to drift by their families. Their schools – if indeed they were still in school – would have given up long ago. Perhaps they had managed to keep clear of the violence – possibly more by luck than judgement. Even if they had escaped it, their young lives would still be anything but easy. Perhaps they will get lucky – but probably not.

A couple of years ago, I was asked to do a talk in Lewisham Library about Barack Obama at a Black History Month event. All went well at first. A sizeable audience of local people turned up and we had a wide-ranging discussion. Then something strange happened. The audience took over and started to talk about how envious they were of America and its ability to move on from its racial past (that was the not necessarily accurate perception they had). The memory of the Brixton riots was still fresh a quarter of a century or so later. There was an angry mistrust of the police and educational institutions. 'Stop and search' was completely corrosive as an issue, seen as the modern means by which the police humiliate certain communities.

Just a few days later, in another similar event, in Hackney this time, I raised the issue of 'stop and search', and asked if the teenagers who comprised the audience had any experience of it. Pretty much all had had a directly negative experience of being stopped and searched. A number of them even got out their 5090 forms, which are given out when individuals are stopped and searched. It had happened recently for the majority of them. (I once received one of these myself when I was stopped while driving on the Embankment in central London – the police officer told me he had to stop a number of white people to balance out the numbers, filled in the form and didn't bother with the search.)

The one story that stuck was from a young black boy who said he was walking down the street with his two white friends. He was stopped and they were not. I asked his teacher about it. She said she was surprised that he would have been targeted as there was nothing to suggest he was anything other than a model student – after all, he had come to a lunchtime lecture on politics and history.

At a focus group session a few months after the riots, I discussed the recent unrest with a group of 16–18-year-olds from the north and east London boroughs of Hackney, Haringey and Tower Hamlets. It was interesting to see what they thought of media narratives attributing the riots to 'hyper-consumerism', brand-driven materialism or a reaction to the cuts. They laughed at these hypotheses, ridiculing their premise, and they gave two alternative explanations.

Those who were from the Haringey neighbourhoods saw it as being driven by a community response to the shooting of Mark Duggan by the London Metropolitan Police's Specialist Firearms Command. Others saw it more as 'freestyling': a moment when order had been lifted and people were suddenly free of the boundaries within which they are expected to operate by social mores and the law. What started as a community's response to a specific set of keenly felt grievances morphed into and then predominantly became an exercise in 'free-styling' as the police lost control. It was a terrifying reminder of the links between basic security and liberty.

The riots wiped out livelihoods, created widespread fear, caused physical harm and tore communities apart. They also revealed something deep and challenging about modern society. The left's easy answer – based on assumptions about class – is to pin every societal ill on inequality. The right is more inclined to point to moral decline. In these debates, everyone tends to have a point but overall fall short in actually understanding what is going on. In general terms, the left opines a loss of class solidarity and the right regrets the loosened binding force of religious morality.

Britain has been through enormous social change since the 1960s, yet both the right and the left want to cling to the certainties of the past. The left still perceives a society predominantly driven by class, and the right sees things through the prism of individual moral failing. Both look back to an imagined bygone age. While class still has an enormous impact on life outcomes, it no longer primarily explains people's dominant outlook on the world. As class has declined as a social and political force, culture, identity, lifestyle and values have risen. Individuals are a complex combination of all these things. It is a paradox that class is central to individuals' life chances, but not to individuals.

As the precious institutions of marriage, community and church have declined, so has the more defined, collective moral sense that they underpinned. There is much that we have lost; where the right goes wrong (as do some on the left) is in thinking that there is a way of turning back. The solution to our present predicament is not to return to idealised versions of the past; it is to think about whether and how those things that are worthwhile and have been lost are to be regained in a society such as our own. We may crave renewed moral certainty – but whose notion of morality will it be?

So, when children are treated like unwanted pets, there is a consequence to that. When anger and mistrust between the police and communities boils over, it is the same communities that are vandalised. Divides in education and employment perpetuate the tensions. Some young kids see nothing good for themselves in doing the right thing, and instead seek the false security of the pack, the gang, the anger and the violence. Gangs are now networked via social media and instant messaging. These networks are new and often destructive forms of organisation and self-expression. We are seeing the rise of a networked generation and a society more influenced by it.

Networks are spreading increasingly across the economy, society and politics. In some senses this networked world is mesmerisingly creative, as new associations mine, in the words of Clay Shirky (the US writer and expert on the internet), the 'cognitive surplus' (the beneficial and creative use of surplus or free time facilitated by networked technology and applications – 'apps'). These networks can contribute significantly to political change as they have done in North Africa. They will also have destructive potential, as we saw in London's riots. A networked future won't be the fundamental reason for political change but it will accelerate and facilitate it in sometimes frightening ways.

The choice is either to be overwhelmed by this complexity or to navigate it and work, despite it, to ensure the security and opportunity that human beings need. If society's ills are simply seen as being driven by class inequality or moral decline, then lasting solutions will not be found. Simplistic solutions will not fit or resolve the problems that many feel they face. Instead, we need to understand the cultures, the identities, the values, the needs, the institutions, the networks, the technologies and the relationships that define our modern society. Society's complexities and dynamics exist beyond political movements and leadership. For the left, its choice is to acknowledge this or face irrelevance.

Traditional social democracy relied on a solid class structure and unity underpinning politics, but the class nature of politics has since loosened. This is one reason why social democracy has found its perpetuation so fraught. What was once a mass movement is now one political 'tribe' among a number, though the historical legacy of its political power remains, as does the legacy of the post-war welfare state – for now. Unfortunately, the old models are ceasing to work. Society is now a series of bubbles and tribes – lifestyle, values, economic position, culture and location all intersect in a myriad of ways. It is no longer possible to build a sustaining governing coalition by putting micro-blocks of support together – there are too many inherent contradictions. It must now be done by combining a nuanced conversation with authentic leadership. People are willing to agree to disagree with leaders to a certain extent – within certain parameters – as long as those leaders are clear about why their vision is the right one.

There are some bottom lines and non-negotiables – for example, on economic management, which must be seen to be competent; tax, which must be fair and measured; crime, which must be controlled; the NHS, which must be well funded; welfare, which must not be abused; and immigration, which must be managed. Beyond these, it is up to parties and leaders to craft a resonant story for our times. Leadership matters.

Once we understand the rich complexity of modern social existence, then some more creative and viable solutions are within reach. Young people such as the three on the Gatwick to Clapham Junction train that day may have something else in their lives: a greater sense of hope and belonging. Instead of 'freestyle' rioting there may be more for potential rioters to lose. Institutions such as the police may become more trusted. The convulsive potential of a networked world may be channelled in the direction of creative rather than destructive change. If we understand why and how our society has changed, then we may be able to create that different future. By understanding change it will enable us to realise that though we may be able to learn from and recover much of what is worthwhile that has been lost, there is no going back. Instead, there are futures that are better and futures that are worse: we have the ability to decide which course we take. This book will suggest some of the economic, commercial, political and ideological paths that might help to achieve the goal of greater social justice in the context of this changing society – and its 'bubbles' of interest, 'networks' of influence and 'tribes' of deeper commitment.

The Paradox of Class – the More Important It Is, the Less Important It Has Become

I was born in 1975. There was a Labour government in office. The party did not win a single further election until I was 22 years old. It then won three consecutively but has now returned to its losing ways. By the time of the next election, I will be 40 years old and only one Labour leader will have had the electoral success of becoming prime minister. Since 1975, Labour will have secured the support of more than 40 per cent of the electorate only twice. It has scored less than 30 per cent twice as well. It has averaged less than 35 per cent in that time. As David Cameron found to his cost, a majority government normally needs to secure somewhere in the region of 40 per cent of the vote.

Since the 1970s, the UK has rapidly de-industrialised; whole industries, such as coal-mining, have largely disappeared. Class solidarity has disintegrated as working people have moved into smaller employee workplaces which are less unionised, more service-based and more casualised. The country now has more degrees per head of population and more of its population is from ethnic minorities. More women have entered the workforce and they are increasingly occupying higher-status jobs. Home ownership has spread and greater inequality has taken hold. Scotland, Wales and Northern Ireland now have devolved power and legislatures. Homosexual couples can now become civil partners and may soon be able to marry. Britain has a rapidly ageing society and there are many more singletons. We have the internet; we use mobile phones; and we watch digital and even internet TV – an unprecedented amount of information and choice is at our fingertips.

As Graeme Cooke wrote in his report for the Institute for Public Policy Research (IPPR), *Still Partying Like It's 1995*, present-day society has a very different feel from even a decade and a half ago, let alone 1975. Cooke points to a society where the left must: 'reach deep into the groups that now dominate the electorate: over-50s; private sector, service workers; and homeowners'.

Such a society has very different demands from that of the 1970s. The problem from Labour's perspective is that the groups now dominating the electorate are not its traditional historical 'base'. What this means is that, without a radical reconsideration of the centre-left's appeal to modern Britain – and this in a mood of economic insecurity and cultural anxiety, then its pretty poor electoral record since the late 1970s could well continue. Cooke rightly rejects micro-targeting as an approach. He argues instead for a 'plural majoritarianism'.

In both electoral terms and in office, the ability of any political party to construct such a coalition determines its ability to hold on to power. It is not just about winning elections; it's about governing relevantly. For the majority of people, politics is like an old radio that is only turned on from time to time. If they switch it on and all they hear is static, off it goes again. Similarly, if they hear music that doesn't appeal, they reach for the 'off' button.

To ensure that the radio stays on, politicians have to be saying the right thing whenever people tune in. Broadly, the leader has to be credible; his or her economic strategy has to convince, including on wages, inflation and jobs; he or she must explain how high-quality public services will be delivered efficiently; he or she must be seen to care about community and personal safety; and a sound approach to managing immigration and combating welfare dependency will be needed. He or she cannot be seen to want to get rid of the armed forces, the monarchy, or want to tax over-enthusiastically. These are the basic political parameters of mainstream Britain.

The problem that New Labour had was in its claim 'there is no other way'. As long as a party has something credible to say in all of the above areas, it may get a hearing. The radio may be switched on for only a few minutes, so the challenge is to articulate a vision within these broad parameters. There is no perfect 'centrepoint'. There is a range of options as long as the basic parameters are respected.

Governing in a complex, pluralistic society is no easy task. It is a case of campaigning with clarity and governing in complexity. Either way, the political-sociological environment in which a party operates is critical. And the class analysis that has tended to dominate the left's view of society is simply too superficial and weak to sustain a winning or governing coalition any longer.

A party that draws solace from short-term opinion poll headlines is destined for a nasty surprise: they are just a measure of inclination rather than conviction. Once the election arrives, support converges on underlying and significant factors such as who is the leader, and economic competence ratings. These are the real polls. This 'real choice' factor explains why Scottish Labour's opinion poll lead evaporated in the last few weeks of the 2011 Scottish election.

The more the left sounds as though it is from a world that has vanished – like the one I was born into – the more the right can get on with dismantling the NHS, reversing the social advances made during the Labour years, and failing to build the right institutions for a better economic future.

So the politics of class is mixed, but the reality of class is not. It is very real and consequential; unequal societies create sharp class distinctions in terms of opportunity. Levels of social mobility in Britain have remained pretty flat since the early 1980s, as research by Dr Jo Blanden and Professor Machin of the London School of Economics (LSE) has shown. The Organisation for Economic Co-operation and Development (OECD) has also found that, by international standards, the UK has a strong degree of social immobility.

Class plays itself out in all sorts of complex feedback loops. The less power you have to build capabilities, the more likely it is you will not be able to meet your needs. Lacking the capability to fulfil your social, financial and psychological needs can lead to severe distress. This can have physical and mental consequences, which in turn further diminish your capability. Class division creates such powerlessness. Despite this, class is actually experienced in a very different and less conscious way in our modern society. The paradox is that, as class has become more consequential, class allegiances have declined.

When, in a *Marxism Today* piece in 1978, Eric Hobsbawm warned that the 'forward march of Labour' had halted, he was describing how patterns of work were changing. In 1961, more than 50 per cent of people were employed in workplaces of 500 or more. The latest figures suggest that number is now nearer 20 per cent, and more than half of people are employed in workplaces of less than 100. This is a completely different social experience and it has political conse-quences. Much has been written of the caricaturing of elements of the working class, such as 'chavs', not least by the commentator, Owen Jones. The fragmentation of a previously homogenous working-class identity allows this marginalisation to take place – the working-class experience of a factory worker in Nissan in Sunderland is different from that of someone who cleans an office in the City of London, and this is different again from that of someone who does not work at all and lives on an estate in the Black Country close to Birmingham.

Not only has there been a fragmentation of class, but the working class has actually declined in number enormously in recent decades – and has decoupled from its very strong allegiance to the left. According to Mori analysis, in 1992 Labour's vote was 11 per cent social classes A and B (professionals and managers), 17 per cent C1 (supervisory, clerical and junior managerial, administrative and professional – middle management in large part), 31 per cent C2 (skilled manual) and 42 per cent of its vote from classes D and E (manual workers, casual workers, state pensioners and those out of work).

By 2005, the proportions were: 27 per cent AB, 29 per cent C1, 18 per cent C2, and 25 per cent DE. This trend towards a swelling of professional classes as a proportion of Labour's vote continued in 2010, as we saw in the previous chapter. By 2005, Labour's vote had become almost a snapshot of the UK population – in this sense the party's support is now 'classless'. If it had not become so, it would be pretty much extinct as an electoral force: Britain is a professionalising society, with the change concentrated mainly among women entering the workplace.

Between 1991 and 2005, the proportion of women in 'classes I and II', according to NS-SEC classes which correspond roughly to the AB social group of professionals and senior managers, increased from 30 per cent to 40 per cent of the female population. The equivalent growth for men was 39 per cent to 43 per cent. Overall, the Work Foundation estimates that the number of 'knowledge workers' defined (not completely satisfactorily) as managerial, professional and associate professional occupational classes will increase from 41 per cent in 2004 to 45 per cent in 2015.

The Conservative lead among professional and middle classes declined from 37 per cent to 12 per cent from 1974–2010. In 2001, they led by only 4 per cent among this group, yet a 23 per cent deficit in 1974 became an 8 per cent lead in 2010 among C2 voters (skilled working class). There has also been a large shift in working-class (DE) support, with a 35 per cent Conservative deficit in 1974 becoming a 9 per cent deficit in 2010. It remains to be seen whether 2010 was an outlier or the first signifier of the permanent decoupling of the working-class vote from Labour. It should be stated that a degree of caution is needed in this regard, as Labour led by only 8 per cent in this group in 1983 but then rebuilt to a lead of 38 per cent by 1997.

Much was made in the UK media of the fact that 75 per cent of people consider themselves to be of the middle class – this percentage came from a survey by the pollster Britain Thinks. Given that, in reality, 75 per cent are not, in fact, middle-class, either in terms of categorisation (though a majority *are* now middle-class) or in terms of their life chances, this underlines the degree to which perceptions about class are incredibly loose (and do, in part, depend on the way that questions are asked in opinion polls!). Class certainties are fragmenting, and within this wider picture the working class have also declined in number in recent decades.

As Hobsbawm put it in *Marxism Today* in 1978: 'It seems to me that we are now seeing a growing division of workers into sections and groups.' This trend has continued apace since 1978. Peter Flannery's powerful 1996 drama *Our Friends in the North* had it down to a tee. It is the story of the decline of traditional working classes – some became wealthier, some became professional, some fell into dependence on the state, anti-social behaviour patterns, and even destitution, but few remained the same. New Labour was one possible response to this – basically, it targeted disaffected Conservative voters, and working-class support held firm for a time. Then it began to fragment. The working classes themselves were fragmented. Politically, they had held together under the Thatcherite onslaught – it was pure defence, but once that threat was removed, what was left of that solidarity dissipated.

This explains much of the haemorrhaging of 'Labour's lost 5 million' votes, which many left-leaning critics of New Labour in office have used as a stick with which to beat the party. A fragile class solidarity that seemed more solid after 18 Conservative years transpired to be illusory. New Labour had been relying on a working-class solidarity that was thin and temporary in its early years – far from the 'core vote' of political myth. It wasn't necessarily a sense of betrayal that was the impulse. It was a sense of disappointment in and disagreement with New Labour – and motivations were multifarious. Despair at welfare dependency or concern at immigration were much more likely to cause dismay than a sense of ideological betrayal, despite the anti-New Labour left's claims to the contrary.

So the 'betrayal' thesis is completely misguided – a return to traditional democratic socialism would have done little to staunch the bleeding; in fact, it would probably have accelerated it. This messy, fragmentary and confusing politics is the natural state for a country that is divided socially through post-industrial capitalism. Political coalitions become more contingent and fleeting rather than loyal and dependable.

In response to this, Labour has begun to make a pitch to people's values – such as with its cry for more responsibility at both the top and bottom of society – instead of their class. It will also need to speak to a sense of identity that is independent of class. It is worth noting in this context the appeal of Alex Salmond's optimistic, civic nationalism as a mobilising political force, as we shall see in Chapter 5. As a nation, Britain is increasingly divided and yet people feel a yearning to belong. We open a newspaper, pull back the curtains, or go to work, and we experience change. Yet we desire security and stability. This is not just in the case of the UK – the same is happening across many Western democracies, and is why social democratic parties – and the mainstream in general – are struggling almost everywhere.

Since the 1970s and 1980s Britain has changed radically: economically, then socially, then politically. There is no going back. The world I was born into has largely vanished. It is this new world – with its bubbles floating, colliding and sometimes merging – in which the left must seek to win people's trust. Neither New nor old Labour is the answer any longer. So what is the good news? The right faces the same predicament. It turns out that national leadership in the post-industrial age is hard. The right can no longer rely on institutions such as the church and the traditional family, and the left can no longer rely on class. It's not enough simply to understand social and economic change; we must also understand people's values. In other words, what it is that makes people tick.

Values

Human beings are not just a set of individuals impervious to external influences. In fact, we are deeply conditioned in ways that we don't realise. One of the most powerful driving forces is our values, and these are driven by our physiological, psychological and emotional needs.

Values are the deep undercurrents of individual motivation. They have a heavy influence on our shopping habits, our choice of partner, our cultural interests, our work and our politics. We do not just wake up one day and decide that we are going to hold a certain set of values; they develop in response to our needs. If we fear not being able to live in comfort then our focus is survival. If our survival is assured, we may then begin to crave the esteem of others, and our values will then guide us towards that end. Once we feel a sense of self-esteem, we may then become more geared towards the attainment of ethical wisdom, which is then what we shall seek.

The Brooklyn-born psychologist Abraham Maslow was right: we do have a hierarchy of needs. Pat Dade has been researching the deep value sets of our society for almost five decades. He is not a conventional social researcher. He was born on the west coast of the US and has that breezy Californian disposition. He first came to the UK when posted here with the US military and decided to come back after he found the election of Richard Nixon was too much to bear. He now lives in Twickenham. He and a colleague, Chris Rose, have put their research into a book, authored by Rose, called *What Makes People Tick*.

They explain how all societies break down into three broad value groupings: *settlers, prospectors* and *pioneers.* These categories relate to Maslow's hierarchy of needs. As Rose explains:

> For Settlers, the deep forces draw people to seek out safety, security, identity and belonging. For Prospectors, it is the yearning for success, the search for esteem of others, and self-esteem, while for Pioneers, the constant drive is for new ideas, the quest for connections waiting to be made, and living a life based on ethics.

Our behaviours, opinions and actions are all in some way linked to these subconscious value sets and the needs to which they respond. For a settler, home is where the heart is. For a prospector, home is for show and keeping up with the Joneses. For a pioneer, home is where you sleep, read and cogitate while imagining a different future for the world. Settlers appreciate tradition. Prospectors respond to fashion and status. Pioneers strive for improvement. Settlers' newspapers of choice would tend to be the *Daily Mirror* or the *Telegraph.* Prospectors read the *Daily Mail,* the *Sun* or the *Financial Times'* 'How to spend it' supplement. Pioneers? The *Guardian,* the *Independent* or the *Financial Times'* main section. As you can see, class correlates only very loosely with these value sets: it is more about people's individual needs and how these can change over time.

As individuals shift their value sets (which they usually, but not necessarily, do over time), so too does society. Understanding these value shifts is the key to understanding politics, business, religion, culture and, ultimately, society.

The Occupy protests which rallied against capitalism in a make-shift camp outside St Paul's Cathedral from October 2011 until June 2012 mobilised around the slogan: 'We are the 99 per cent'. The simple fact is that there is no 99 per cent. There is no 99 per cent behind any given position: we have a divided and plural society in terms of our values and that is how it will remain. This creates problems for anyone looking to construct political movements and coalitions of all types, not just for the protestors. In the post-class-politics era (but not, please note once more, post-class) political motivation and allegiance are more contingent, fluid and free-flowing.

Many on the right who see our society's ills as the moral failings of a liberal elite that have spread to others have missed the reality of this dynamic of human psychological change over time. Some, such as the American sociologist Charles Murray, see a cultural inflexion point in the social liberation of the 1960s. These sociologists are right to a certain extent. But what happened was less a 'choice' than a reflection of the reality of post-austerity societies enjoying a consumer boom and the expansion of 'knowledge work'. The first post-war generation, with its access to better education, was inevitably more inclined to express its individuality – and this happened across advanced societies.

As societies became more prosperous, and as the threat of cataclysmic war receded, then social, economic and political freedom became highly desirable. We give the baby boomers – the first post-war generation, who came of age in the 1960s and 1970s – a hard time, but they were the first generation who were able to enjoy social, sexual, political, cultural and economic freedom as the historical context shifted. In the long shadow of the horrors of the 1930s depression, the Holocaust and World War II, it is not surprising that they wanted a different future. This shift was not 'done to us' by a liberal elite. It happened and we need to be aware of what happened and why. The number of prospectors and pioneers increased as settlers became fewer. Chris Rose quotes the work of Ronald Inglehart on the rise of post-materialist and secular values approvingly. Inglehart's World Values Survey explains the changes we have seen quite neatly, while counter-weighting social change with cultural and social institutions.

For over four decades Ronald Inglehart has been collecting and systematically analysing data about societies across the globe. He was instrumental in establishing the World Values Survey, which has gathered data in nations covering 90 per cent of the world's population. It is the definitive dataset on comparative values and value change over time. Inglehart correlates value sets in accordance with different economic systems. In the spirit of the great Max Weber, his argument is not deterministic. Values are mediated by tradition, institutions and culture – religion being the most obvious factor. Nonetheless, the correlation of the development of self-expressive values and the expansion of the service-industry-based, post-industrial economy is striking. This is not a linear pathway, as each nation has its own traditions and institutions. Nor is it irreversible – societies can degenerate economically. However, it is a very strong correlation.

When Inglehart and his colleague Christian Welzel plotted the concentration of the service sector against the types of values that Pat Dade looks at – survival (settler) versus self-expression (pioneer) – they found a significantly higher concentration of the latter type compared with more industrial societies. The more a society has services at the core of its economy, the more that society demonstrates strong values of self-expression. Services tend to be more information- and relationship-driven. They employ smaller numbers of people on average in a place of work and are incredibly diverse in terms of their business.

Survivalists (settlers) tend to be dissatisfied with their financial situation, believe women need children to be fulfilled, or be anti-technology. Self-expressionists (pioneers) tend to be the opposite on these and scores of other attitudes. The greater number of self-expressionists (pioneers) there are, the more individualistic the society. That is one of the key sociological stories of the last 50 years. Back in the 1960s, the UK had many more settlers than pioneers. Industrial society at that time was less prosperous, people worked together in common activities in large workplaces, and they lived in communities with a greater degree of shared local life. By the late 1980s, there were approximately equal numbers of settlers, prospectors and pioneers, and as of 2010, the UK was made up of 41 per cent pioneers, 31 per cent settlers and 28 per cent prospectors.

This value change – towards expressive individualism – is one way in which the collective spirit has weakened, but it has not prevented people from coming together in collective action. It has just undermined the coherence of disciplined mass organisations. It was the discipline, coherence and large scale that enabled labour movements to exert political pressure for their social rights to be respected, and for a redistribution of wealth and opportunity. Today's new political movements are more fragmented, temporary and networked.

They rise around issues and are often gone before they've had time to become part of the establishment. The conventional political forces occupy traditional democratic institutions; but the real democratic energy is elsewhere. It is both an expression of post-industrial individualism and, as we shall see in Chapter 4, a reaction to it.

As Chris Rose says of Inglehart in *What Makes People Tick*:

> Inglehart predicted in 1977 'declining rates of elite-directed political mobilisation and rising rates of elite-challenging mass activity among Western publics' – in other words, declining participation in formal elections, and rising participation in things like campaigns, boycotts and petitions. This is, of course, exactly what has happened, as these are the activities of the Pioneers, with their latest expression found in new powerhouse groups such as www.avaaz.org, www.getup.au, www.moveon.org, and www.38degrees.org.uk.

Political actions are often attached to particular value sets. The Greens and the privacy-and-freedom-motivated Pirate Party, which has been successful in Sweden and Germany, are full of, to use the Pat Dade terminology, pioneers. The far right is a mix of settlers – which needs certainty, stability and is more focused on locality – and power complex clusters of prospectors (the latter are more likely to be the activists). An unfulfilled desire for power and status leads to anger, and this provides fertile ground for the far right. The rioters were concentrated in a particular group within prospectors. What this means is that when class weakens, these value sets motivate political action.

Understanding people through their values is key to explaining political behaviour and much more. It also serves to remind us that it's not just clever marketing that achieves political change. Once we understand people through their values and needs, we are able to see why the context has shifted so markedly for traditional social democracy. These values are part of the reason why any class analysis of Labour's defeat in 2010 is deeply flawed. Labour lost much of its 'core' vote – but not for reasons that many on the left have claimed. In fact, it was far from being predominantly a class protest.

Attitude Problem

A poll conducted by YouGov for Demos in 2010 showed a stark contrast in attitudes towards the state and spending between the voters Labour kept and those it lost in the last election. The poll asked whether the state was a help or a hindrance in the lives of the respondent and his or her family. By a margin of only 33 per cent to 27 per cent, lost Labour voters considered the state to be a help rather than hindrance. The comparable figure for Labour's loyal voters was 54 per cent to 14 per cent. Only 14 per cent of Labour's lost voters believed the priority was to avoid cuts in NHS spending as opposed to efficiency gains.

What is more, in these overall attitudes, Labour's lost voters were very close to the national average. It was actually the loyal voters who were at a distance from the mainstream. As noted earlier, Labour lost C2, D and E voters disproportionately in the 2010 election. Despite the fact that these voters were reflective of Labour's traditional 'core vote', they were actually fairly sceptical about public spending and the state. YouGov conducted a similar poll at the time of the 2009 European elections. On issues of welfare, immigration and trust, its findings were similar. The voters Labour have been losing had the *social* characteristics of Labour's traditional 'core' vote but their *attitudes* were much further to the right than those of pro-state, liberal, redistributionist social democrats.

Overall, attitudes towards welfare have hardened significantly, partly as a result of the media-political climate. The wind seems to have been blowing pretty consistently in one direction for some time. In 1983, according to British Social Attitudes (BSA) data, people thought benefits were too low by a margin of 46 per cent to 35 per cent. In 2010, however, people thought they were too *high* by a margin of 62 per cent to 19 per cent. If there was now the type of deep solidarity that existed in the immediate post-war era then the media would be less capable of driving an anti-welfare narrative, and if it did so it would be less effective. Even if the media-political narrative could be reversed, the simple reality is that the social support for extending the welfare state just is not there; a party or media force would always be able to step into the space. Public support for the Coalition's welfare cap underscores this point. With the exception of a recession in the early 1990s, there has been pretty much one-way traffic in terms of more scepticism towards welfare. And the recession that began in 2007, unusually, has not as yet reversed the flow towards welfare scepticism.

In 1997, 62 per cent of people wanted to see more taxes and spending, according to the BSA data. By 2008, following a period of sustained increases in public spending, this percentage had fallen to 39 per cent. In 2011, the proportion was 36 per cent, though this was a 5 per cent increase on 2010. It remains to be seen what impact a prolonged period of austerity will have on these attitudes, though there has been a slight shift. A shift back similar to the post-recession period of the early to mid-1990s could occur, but the early signs are that people accept the necessity for cuts (though they differ over the pace of these). According to YouGov, at the end of 2011, 59 per cent considered that the cuts were necessary, while 27 per cent did not. Attitudes are short-term, however, and can change. However, the deep undercurrents of social change and values will shift political attitudes over time.

The left's problem is that it is stuck in the old ways of under-standing this political and social change. Its models are outmoded. Commentators and politicians on the left have a habit of starting with the position they want to argue. They then cobble together something that on paper looks like sufficient backing in terms of blocks of class support. But people are no longer strongly driven in that way. Old left views are subject to heavy 'confirmation' and 'optimism' biases – they see their own viewpoints in the evidence. The allegation then is that the alternative is just to switch around tactically to follow public opinion. Again – and this argument comes mainly from commentators on the soft and hard left – this misses the point. A viable and sustainable political strategy understands where the parameters are, then crafts a viable vision backed up by sound policies within those parameters. There are choices; there is not only one 'centre ground'. It is just that it's not a free-for-all. You have to reach to where people are to engage them, and then lead them, while also responding to their needs and concerns. It is conversation, not capitulation, that is required.

An argument for greater social justice is not lost as long as it is cast in the right way. A case for the future of welfare that does not depend on contributions – what you get out is in relation to what you put in – will be likely to fail. Generous Scandinavian welfare systems depend on a strong sense of collective and individual responsibility, as did the original insurance-based Beveridge model. A discussion that centres on playing by the rules – applicable as much to the wealthy as to those on welfare – and security in an increasingly risky world, rather than on redistribution and welfare, is more likely to succeed in tackling the significant injustices that remain in British society.

It is little wonder that welfare states across Europe have similarly retrenched in recent years: including in Germany, the Netherlands and Sweden. European societies are facing many similar changes to social structure and values as the UK – welfare states are seen as increasingly inflexible, marginal and open to abuse. This means that attitudes towards welfare, immigration, public spending and criminal justice have tended to shift away from the social democratic defensive view. There is renewed interest in 'framing' as a device to counteract this: in other words, finding a visual language to appeal to people's innate empathetic sense. The obvious framing is the battle to frame government spending as 'waste' (the argument of the right) versus 'investment' (the argument of the left). Another one might be welfare (bad) versus social insurance (better). The problem is that, in order to be heard, you have to be taking part in the conversation. Unless you at least acknowledge people's starting point you may not even be invited to participate in the conversation. Greater political empathy with where people are coming from, and why, is required.

By failing to acknowledge these shifts of demographics, values and attitudes, the European left has too often been outmanoeuvred by the right – who have projected themselves as compassionate reformers. David Cameron brought himself into greater public favour in 2010 by claiming that his priority was the NHS (though he has since inflicted an injury on himself on that front with the chaotic Health and Social Care Act). Angela Merkel intervened with state support to prevent any rise in post-crisis unemployment in Germany. Fredrik Reinfeldt's centre-right coalition has reformed Sweden's welfare and education systems and has won middle-class support from the Social Democrats as a result. In the case of Merkel, she has deployed social democratic means to support her own position. Cameron and Reinfeldt reform traditional social democratic institutions while articulating their commitment to them. Both strategies have been effective at various times and in various ways: they either move on to the left's political territory, or adopt the left's commitment while challenging its defensive status-quoism.

In the 2009 European elections – the first after the crash – the major parties of the left suffered a trouncing in France, Spain, Germany, Italy and the UK. The global financial meltdown might have been expected to usher in a new social democratic renaissance. Neo-liberalism as a creed was deemed to have failed. Admittedly, many parties on the left, including Labour, were tied into neo-liberalism and seen to be so. Regardless of that, we are no longer in a situation with only two choices: neo-liberalism fails, so people turn to social democracy, and vice versa. Social change – and the more pluralistic and complex politics it has provoked – suggests many of the reasons why.

The question for the left is, if people want welfare reform, a more efficient state and better-managed immigration, how can they change the 'frame' of that? With difficulty, in reality. If the 'core' has crumbled and loyalty declined as the old social structures decay, where is the left's foundation? Across Europe, the left too often rests on old institutions and social structures. In the meantime. people feel less bound by tradition and are less deferential to hierarchy and established institutions. Values influence attitudes; and networks and institutions mediate how we interact. Increasingly, networks – organic, often fleeting and based on interest – are challenging traditional institutions. This accounts for much of the political and social change we are experiencing.

The Clash of Networks and Institutions

What links the democratic movements in North Africa and the Wisconsin union resistance in 2011 to the British student protests at the end of 2010 and the anti-cuts movement? They all – in very different ways – alert us to the shift from more rigid institutions to more flexible networks as a form of political and social interaction. Institutions establish the norms and rules of interaction. They are value-heavy and deploy incentive and sanction. Networks, initially at least, are formed to bring people together around some shared interest or pursuit. Networks can become institutions over time, as the links become deeper and more established, but in their infancy at least they are more contingent, less permanent, more open and faster-moving in essence. Driven in part by technology, but also the social fragmentation that has been identified, networks are increasing in influence relative to institutions. Governments, companies, collective institutions, traditional cultures and practices are falling as a result. The swarm is flying over the moat and the castle is no longer impregnable.

Both in and beyond the developed world, we are seeing not simply a global struggle for economic justice and for democracy, but tectonic friction between two different forms of society: the network society and the institutional society. This clash may well define much of the next phase of human history. Now that modernity travels through thin air, transmitted from space, travelling through distributed computer networks, accessed through a metal or plastic box in your pocket, available at a price affordable by most, the technology of the network society is relatively freely accessible. Networked mobile telephony has become a primary tool of protest, riot, revolution, organisation, social action, social interaction, criminality, humanity and consumption. It is not replacing human contact; it is hyper-activating it.

Over a decade ago, in 2000, Jeremy Rifkin argued, in *The Age of Access*:

> The fast pace of hyper-real, nanosecond culture shortens the individual and collective temporal horizon to the immediate moment. Traditions and legacies become fading interests. What counts is 'now', and what's important is being able to feel and experience the moment.

At the time, it seemed like science fiction. It now seems very real. The crisis of a financial system driven by the moment, by mathematical models and automatic trading, prioritising short-term gain over long-term value, is just one demonstration of the potentially destructive power of networks. Democracy is beginning to bear some of the hallmarks of a system driven by a series of populist spikes. Western culture is disposable, as are too many of our relationships. While this seemed *Bladerunner*-esque a decade or so ago, it seems frighteningly real now. In *Viral Politics*, published in 2001, I wrote: 'Faced with multiple networks of interest and shared culture [people] treat their life as a process rather than an event, continually inventing and re-inventing themselves.'

Any politics of power redistribution – which should be the left's fundamental argument – relies on more than the here and now. We are more likely than ever before to think in societal and even civilisational terms – about our long-term needs and future – but, equally, we are living more and more in the moment. We are becoming at once more global and more immediately local – or personal. We crave a long view but we increasingly operate from one nanosecond to another. The economic and financial rupture we are facing provides a crying need for us to break free from this psychological and cultural short-termism. The question is whether we can, and how. The answer will require an understanding of where and how a networked culture can work in favour of creating an energy behind long-term change – as it has, for example, in the case of the green movement – and where, conversely, it might be destructive of it. Ultimately, creating new institutions will require the active mobilisation of networks of interest, values, ethical concern, culture and lifestyle. This entails a degree of humility for the traditional forces of the left – the old solidarity approach is no longer effective.

Networks are fast, disruptive, asymmetrical, convulsive, mesmerising, and aggregate quickly. The economist Paul Ormerod points to the fundamental concept of influence in his 2012 study of networks, *Positive Linking: How Networks Can Revolutionise the World*. Traditional economics relies on incentives. If Coca-Cola reduces its price it will sell more units. But in a world of overflowing information and advertising trickery, where consumers and producers can interact in a myriad of ways to influence one another, and the 'rational' strategy is to copy others, the actual outcome becomes skewed away from a 'normal distribution'.

Coca-Cola could have reduced its price in response to the success of the marketing of the Pepsi brand. If Pepsi is cool – a status or a 'Veblen good' (which people buy more of, the more it costs, in other words) – then Coca-Cola's price cut might have no effect at all. Indeed, it could be completely counter-productive, not only in terms of revenues but also in terms of maintaining its position of influence within the network of people who want to look cool drinking a certain drink.

Skews, influence, copying, crowd-behaviour, influencers, network hubs – real life in other words – all distort the explanatory power of conventional economics. Ormerod likes to turn things on their head, as he does when he cites John Maynard Keynes as a guru of network theory – what else are those 'animal spirits' of which Keynes talked? Keynes' primary concern was the influence of people on one another, and the periodic collapses in confidence of economic actors. Ormerod sees the current economic predicament in precisely these terms – a fatal collapse of confidence rippling through networks, starting with the banks ceasing to trust one another from 2007 onwards. These network effects occur throughout politics, economy and society.

Networks can be utterly destructive, as in the case of Al Qaeda. They can help to bring down governments, as President Mubarak of Egypt discovered. They can facilitate mass and rapid protest, as was seen in London with the 2010 student protests, and the UK Uncut's direct action since then; they can facilitate riots that spread like wildfire. The point is that institutions struggle to keep up with the speed of communication: London was victim to mass rioting in August 2011 as a result of the Metropolitan Police being very slow off the mark.

Markets can be network-like or institutional. The market for energy generation (though not the wholesale trading of energy units, which is network-like) is heavily institutional, whereas the hedge fund market is network-driven. The more a market is defined by rapid interaction and exchange rather than institutions with transparency and regulatory rules, the greater the potential risk. It is because when modern financial markets became more networked – driven by global technology and communication – and less institutionally constrained, they became more uncertain and risky.

What applies to networked financial markets also applies to social networks – the less constrained by norms and accepted rules, the more risky and potentially convulsive they are. Networks are convulsive in both a creative and destructive manner. They can spread democracy and justice, and they can spread terror and violence.

The focus on the branded element of the network society – such as Twitter and Facebook – has missed the point. There is nothing particularly special about these 'apps'. There have been dozens of Facebook equivalents. It won not because of great technology or ingenious innovation. It won because it stumbled on a marketing strategy that worked: the college campus network dissemination. If it had not prevailed, something else would exist in its place. It was nothing fundamentally innovative – networks have existed from the moment in evolution that organisms began to socialise.

Even networked protest and revolution is not new: the civil rights movement and the Russian Revolution alike relied on the power of networks to cause disruption. They were just slower-paced, relying as they did on the 'technology' of word-of-mouth, the landline telephone or leafleting. Now the pace, cost and consequent availability of the means of networked communication, is greater. That gives networked organisation a greater ability to influence – even if it is short-lived. This shifts power – in the short-term at least – towards networks and away from institutions.

Networks can often be better at destroying things down than finding an alternative. Institutions are better than networks at preserving standards, maintaining stability (which can also mean oppression or inflexibility) and achieving desirable outcomes over a long period. Japan's Tohoku earthquake and ensuing tsunami in early 2011 demonstrated both the strength and weakness of its institutions. Though the earthquake was 900 times the magnitude of the one that hit Haiti in 2010, the loss of life was a fraction of the 200,000 lost in Haiti. This was down to brilliant preparation, training, regulations and engineering.

Japanese people accept that earthquakes are part of their island experience, but far from being fatalistic about it, they have built an effective institutional response. Networks helped in the aftermath, but it was the endurance of Japan's institutions that saved many lives. Unfortunately, though, their regulation of nuclear power safety standards was less than successful; it is clear that the regulators had become captured by the regulated. Over time, institutions can become infected and corrupted. As a result of regulatory failures concerning the nuclear disaster at Fukushima, the head of Japan's nuclear watchdog, NISA, was fired, alongside the head of the agency for natural resources and energy.

So the types of institutions in place matters as much as creating the right network dynamism, and Japan is an institutional builder par excellence. The Japanese earthquake experience is also a cautionary lesson in the potential for corruption of institutions over time – that in itself can provoke a sudden networked reaction. The revolutionary fervour in Egypt, Tunisia, Bahrain, Syria and Libya are all examples of this – corruption mobilises discontent. When things work well, networks and institutions can balance each another: one serves as venture capital, the other as insurance; one exploits the present, while the other builds for the long term. The ideal is to balance the creative energy of networks with the long-term logic of powerful institutions. Get it right and you can combine energy and stability. Get it wrong and stability blocks adaptation, or energy destroys or ignores things of long-term value. To create a different future, the left will have to both tap into the energy of networks and galvanise that energy for institution-building.

Networks are at their best when they not only disrupt present injustices, but move rapidly to build institutions around more just and democratic alternatives. It is easier to organise a protest – even a large one – than to build a new economy, democracy or society. A networked movement of protest in defence of publicly valued institutions is elegant and powerful. Collectively, this networked momentum must be harnessed to create the new institutions – economic, social and political – of social justice and democracy.

Along with vast inequality, the present age will be shaped by environmental degradation; the global economic and political power shift from north and west to east and south; the battle between open and closed societies and markets; and the conflict between networks and institutions. Where the energy and innovation of networks is used to build enduring institutions of long-term public value we shall succeed collectively. In the case of the Coalition government, it is hoped that this will occur spontaneously – and this is at the centre of the Big Society (which we shall meet more intimately in Chapter 6). This may work in some places and certain contexts with already existing networks of huge resource and capability – generally better-off places that already enjoy a depth of social and human capital. Too often it will not, however, and instead of new institutions and networks only chaos, desolation and insecurity will result. This will happen primarily in places that are already materially, socially and institutionally deprived, and could entrench powerlessness further.

The shift of balance from an institutional to a networked society will topple dictators, bring down governments, occasionally create terror and mayhem, create economic risk and opportunity, and quickly eliminate some traditional civic and state institutions. Things will seem stable one minute and unstable the next. Sometimes institutional power will out: for good or evil. Networks' weaknesses are often exposed by the hard power of institutions. The Syrian military and the Assad dictatorship is one such example – not least because of the weakness of international institutions. Networks of resistance have sometimes lacked the hard power to prevail without outside assistance. Often, though, institutions and their leaders will be crushed by the power of networks. New possibilities are created alongside new risks.

Such was the case in Egypt. Protestors were drawn to protest in Tahrir Square via social media networks at the end of January 2011. Security forces expected just a few thousand people. Demonstrators communicated word of a far more significant demonstration than the reality via the very same social networks and managed to present a more formidable picture. The Mubarak regime panicked and shut down internet access both over the landline and via mobile phones. The demonstrations swelled to include more than a million people. Mosques became involved. The Mubarak regime collapsed and the army took control, with a promise to shepherd Egypt towards a new democratic constitution. It remains to be seen what will be the result of Egypt's revolution: an uneasy balance has been struck between networked protestors and the traditional institutions of the army and Islam. Nonetheless, an oppressive, corrupt and authoritarian regime was basically removed from office in 18 days after decades of misrule. This is the power of networks to disrupt – which can be positive or, as in the case of riots, gang activity and violent protest, it can be exceedingly negative.

Networks can also be creative. Such a network energy is seen in Silicon Valley and in East London's Tech City. People with skills, ideas and creativity come together with people with resources, know-how and organisational capability. They agree contracts, develop intellectual property, market their products and services, build companies and create wider networks of value. It's an extremely dynamic process that can become institutionalised over time – through universities, skills provision, funding support and ideas networks. Open communication networks make this dynamic possible. The challenge, as we shall see, is to get the right institutions working with the right networks in the right way. Getting the balance and interaction spot on is critical: so that institutions of value are not destroyed, new ones are created where they are needed but networks are allowed to flourish where they are creative rather than destructive.

Class has fractured and declined. Individual values and needs have risen as a plural political force. Attitudes no longer follow predictable pathways on the basis of social categories. Networks and institutions clash, with the former becoming more forceful. This is the nature of social change in modern democracies. And it is a process of change that cascades down the generations.

Generation Game

In a collection of essays entitled *The Labour Tradition and the Politics of Paradox,* Maurice Glasman, the intellectual force behind 'Blue Labour' – traditional labourism set in a contemporary context, which will be revisited later – and his co-authors treated the left's dilemma as a family dispute. Glasman's essay 'Labour as a radical tradition' was a story of nationhood and identity in which the radical impulse is intrinsic. The two members of the family were a 'middle-class' mother who was interfering and knew what was best for everyone else, and a 'working-class' dad who was unassertive and deeply frustrated. Beatrice Webb was the 'mother' and Keir Hardie the 'father'. It was, of course, a metaphor for the rise of the statist and elitist 'Fabian' view within Labour, and the decline of the traditional Labourist outlook which emphasised local bonds of community and politics to a greater extent.

Glasman argued that 'pluralism and diversity, without strong forms of a common life, undermine the solidarity necessary for generating a welfare state and redistribution'. This is the left's predicament: it is stranded between the solidarity of old and the greater individuality of the present. The problem is that turning back the tide will not resolve this contemporary dilemma. Humanity has enormous capacity for generosity in the context of the trust that comes with a common understanding of ourselves and our condition. Yet we live in times where that trust is eroding in old institutions: the church, the media, Parliament, and, indeed, the political parties themselves. On what basis does the left make its plea for common action in such a context? The reality is that it becomes a sectional rather than a transformational appeal. Just as religion in many places still insists on its transcendent voice despite its decline, so class-based ideology hoists the flag of social democracy.

Perhaps near financial meltdown was an opportunity in this regard; but if it ever was, the moment has gone. We are seeing the opposite process at play. Not only is Britain becoming more divided as a nation – financially, culturally and socially – the populace is becoming antagonistic towards one another, encouraged by the statecraft of a ruthless Coalition government led by the Conservatives and backed by elements of the media. There is fertile ground for this approach, as we have seen.

The problem with Glasman's 'middle class'/'working class' family metaphor, however, is that it works as a kind of a political version of the Two Ronnies' and John Cleese's 'class' sketch but does not reflect the reality of the society in which we live. This is a perpetuation of the left's problem. It has a bad habit of seeing the world in primary colours when the reality is more complex. The working class is its 'base' in this view, and public sector professionals are also increasingly forming a part of the base. Working-class dad; professional mum, so then the battleground becomes the middle classes. If this model of political society ever worked convincingly it no longer does so. It contains faulty assumptions about who people are because of where they have come from socially; increasingly this has separated the labour movement from where – and who – people actually are. There has been a papering over of the cracks with micro-targeting, focus-grouping and poll-driven strategising, but this has only made matters worse, as politics on the left appear to be simply a series of tactical adjustments.

James Purnell's essay in Glasman *et al.*'s *The Labour Tradition and the Politics of Paradox* added the 'progressive son' to the discussion – a Generation X entrepreneur and public sector reformer. He is recognisable. But what about his daughter? She is involved with the ethics of helping the developed world and fighting off climate change, willing to take to the streets or volunteer for a charity overseas as a means of self-expression. As a consumer, she is materialistic but not a patron of the mass market. She has the intellectual self-confidence to tie an opponent up in knots, and participates socially on- and offline, near and far. She is networked in and, graduating in 2012, just learning that things are going to be a far more uphill task for her than she was ever promised. She now thinks Generation X and the baby boomers both failed.

The New Labour son is just as bewildered when it comes to his sister as his mum and dad are with him. She is certainly socially liberal and she also may become radically liberal – activism in the pursuit of interest and ethical outlook should come naturally. Politically, Liberal Democrat seemed like a good compromise for her but is no longer following the tuition fees debacle and other swiftly broken promises of office. How she – and her younger brother, who is facing monumental tuition fees – are now engaged politically will determine much. Their pathways are by no means established – they could end up as liberals, liberal conservatives, greens, reformist social democrats, or even as

Pirates, as that party's success in recent city elections in Berlin shows. Things are not getting any easier as we cascade down the generations.

As the left looks to build a new governing coalition it will be tempting to talk Dad's language while offering Mum's solutions, but that will be seen through straight away. Besides, the Labour dad versus the Fabian mum metaphor seems strangely anachronistic to the other two generations in this story. Indeed, this is the central conclusion of this chapter. The left needs to reach beyond these constraining traditions and create a new argument for enduring social justice – one that is grounded in the pluralistic society of the present. Understanding the social change that has been experienced since the 1970s does not provide answers but does suggest an urgent need for radically re-crafting what it means to be on the left in the twenty-first century. The familiar social democratic and Labour arguments rely on societies that less and less resemble our modern societies.

There will be no future for the left if it cannot rebuild a majority. The decline of the working class in number and in intensity of allegiance suggested a New Labour-style strategy of pitching to middle-class sources of support. But when we look at British society as a series of classes, bubbles, tribes and values, then a simple process of re-positioning is no longer adequate. The converse risk is that, in an attempt to micro-target, the left speaks with anything but a clear voice.

Tony Judt, as we saw in the Introduction, spoke of a need for a language of ends rather than means. There is a great deal in this. The right response to this complex and fragmented environment will instead involve campaigning with clarity, and governing for complexity. There is no clearly defined centre-ground; instead, there is a set of parameters within which modern politics operates. There is no ideal solution but there are some routes that are impossible – beyond the parameters of potential success. The possible solutions vary across societies and political contexts: one size does not fit all.

In a complex environment, leadership acquires an even greater premium. Effective leadership works in two ways. First, those voices that are able to map out a clear and coherent vision of the future will capture people's attention, but those that get locked into the tactics and manoeuvres of the here and now will fail to cut through. Even where people disagree they will have a certain tolerance as long as the leader is honest about why there are differences. A humanistic discourse, which naturally builds a political argument around personal stories, experiences and identities, including nationhood and values, is the most powerful.

Second, in office, a different type of leadership is required. This is a more conciliatory process, which acknowledges the pluralism of needs and demands. This leader will be a navigator. It is no longer enough for centralised administration to impose its will on those who demand a voice in the things that affect them. The utter chaos and destruction of the NHS reforms instituted by the Coalition is an example of what happens when modern administration becomes directive. Passing legislation in the UK parliamentary system is relatively easy compared with actually securing public legitimacy. It is the opposite of health care reform in the US, where passing legislation was harder than securing consent. In a sense, such a hard-fought process can be a better way despite the frustrations it imposes: it accepts the reality of political pluralism and thus attendant social complexity. In a pluralistic society, with an assertive disposition, engaging and securing consent becomes even more important. This is what is meant by 'governing for complexity'. Political leadership accepts its limits. It becomes discursive, devolved, persuasive and pluralistic. Its authority and legitimacy are earned through brokerage rather than electoral success. It is transparent and open.

Understanding society is necessary not simply to acquire electoral success but to secure real change. It enables a better understanding of people's real needs. It is unfortunate that this type of analysis has been seen simply as a tactical means of building short-term support. That is not the real value. Meeting the needs of a complex society is the real value. These needs are economic, social and democratic and they permeate our collective life: civic, market, local services and central administration.

Those three teenagers on the Clapham train that morning need more than politics has been able to offer. Like all of us, they need love and support, and there is no national programme that can supply those things. There is no purely administrative solution to neglect.

The modern state can cope bureaucratically but not personally – and this is a considerable flaw. These young people's isolation and alienation is an extreme case of what happens when politics thinks of people as a mass rather than case by case. We all want and need that politics of personal engagement – one that nourishes rather than ignores human needs that are beyond the material. The choice now is how politics, the state, the constitution, the economy and civic life have to adapt to achieve that. Paradoxically, getting to the bottom of what's gone wrong with the economy – as one element of promoting our humanity – is a good place to start. It is a necessary starting point but far from sufficient, as we shall see.

CHAPTER 3

Economy

Economic policy does not come from nowhere. It rests on ideas. Two big, broadly defined economic ideas have dominated discourse in recent decades: neo-liberal economics and Keynesianism. The former, in very broad terms, contends that markets should be able to operate freely and without constraint in order to achieve a more efficient economy. It has been, and still is, the dominant economic idea. The latter sees markets failing, to which there needs to be a response from the government to boost aggregate demand. These two ideas operate as a kind of see-saw: when one is up the other is down. Unfortunately, both have significant limits and flaws. In the world of politics and public policy we have to understand the limits of these ideas to avoid many of the mistakes of the past. Just because one set of ideas is wrong, it does not mean that the other is automatically right in all respects.

There are few immediate solutions to the predicament in which we find ourselves. It will be a long road to real recovery. If we just do things the same again we shall be in a similar predicament within a short time. So a different type of economy is necessary. This will not be built overnight. We cannot simply decide to transplant, say, German institutions and culture into the UK. That is not to say that we can't learn from others. But we have to understand this economy and society and not look to some magic alternative from history, overseas or from economic theory. It is a careful building job that is needed; and it must be sensitive to the pressures and opportunities presented in an economy such as that of the UK. This is about crafting a different future rather than settling economic and political scores. To do that, we need to both understand where economic approaches have let us down and carefully weigh the responses that might have a chance of success.

The fingerprints of the Chicago school of economics – a belief in free markets and minimal state intervention – are all over the Great Recession we are currently experiencing. The home of efficient market hypothesis, rational expectations and Milton Friedman has dominated the economic universe of both Anglo-Saxon nations and international institutions since the 1970s. Bad ideologies sow the seeds of their own destruction. The structural imbalances that emerged as a result of neo-liberalism – low wage levels, inadequate investment, the wrong sort of investment, 'irrational exuberance' – were its undoing. Wages have fallen as a percentage of GDP since the 1980s. They were near the 60 per cent mark at the end of the 1970s, and are below 55 per cent of GDP now. According to the Centre for Economic Policy Research (CEPR), an economic thinktank, one in five UK workers is now on low wages (less than two-thirds of the national median wage). Among the advanced industrial nations, only the US has more than the UK, with one in four. The Resolution Foundation has shown how low- to middle-income earners (those between the tenth and fiftieth percentiles of income) saw their earnings share drop from 30 per cent of national income in 1977 to 22 per cent in 2009. This is even starker in the US context, where median wages have not increased since the mid-1970s. At least they were increasing in the UK until the early 2000s, but have remained flat since 2003. Wealth is concentrated in the hands of the few. The top 5 per cent of the population held 40 per cent of the total asset wealth in 2005. Those with low incomes are also asset poor – the bottom 50 per cent own just 7 per cent of all assets. Their wages are stagnant and so is their asset base.

Why does this matter? It certainly matters from a social justice perspective. However, it matters equally from an economic perspective. Low wages have an economic cost. They lead to indebtedness, instability, sap demand for goods and services, and lower productivity. None of this would have been predicted by the Chicago school. An economic ideology has been adopted – as a political choice – that is both destructive and unstable.

Open trade, technological advances, and low-wage competition from developing nations have eaten away at the good wage centre. The highly qualified – who are part of an international talent pool – have not only been insulated from this, but have secured ever greater rewards. The expectation of skills, even in those on relatively low wages, has increased as a result, which has led to the loss of employment completely for many without qualifications. The decline of manufacturing has meant the loss of the type of good, middle-income jobs that are essential to maintain a well-balanced economy.

The real challenge is to provide better wages for the majority. Attention has been focused on the extremes: the exorbitant earnings of those at the top, and a 'dependency culture' at the bottom. The easy but unsustainable and expensive answers are welfare reform and redistribution, but these will only go so far. Instead, the task is to ensure better wages. It is not just about how to make welfare work better; it is also about how better work can be created.

Instead of an economy driven by shared prosperity we have one characterised by inequality with financial wizardry filling the gaps. The consequence of this way of doing things is low savings rates, high levels of household debt, asset price bubbles, high-risk finance, followed by a crash, and then sovereign debt and stagnation. For a time the UK economy will, if we are lucky, gain from currency depreciation that makes our goods and services competitive, and exports will begin to lead us out of the present Great Recession. It should be said that Britain has largely been out of luck up to now, as the Eurozone is stagnant. Moreover, a similar pattern will resume until the next crash. Even if we are sensible enough next time to deflate asset price bubbles before they pop, we shall be back to stop–go economics and low average growth. The majority will face perpetual insecurity driven by indebtedness, low wage growth and periods of economic inactivity. And yet, there is another possible approach: build the institutions of a higher wage economy.

The political response on the left has tended to focus on inequality per se rather than low and stagnant wages. This has given the argument an ethereal and abstract tone and has made it difficult to grasp. Two major narratives – one on the social consequences of inequality and the other on the moral failings of the wealthy – have tended to dominate. Neither provides a cut-through argument for change that can be sustained.

Richard Wilkinson and Kate Pickett, in their popular book *The Spirit Level*, make a powerful case for an association between inequality (as described by Gini coefficients – a statistical measure) and a series of social and public health ills. Even if one accepts the strength of the raw correlation it is difficult not to consider that different cultures and traditions have different degrees of solidarity – with inequality being one of the consequences of this. As we have seen, Western European societies, including Scandinavian societies in general, are becoming less infused with an ethos of solidarity, so to rely on such a pitch elsewhere is politically daring. More solidaristic societies tend to spend more on high quality public services – and tolerate less inequality – and this is a key factor in their better social outcomes.

We could spend our time and political capital aiming to reduce a mathematical measure of inequality, by, for example, attacking the earnings of those at the top – thereby securing a 'better' Gini co-efficient. Encourage millionaires to move overseas and the objective could be met, but are we really suggesting that would improve the lot of those at the bottom as per the implications of the income inequality argument? In fact, it is worth a wager that it could make things far worse for them. Instead, why not concentrate on people's lived experience rather than some statistical abstraction? In other words, provide better services such as child care, and work out the policies and institutions that support better wages at the bottom and in the middle. Those who wish to target income inequality would propose many of the same solutions, but the explicit objective is important so as not to lead to wasted resources and political capital. The inequality analysis takes us back towards the orthodox social democratic perspective that is, as we saw in Chapter 2, more difficult to sustain in this social and political context. It may not even be necessary, as there are other ways and means that achieve even better outcomes.

Others on the left have pursued a politics of moralising populism aimed at elites. This includes the Occupy movement. It makes good headlines to go after those at the top. Away from shrill political discourse, there are two good practical reasons to question unreasonably high rewards. First, as the excellent High Pay Commission has shown, large pay disparities damage trust, and therefore productiv-ity within firms. The management guru Peter Drucker thought anything more than a 20:1 ratio of top to average pay to be destabilising, but ratios of 50:1 or even 100:1 are not unusual in FTSE 100 companies. There is enormous productive potential within a firm if senior management shows restraint and binds their remuneration to that of everyone within the firm. We shall re-visit the issue of trust in human organisations such as businesses in Chapter 7, but this is an issue for firms and their investors as well as the workers themselves and the government. Transparency, research, changes to company law, and challenge are the best antidotes to tackling market failure in this regard. The second good reason to intervene is when large bonuses create perverse incentives for financiers or chief executives to prioritise the short term over the long – this is as much an argument about structures of remuneration as it is about their levels.

What should concern us more is what causes high pay and the increasing inequality of recent decades – it is a *symptom* of deeper, more structural problems. Wages are depressed, which then allows senior executives, shareholders and other investors to secure the gains. The neo-liberal view is that this should be good for investment. The returns will be re-invested, thereby growing the pie and everyone benefits even if the gains are more unevenly spread: trickle-down.

Unfortunately, it is not working out that way. Duncan Weldon, an economist at the TUC, pointed out that:

> For decades in Britain the safest bet for a bank manager to make, and the easiest way to 'fail conventionally' as Keynes might have put it, has been to lend against property, either commercial or residential. Between December 1997 and December 2007, the pre-recession decade, UK banks advanced £1.3 trillion to UK residents as loans. Of this lending, 46 per cent went to financial companies, another 12 per cent to commercial real estate companies, and 23 per cent to mortgages for households. Very little found its way into the productive economy.

In fact, just 9 per cent of the investment between 1997 and 2007 found its way into the productive economy. It is little surprise that wages began to stagnate as a result. During the whole of this time people were increasing their borrowing; household debt increased by 28 per cent between 2000 and 2008.

Money was available because China, with its surpluses, was happy to invest in debtor nations such as the UK and the US. Meanwhile, financiers on Wall Street and in the City of London were finding ever more sophisticated ways of packaging up household debt in collateralised debt obligations, triple-A rated by the ratings agencies, enabling ever more risky loans to be extended. It was the sub-prime mortgage market that eventually popped. It could have just as easily been the UK housing market. The banking system was over-leveraged, over-exposed, and too interlinked to fail. The regulators failed to act pre-emptively. The governments of both the UK and the US were happy to ride the political wave of easy taxes and bubble popularity and also failed to act. Oppositions were silent. The Conservatives in the UK were ideologically predisposed to de-regulation and steeped in neo-liberal efficient-market hypothesis. The Democrats in the US were happy to see middle-class families invest in their homes. And the populace borrowed like there was no tomorrow.

Yes, we were all in it together – politically, economically and psychologically. We were locked into a world of false trickle-down, a weakening middle-class, low savings and high debt, and enormous risk. Simply going after inequality and high pay are inadequate solutions to this mess. Before we look to build a different type of economy there is the small matter of how we get out of the economic chaos caused by the collapse of the pre-bubble economy. Unfortunately, there is no easy, short-term way out.

The Economics of No Way Out

This recession should serve as a warning. We need new institutions to avoid just simply re-running the same distorted economic logic. It is in all our interests to do so: for business to align incentives with long-term value; for individuals to mitigate risk; and for governments to spread wealth and diminish the risk of economic catastrophe.

Before we get to the major task of rebuilding, however, there is an economy to fix. The UK is stuck between two orthodoxies. On the left, there are those who see the state as virtue itself, while on the right, there are those – including the chancellor, George Osborne – who see it as vice. But the state is neither virtue nor vice: it is a tool. It is necessary and it will be fundamental to building the institutions of the new economy – and challenging concentrations of power where they gather. It is neither all-powerful nor intrinsically destructive. It is available to be used carefully and wisely. For now, we need to use it to help get us out of an economic hole.

This economic debate oscillates merrily between those who reach for Keynes and those who turn to the neo-liberal school of economics. It is a fascinating theoretical debate – and the Keynesians have had a stronger case in the current circumstances. But what if both outlooks are limited in their ability to get us out of this mess in practical terms?

If there was a strong Keynesian route out, in all probability it is now off the table – politically at least. In a sense, while not conceding an inch on the theory, even the Nobel-Prize-winning and stylistically brutal Paul Krugman has admitted this defeat. In his 'Keynes and the Moderns' lecture in June 2011, he lamented: 'But watching the failure of policy over the past three years, I find myself believing, more and more, that this failure has deep roots – that we were in some sense doomed to go through this.' This is the problem. The preferred Keynesian response – debt-financed demand expansion – has hit three simultaneous buffers. The first was intellectual. The neo-liberal response has been robust. It is politically powerful as it has become deeply embedded in the institutional logic – central government, central banks and elite default wisdom – of major industrial powers such as the US, Germany and the UK. Keynesians have a serious rhetorical deficit. The rhetoric of 'borrow and spend' has even less chance of working in anxious times. That leads to the second limit – political. It is mighty difficult to get politicians, the media or voters to be relaxed about budget deficits of, say, 10 per cent of GDP or more for a prolonged period of time. Keynes never had a mobilisation strategy, and his modern-day disciples still do not have one. The objection of the German leadership to this route in either monetary or fiscal terms has been particularly intractable.

The third buffer is financial. This is the buffer that Keynesians began hitting as the Eurozone debt-financing crisis took hold. It is difficult to find people to fund deficits and debt on the scale that is required. It becomes more costly to do so and, what is more, ever greater levels of interest debt are stacked up. There is an important caveat here – if a country controls its own currency there is more room for manoeuvre. The UK is in that position and we shall revisit that point.

Credit-rating agencies are easy targets in all this. There is no doubting their incompetence given that they merrily AAA-rated sub-prime sewage for many years. Equally, there is no doubting their perverse incentives. They were paid by the (cleverer) people producing the sewage to rate it. Their interests were aligned with those of their clients': the investment banks and insurance companies producing the stinking effluent of toxic debt. This is all fair criticism but it does not get around the reality that large-scale, prolonged, debt-financed stimulus – as recommended by ultra-Keynesians – is just not on the table. It is, as Roberto Unger has argued, a 'vulgar' approach.

The sovereign debt markets want austerity and growth. So does George Osborne – in accordance with his bizarre creed of fiscal expansionism, which argued that growth would come as a natural consequence of austerity. This was nonsense. Growth has come to a shuddering halt and austerity has, in part, contributed to that. Worse austerity is yet to come. The bond markets are just as irrational as the British government: they seemingly have growth and austerity objectives that, as things stand, are mutually exclusive and make little sense.

The current Coalition government sees its inflexibility as a virtue. It is, of course, no such thing once you realise that growth and fiscal sustainability have a relationship. The Institute for Fiscal Studies (IFS) has calculated that a short-term stimulus of £9 billion would be achievable without harming medium-term fiscal consolidation. With a need for capital investments ranging from house building to energy supply to skills and human capital, there is an argument for bringing forward plans to invest. Instead, government investment is scheduled to fall year on year: it is easy to cut yet it is the last thing that should be cut. That is not austerity; it is masochism.

There are four sources of potential growth: exports, government expenditure, households and private businesses. Households are economically insecure and heavily indebted. Private business has no confidence. Our export markets are in a dire state. Fiscal restraint has eliminated government as a driver of growth. Essentially, the UK economy is a jet with all its engines stalled. Jonathan Portes of the National Institute of Economic and Social Research (NIESR) has been arguing for some time that very low interest rates would not be in jeopardy if the UK government decided to borrow more in the short term. In a floating exchange rate environment with control over the money supply you have more flexibility over fiscal policy.

Basically, holders of pounds sterling – many UK pension and investment funds among them – are fairly locked in, given other global investment opportunities and exchange rate risk. It is easy to get your capital out of Greece, Italy and Spain, as we have seen – hence negative interest rates on German Bunds. Moreover, there are not many AAA investment opportunities in the UK other than government bonds. Strangely, Eurozone risk and lack of confidence in the UK economy have worked in favour of a more active fiscal policy. The inflation risk is minor in the short term, given spare capacity – assuming the UK's productive base is not too damaged.

That does not give unlimited scope to fiscal activism. There may be an inflexion point that has not yet been spotted, or a currency crisis if things are seen to go too far. Also, the flipside of low growth/ low interest rate yield is the return of higher yields as growth returns. The UK is still going to have a great deal of interest to pay on its debts after growth returns. So it makes sense to invest in a way that is time-limited, brings forward investment that is needed in any case, and adds to the productive potential of the economy. The argument is given more force by analysis from Brad DeLong and Larry Summers in their seminal paper *Fiscal Policy in a Depressed Economy,* which argued that fiscal multipliers were higher in a depressed economy – that is, government expenditure has a bigger impact on growth in the current climate. This was further backed by the IMF's *World Economic Outlook* in October 2012, which came to a similar conclusion. There is a strong argument for bringing forward discretionary one-off capital investments – widely defined – with low interest rates available, and higher than supposed fiscal multipliers. Alongside this, current expenditure and tax rates will need to be controlled tightly.

There is more that can be done that is fiscally neutral: Ian Mulheirn of the Social Market Foundation (SMF) has, for example, argued for shifting resources from expenditure that has a 'low multiplier' (i.e. economic impact) such as pension tax relief for higher earners to activity that has a higher impact like capital investment. This is sensible.

So what about defaulting on debts? This is not currently a major concern for the UK, but after another two or three years of very low growth, barely moving deficits and political impotence, we may be looking at a very different picture. The problem with a default is that it is simply austerity by another name. The economy is starved of credit for a considerable time, but it can bounce back eventually and that is why this is an option. In the short term, though, the human and economic costs can be immense.

That leaves inflation as a final option. Essentially, this involves printing money – or permanent quantitative easing – to the extent that the dam bursts and prices start to rise as cheap credit, or even free money, floods the economy. Very serious economists such as Professor Kenneth Rogoff argue for the inflationary approach. He argues for inflation in the 4–6 per cent range for the US. The reality is that this is default by another means, which, as already argued, is austerity by another means. It may be a better way of defaulting and pursuing austerity, but do not think for a moment that it is a cost-free option – or necessarily controllable.

The problem with inflation is that we do not get to 'choose' the inflation rate: we can aim for 6 per cent but find ourselves with 15 per cent. It corrodes the income of those who live off their savings and of the poor, whose wages fail to keep up with price rises. It might also affect the flow of credit after a time, as unpredictable inflation makes loan valuation difficult. In reality, this is a strategy that must be treated with caution. Besides, independent monetary authorities such as the Bank of England have a legal duty not to permit this course.

So ultra-Keynesianism has hit the buffers; austerity is failing but is supported by the major bond players such as Pimco (while they also claim to support growth strategies); default has horrendous short-term costs; and inflation is a highly risky and costly strategy. A capital-intensive stimulus is sensible – the opposite of the Coalition approach. But retrenchment will have to be rapid as soon as growth returns, as interest rates will start to rise again at that point.

The Autumn Financial Statement of November 2011 outlined in full the dire economic situation that Britain will face for much of the coming decade. Squeezed living standards, high borrowing, cuts in public services, the shrinking of the welfare state, ongoing uncertainty and high unemployment will define the 2010s: the austerity decade. More worryingly, there is a greater chance that things will get worse rather than better.

George Osborne has made the situation worse – unnecessarily so. Cutting short-term programmes and investments such as the Future Jobs Fund and Building Schools for the Future, which do not add to the structural current deficit, was myopic. Once his model of economic recovery – driven by exports and private sector investment – was faltering he should have intervened. He did not do so, and therefore the economy double-dipped into recession. We are all paying a price as a consequence.

The choreography of the party political dance is for the Tory–Lib Dem government to blame the last Labour government for all the country's economic ills, and for Labour to blame the government for the austerity situation. The reality is far more complex. The government bears some, but by no means all, of the blame. Value Added Tax (VAT) increases took the pace out of economic recovery (though one of the 2.5 per cent increases was under Labour in January 2010) from Spring 2010. However, a strong stance on fiscal consolidation reduced the risk of government debt in the eyes of investors; world oil prices and food prices that increased by 30 per cent in a year were also a drag on growth; and the Eurozone crisis reduced confidence – 50 per cent of UK trade is with the EU. Nonetheless, the Office for Budget Responsibility's (OBR) revised forecasts made the economic choices clear: between austerity minor and austerity major. And every time the forecasts are revisited, the challenge seems to be prolonged as growth is underwhelming.

Labour's proposed short-term stimulus focusing on investment and jobs is a reasonable gamble to take, but not if it was to become a permanent stimulus, and only if it also involved cuts in current and recurrent spending alongside the stimulus. It could only be a short bridge to recovery and little more. Persistent borrowing at around 10 per cent of GDP is just not feasible, particularly when so much has been borrowed already. Even under current projections, Britain will be spending around the same amount on interest as on the entire prehigher education budget by around 2014–15; and interest is likely to overtake education a year or two later.

It was in response to this debate that Cooke *et al.* wrote *In the Black Labour: Why Fiscal Conservatism and Social Justice Go Hand-in-hand*, which was published by Policy Network in 2011 and created something of a stir in Labour circles. Its core argument was that a reputation for fiscal responsibility was fundamental to any party aspiring to national leadership. What is more, by accepting that there are fiscal constraints, it provokes a more creative and less resource-heavy approach to advancing social justice. *In the Black Labour* advocated an 'enterprise' state over a 'welfare' state, which is, naturally, the approach adopted by this book, as will be seen in later chapters. This means that those interventions that create future growth should be prioritised over those that simply redistribute resources – unless they are properly funded and politically sustainable.

The Autumn Financial Statement in 2011 contained an HM Treasury calculation that the Darling plan, which had hitherto been the Labour Party's defined approach, would mean an extra £100 billion of borrowing over the course of this Parliament, with an extra £21 billion in 2014–15. The IFS green budget in February 2012 calculated it to be even greater. It was right for March 2010 but has long been overtaken by events. While the Conservatives and the Liberal Democrats avoided defining a clear deficit-reduction plan prior to the election, it is unlikely that Labour will be able to get away with a similar omission.

A fiscally sustainable and economically sensible alternative is needed. There must be a degree of flexibility: economic forecasting is far from an exact science. A sustainable alternative is fundable without a greater risk of default, it can maintain public confidence, and does not keep replacing large volumes of future services and investment with interest repayments. The country cannot continue to spend the future on the present. A sensible policy responds to the economic needs of the moment – some stimulus, particularly high-quality capital investments, is advisable. However, it cannot be of a level that would provoke a Bank of England response, which would be counter-productive. In other words, fiscal responsibility recognises the real constraints that are facing the government. Neither ultra-Keynesianism (too risky) nor extreme austerity (too (sado-)masochistic) fall into this category. All that is left is to maintain a grip on current public expenditure while seeking new taxes to support this tight control of the current deficit – and a mansion tax would seem like a logical step.

The economic ideas at the policy-makers' disposal are either wrong, as is the case with George Osborne's 'expansionary fiscal contraction', or just not practical, as is the case with ultra-Keynesianism. In the short term, it will be a case of doing the best that can be done within very tight constraints – especially if that involves growth-enhancing capital investment. In the medium term, it is about erecting the institutions to promote the types of economic behaviour that can support more sustainable growth shared by greater numbers of people.

Higher Wages; More and Better Investment

Two baristas serve in a coffee shop. One is pretty miserable and inattentive. She serves 50 coffees per hour. Her colleague is brilliant with people, and customers love her. Yet she too serves 50 coffees per hour. Who is the more productive barista? The answer, of course, is that they are equally productive. As a result, they both receive the same wage of £7.50 per hour. One of the baristas is adding value to the coffee shop. Customers develop an attachment and keep coming back. The other is adding little, and may even be subtracting value (it may be better just to put a self-service coffee machine there instead). But in this scenario they are equally productive and have the same incentive – their wage – to perform to this standard.

The reality is that the friendly barista's additional value is extracted by the brand and is paid to senior managers and investors – they cream off the surplus. This same process happens across much of the service economy – or at least it does with lower-paid workers. They have little incentive to improve the standard of their service other than the threat of dismissal. More qualified workers, especially those with high-level qualifications, skills and experience are more immune to this, and may even achieve greater earnings rewards than their measured productivity. This process is one of the major factors behind the low-wage vortex at the bottom end of the earnings spectrum and rocketing rewards at the top.

These effects are even more consequential in an economy less dependent on manufacturing, with weaker trade unions and weak labour market regulation. Manufacturing represented 35 per cent of economic output in 1960; it is now about 13 per cent or so as a proportion of GDP. Manufacturing was unionised, so there was a back-stop to low pay. Its outputs were rational – productivity could be measured in 'units' rather than intangibles such as value (though quality was also an under-measured element). As a consequence, pay reflected value more closely through the wage distribution. It is very different at the lower end of the service economy, in which approximately 80 per cent of people are now employed.

As the Israeli management guru Eli Goldratt put it: 'Tell me how you will measure me and I will tell you how I will behave.' So we need to learn how to measure more of the right things – real value, contribution to long-term growth, impact on the natural environment, and human capability. The traditional model focuses on quantity of product; there needs to be a deeper appreciation of quality as an aspect of value in a service-based environment. Once we have understood how to measure more of the right things, then, as governments, individuals and companies, we will need to recognise how it is in our own interest to pursue them.

Services find it more difficult to transmit 'productivity' increases into improved wages. In 1966, William Baumol and William Bowen demonstrated in *Performing Arts* how there was a productivity lag ('cost disease') in the performing arts sector, which meant that it could not keep pace with productivity increases elsewhere in the economy. A performance of an opera could be completed more efficiently with fewer performers or by taking less time over it. However, would this 'productivity' increase be desirable? Baumol and Bowen's observations on productivity and the performing arts can be applied to a range of service-based industries.

Businesses and, indeed, national accounts are still focused on tangible, output-oriented measures – quantitative measures. What would be expected in such a situation is that those with market power – senior managers and shareholders – would capture the generation of surpluses within the firm, and that is precisely what has been experienced. We are seeing a lag of service wages. Neo-liberal ideology under the Thatcher/Major governments broke unions, re-cast the rules of finance, abolished institutions such as the wages councils that maintained pay, and failed to direct investment towards UK manufacturing. This matters because wages enable people to meet their own needs. It also skews business incentives: they are rewarding outputs rather than value. So this industrial age mentality harms both workers *and* businesses, as there is a mismatch between real value and incentives. Smart businesses have realised this. As Diane Coyle argued in *The Economics of Enough*: 'Profit-oriented capitalism has always drawn on support from other institutional values. The policies of the past thirty years have lost their anchor in values outside the market.'

The UK's economic institutions are either under-developed, have failed to adapt or simply do not exist. Coyle articulates a pluralism of values, and on that basis argues for a balanced economy that allows for the achievement of a mixture of fairness, efficiency and freedom while being honest about the contradictions between them. The easiest trick to pull off is to say that fairness equals efficiency equals freedom, and that's the 'trilemma' resolved. Generally, when things are too good to be true they *are*. There are choices to be made. To create a prosperous and sustainable economy in the future, it will be necessary to build institutions that transfer wealth and power to the majority, but this may be at the loss of some efficiency. It is necessary to consider how much and in what ways this can be minimised.

Government-imposed minimum wages and living wages can address some of this problem at the low-wage end where they do not destroy employment, but the fundamental issue remains – highly 'productive' workers can be either systematically underpaid or not invested in properly, thereby decreasing the real value they offer. It's a vicious circle: low pay means low investment, which means lower value and fewer profits. So, many service companies, including even such giants as Tesco, are starting to feel the pinch as a focus on holding wages down creates a poorer service which in turn hits profits.

There is a higher road to business success. A focus on creating higher wages, greater value and better jobs will mean challenges to public as well as private services. Carried out correctly, it can improve quality, as work that adds real value can begin to be rewarded. The end of this story is that, because so many are underpaid and under-invested in, there is an insufficiency of demand, which means that the coffee shop introduced at the start of this section does not have enough customers. Higher pay can drive more investment, support jobs, incentivise decent training and increase profits in a competitive economy. Henry Ford understood the circularity of a successful economy – his workers were also his consumers, so he paid them a decent relative wage for their work.

Zeynep Ton has been studying 'bad jobs' in retail empirically since the 1990s. She has found that the assumed trade-off between wages and prices is a myth. Studying large retailers such as QuikTrip, Trader Joe's (of whom more in Chapter 7), Costco in the US and Mercadona in Spain, she has found that the mooted wages–price trade-off applies only at a certain level: and most retail workers are paid far below that level. Employees of these stores have higher pay, better training, higher benefits and more convenient schedules than their counterparts.

Employees at Costco earn about 40 per cent more than at its largest competitor, Walmart's Sam's Club. Staff turnover is less, employees are better trained, more focused on providing a good service, committed to eliminating waste, and they make micro-decisions proactively that improve the process, just as workers in Toyota's factories have done for decades. Research by Fisher, Netessine and Krishnan has demonstrated that for a $1 increase in payroll, a store could see between a $4 and $28 increase in sales. Imagine that effect across an entire economy. Ton argues that her findings are also relevant for hospitals, restaurants, banks and hotels – and, one could suppose, coffee shops also. Ton recently wrote in the *Harvard Business Review*:

> Highly successful retail chains … not only invest in store employees but also have the lowest prices in their industries, solid financial performance, and better customer service than their competitors. They have demonstrated that, even in the lowest-price segment of retail, bad jobs are not a cost-driven necessity but a choice.

Diane Coyle argues for measurements that take into account more than material wealth but do not ignore it; the right mix of values arrived at through open discourse and dialogue; and the right institutions that prioritise the long-term over the short-term without sacrificing too much of the latter in favour of the former. That, for her, is the economics of enough. Building on this approach, it will be necessary to change the way we understand economic value. Government can take the lead in this by, for example, measuring the stock of human capability in the economy. It could ask firms to report on the contribution they make to their workers' capabilities. As significant economic benefit comes from investment in people, it is conceivable that investors will start to take note of the firms that exercise good practice when it comes to rewarding and developing the skills of their employees. The government can provoke this debate and help us to understand how good practice can be measured and communicated. It can also begin to do so with regard to public sector workers, though with constrained resources this could take some time.

The underpinning element of a shift to how the UK runs its economy, to the basic logic underpinning economic activity, is an ideological shift. Inspired by neo-liberal economics, the UK economy has followed a credit-led economic approach. In such an economy, the good times can be very good but structural economic weakness – low wages, high debt, and inappropriate and periodic under-investment – soon assert themselves. The other major model that is pursued in the global economic context is the export-led model. This has far more resilience, but the problem is that not everyone can pursue it simultaneously (the world will remain a closed economy until the trans-galactic trade routes have been established!).

Instead, now is the chance to put credit-led 'growth' to one side and seek an economy with higher wages, and more and better investment. The economic ideology that has been dominant since the 1980s would see this as madness. It would create unemployment and inflation, and result in lost output. This cannot be disregarded, but the gains from pursuing a very different approach, if done sensibly, would be considerable and shared more evenly.

Scores of studies, collated by Servaas Storm and C. W. M. Naastepad for the *International Journal of Labour Research* in 2011, demonstrate that an increase of wages also result in increased productivity. As average wages increase, demand picks up, and this raises the usage of existing capacity. Higher wages increase demand as well as expectations of profit. These then incentivise new investments in organisation, skills and technology. Studies in countries ranging from France to the US, the UK and Germany, have shown the positive productivity impact of higher wages. Averaging across six major economies/economic blocs, the Storm and Naastepad collation of available data shows a 0.38 per cent increase in productivity for every 1 per cent increase in wages. Higher wages increase demand and therefore also the utilisation of labour. They also encourage investment in labour-saving and operations-improving technologies and techniques.

So what is the catch? There are two, in fact. There is a possibility that profits could fall. This is subjective, however. Storm and Naastepad find that in relatively closed economies where there is a stronger impact of wage increases, the combined impact of higher profits from stronger demand and labour productivity increases means that actually there is no impact on profits. In more open economies such as the UK, however, there could be a profit impact that is more significant – about an 0.4 per cent decline for every 1 per cent increase in wages. But remember, this model leads to less indebtedness and less reliance on risky financial innovation. Because the benefits of this reduced potential volatility are diffuse rather than concentrated, this suggests the need for some government, as well as firm-level, intervention. Greater stability would thereby be a corrected market failure. It would enable some of the volatility to be taken out of the system in comparison to the current credit-led approach.

Second, given that this is unlikely to happen spontaneously, it may be necessary for there to be a degree of intervention. Doesn't intervention in free labour markets cause unemployment? It can do – but only at very high levels of intervention according to the empirical evidence. OECD data shows that the three countries with the lowest employment protection among advanced economies are Canada, the US and the UK. Their unemployment rates were 7.6 per cent, 8.3 per cent and 8.4 per cent, respectively, in February 2011. Three countries representative of moderate levels of protection are Germany, Denmark and the Netherlands. Their unemployment rates were 6.8 per cent for Germany, and 6 per cent for the other two countries. So, in tough economic times they are performing well. The low regulation countries can perform better in good times – volatility is one of their characteristics.

However, when we look at countries with a high degree of regulation – for example France, Portugal and Spain – we then see unemployment rates that are much higher: 10 per cent, 14 per cent and 23.3 per cent, respectively. So a high degree of employment regulation is associated with high unemployment but a moderate degree is not, and indeed may help protect employment and raise productivity. Germany reduced its degree of employment regulation from high to moderate during the 2000s and its unemployment rate declined significantly as a result. The gains of moving to a low level would at best be negligible, and in all probability negative. It would certainly become a more unstable economy.

There is also a major public sector dimension to this argument. When controlled for education, age, region and qualifications, the IFS has shown a public sector pay premium of 8.3 per cent. This increases to a much wider gap for the lower paid, for women and for those in less well-off regions. The neo-liberal response – and George Osborne is seeking to pursue this – would be to reduce public sector wages. But this would simply compound the problem in a further race to the bottom. It would hit women hard and depress already suffering regions. It is precisely the wrong response. Instead, it is worth looking to how to ensure better pay overall. Local flexibility can be introduced into the public sector but the economic impacts are great so this should be done over time. Closer alignment of pay with public service outcomes is also sensible as a public service reform strategy.

Living wages, local wage agreements and new measures of productivity to help inform corporate decision-making are the sorts of reform that will start to bend the economy towards a higher wage environment. This requires a shift towards what Peter Hall and Daniel Gingerich term a co-ordinated market economy as opposed to a liberal market economy. Interestingly, in their 2007 paper 'Varieties of Capitalism and Institutional Complementarities' they find little difference in overall performance between the two types of economy, but the co-ordinated market economies have kept trade union membership up, wage bargaining strong, CEO salaries rises relatively low, and inequality at a much lower rate. Once more, there is a high and low road to economic success.

Some additional regulation of wage levels will be necessary, but this is better achieved by market-sensitive institutions, not by the state in general. In particular sectors there could be scope for work associations – new local institutions that are designed to analyse where there is economic benefit without significant harm from increasing wages. A number of stakeholders would take part in decisions made by these associations and these decisions could have the force of law if certain employers did not comply. They would be regional in scope. The incentive for employers is that this could be a means of preventing free-riding and encourage the pooling of resources for training and so on.

In both the public and private sectors, work associations could improve outcomes for workers, services and businesses alike. The impact on employment and businesses' chances of survival are factors that cannot be ignored, as is the affordability of any public service. So to begin with it may apply mainly to sectors with larger employers. These challenges will be treated by opponents as deal-breakers. They were articulated as such when the minimum wage was introduced. It proved to be special pleading. It will be necessary to distinguish between such pleading and genuine business concerns; and that is best explored in trust-based dialogue rather than through onerous legislation if at all possible.

The imposition of a living wage could be one sanction that could be applied in the absence of co-operation. These work associations can be facilitated by national, local and regional government bodies and backed by legal authority, albeit designed to enable both workers and employers to find a better relationship and confront free-riders on the system. They would have a statutory requirement not to damage employment. When firms are subject to international competition there can be a strong argument for keeping wage levels competitive, but this is also achieved by increasing productivity (output per worker) via investment and innovation. However, more than four-fifths of the UK economy is in service provision – which is far less exposed to international competition than manufacturing. Special care should be taken with small firms.

In time, these work associations could develop a role in promoting training of workers – and skills providers would have a place in the associations. They might also develop a role in supplementary contributory unemployment or sickness insurance. Trade unions were key players in the industrial economy. They have not been able to transfer this influence to the private service economy: market-sensitive institution-building by a smart state at the local and national level will be crucial. This is very different from the corporatist bargaining of the industrial age.

There may be sense in reducing employers' national insurance contributions when they increase wages as an incentive. As they do, the state will reduce the amount of tax credits it pays out. It is perverse to tax firms only to pay that tax back to their workers on low pay in the form of tax credits. What is more, the relationship with tax credits is between the state and the individual, with the employer simply acting as the intermediary. Is it not better to have a higher wage for the individual so that the employer has the incentive to invest in them, thus increasing their value to the firm? So tax credits not only subsidise low pay, they also indirectly discourage investment in people. Higher wages are better for business, individuals, the economy, public finances, savings, stability and the country's economic future.

Further tax incentives to encourage productive businesses to invest are also necessary, as are new institutions designed to put both debt and equity finance into high-growth potential firms. Tax relief should apply to human as well as fixed capital. Investment in people and their skills should be reclassified as an investment rather than a cost, and tax credits and further subsidies attached to it – as long as the qualifications were portable, of a high quality and constituted a genuine upskilling. Many current apprenticeships fall short in this regard. All this will help to raise productivity and value-creation alongside wage increases dampening any potential price rises. It will also limit the inflationary impact.

Interventions to promote true competition in major sectors of the economy could also keep a lid on price rises – this applies especially in sectors such as retail or utilities, where the market is domestic rather than international. People with higher wages will have a greater ability to build up their asset base, and this will increase the pool of capital for productive investment.

All this takes time, though. The direct negative impacts on profits may be immediate; but the indirect positive impacts could take longer. The shift from a Keynesian welfarist to a neo-liberal economy took a couple of decades in reality. The point is to act with care and attention, and to persuade business of a case for change. It is in its interests too, if the government gets this right. It requires a Niebuhresque sense of care and determination not to overreach. It is likely to take a decade or so at least to assemble a critical mass of institutions – all the more reason to start now. What it would also mean is a more rational basis on which to plan public services, as there is a stronger tax base upon which to sustain services – and less being diverted into tax credits. People will have more incentives to work, as better wages will remove benefits traps.

The UK cannot just become like Germany, Japan or the US, because their cultures and institutions vary considerably. We can learn from them all but only in the context of the modern UK economy. The institutional innovations suggested here have been drawn from some of the best practice across the world, but the lessons are to be applied in the largely service-based economy of the UK. Principles are the most transposable things and these should underpin new institutions. What is more, there is no going back to the economy as it was. Globalisation is not simply about production; it is also about technology and expertise transfer. As a result, winning back what has been lost is almost impossible. Manufacturing should be promoted wherever possible because it does provide good jobs, with wages that rise in accordance with measurable productivity. But this has its limits. For those in the services sector whose value is less easily measured, institutions need to be built that enable the situation to change, and create understanding about how it is in the interests of all of us to do just that.

A largely service-based economy in the midst of a technological revolution in the context of intense global competition, austerity, social anxiety and ecological threat creates a very different set of challenges compared with those faced by an old-style industrial economy. If the nice barista is to get her just reward, if the 'squeezed middle' are to get theirs, we need a smart economy of shared reward. How we are measured determines how we behave, and at present the right things are not being measured. As a consequence, we are in an economy of both too much and not enough. With new and better institutions we will have a better shared and sustainable future.

Building Better

Creating new institutions to drive economic change is a project that will take longer than one Parliament. Political culture is shaped by the day-to-day and the instantaneous. It is just as adrenaline-driven as share-trading. Yet what is required is precisely the opposite: institutions that create long-term value. Later chapters will explore further how to create a political coalition for change, which will require a deft response to social, cultural and economic change combined with a different type of political argument and organisation. The concern at the heart of all this, however, is how to create enduring social justice. There is an economic logic to the analysis. Underpinning this logic is a set of ideas – a new political economy.

British capitalism is entrepreneurial. It is dynamic. Its innovations – in biotechnology and pharmaceuticals, energy, semi-conductors, high-end manufacturing (including aviation and motor vehicles), design, technology, the creative industries, business and financial services, higher education, science and research – should be sources of pride. It is easy in the current economic context to forget this. The major problems the UK is facing are a result of risk and low wages for too many. If these issues were addressed it would become both more stable and more productive. It would also be more socially just.

A new fiscal approach is needed immediately. The Office for Budget Responsibility (OBR) should have enhanced independence to assess the government's fiscal approach, as argued for in the report *In the Black Labour*. It should be able to assess alternative policies for their impact on fiscal outcomes – though its models do need to be refreshed as it has had to adjust its forecasts on a very regular basis. To increase the independence of the body even further, it could become attached to Parliament as a UK version of the US Congressional Budget Office (CBO). It would measure fiscal policy in the context of defined rules: running a current budget surplus when the economy is growing. Long-term confidence relies on sound long-term fiscal rules and institutions.

Beyond that, clear priorities are necessary. Jeffrey Sachs, in *The Price of Civilization*, has argued for shifting the US budget towards long-term investments and an expansion of social provision. This is also necessary in the context of the UK. Sachs does not suggest doing this by ignoring the budget deficit. In fact, he argues that both stimulus spending and unaffordable tax cuts are 'gimmicks that distract us from the deeper reforms that are needed in our society'. He proposes a reduction in the deficit in the US to 2 per cent by 2015.

Sachs argues for tax increases: a new value added tax, a reversal of the Bush cuts, and a new wealth tax. He seeks to divert spending from bombs to roads and child care. The focus is the long term. His case for new welfare outlays reflects a different baseline for the US compared to the UK. Overall, though, he makes a powerful case for institutional, political and economic reform. It is an approach that influenced the Obama Budget of 2012: investment and efficiency, with tax increases for the wealthy and deficit consolidation.

In all of this there is a clear role for the state. It is a fashionable – and wrong – view of the right that the public sector does not 'create' jobs. It absolutely does. Tyler Cowen is one economist who falls into this trap in his book *The Great Stagnation*. He is sceptical about government investment and sees public expenditure almost as a false economy. He also makes some pretty debatable claims, such as this one on the stimulus: 'Replacing private debt with public debt won't restore prosperity because it doesn't create anything.'

If the stimulus – or government – is used to build roads, bridges, renewable energy, transport infrastructure, housing, schools or universities and so on, then clearly something is being created. The production horizon is being raised. Public-sector workers do produce services that have measurable value – why would a private refuse collection service represent real job creation and a publicly provided one would not? So, to describe the state almost as not a real economy seems perverse. The fact that it is funded by tax revenues is neither here nor there – unless the government was raising tax, and then burying the cash at the bottom of the ocean. Those same tax revenues are themselves supported by government services and investments; it is a mutual dependency.

What is even more perverse is that, in trying to restore budgetary balance, it has been capital investment that has been cut. Such investment, as long as it is of a high quality, increases economic growth. Under Coalition plans, net investment will decline from £38.6 billion in 2010–11 to £20 billion in 2015–16. This is crazy, when investment could support the economy in the short term, raise productive potential in the medium term and help to pay down the deficit over time. The country needs a better digital, transport, energy, educational and health infrastructure as well as more houses to help alleviate pressure on house prices in the future. And it needs further investment in skills. Yet these are precisely the types of things that are potentially being cut – notwithstanding a multi-billion-pound national infrastructure 'plan'. Again, the solution is institutional: dealing with capital investments in a different way.

First, the government has to re-define what is investment and what is not. For example, investment in higher and further education that genuinely adds to the productive potential of the economy should be re-classified as capital investment. This will mirror the way such expenditure would be dealt with at the level of a firm. Second, the actual impact of different types of investment – such as investment in transport over digital infrastructure – for every pound spent should be calculated and published. Third, fiscal rules should concentrate on current rather than capital expenditure; when the economy stagnates, capital investment plans should be brought forward. An overall target for national debt is needed to prevent undue risk to public debt financing and to maintain headroom should future fiscal interventions be required in the event of a sudden slump. An annual statement on the investments that the state is making and their impact on future growth could be published. Bonds to finance that investment portion of government debt in particular are attractive to pension funds and the like: they would be available at a low rate as long as the overall picture was stable.

Finally, establishing a national infrastructure bank to support large-scale public investment is a no-brainer. The UK is already a shareholder in a public investment bank, the European Investment Bank (EIB), in which it has a 14 per cent stake. It makes a range of investments in the UK, particularly with regard to energy projects, though it also contributes to housing projects, car makers, banks and a range of other investments. In total, the EIB raises around €70 billion a year. An arms-length capital investment bank with a government capital reserve could have a similar ability to raise AAA-grade finance. It would prove significantly less costly than the private finance initiative (PFI) to build new infrastructure. The risk would be minimal for investors, as the government would pay for the investments over time out of its current spending. For example, it would lease back a new hospital built to its specifications but funded through capital raised by the national investment bank – but at rates that did not attract a huge interest rate premium, as was the case with the PFI. The Obama administration intends to create such an institution in the US.

These investments would be attractive to those who require long-term and stable returns, such as pension funds. The risk would have to be quantified, but in a reasonable way – HM Treasury is effectively underwriting the bank, but not everything it borrows would be at risk. It does not make sense to count every pound borrowed as contingent expenditure, as HM Treasury rules currently insist. The bank's borrowing from long-term saving and its returns from long-term (mainly) state expenditure would be aligned, further reducing risk. The objective is to increase the level of capital investment for any given fiscal situation. It must be a low-risk institution for that to happen – it must be AAA and infrastructure-focused.

A long-term investment logic requires a pool of savings from which to draw. During the last few years, as median earnings were frozen, the UK savings ratio plunged to lows of below 2 per cent – whereas the average since 1970 has been over 7 per cent. This means that the pool of domestic long-term savings available to invest is low. The introduction of the National Employment Savings Trust (NEST) in phases from October 2012 will create a new pool of pension savings. The 'nudge' of auto enrolment is a neat way of getting people to save without coercion. Public sector pension funds – for example, the Local Government Pension Scheme – might well also be attracted by certain returns over the long term.

Alongside this, there is a case for short-term approved products that have more flexibility. Schemes that allow individuals to invest pre-tax income in low-risk savings products would be one such incentive. If they subsequently were to draw on the savings, the amount they withdrew could have the tax deducted if the amount saved had been in the account for less than ten years, say. Again, this has to be a long-term policy. To implement these changes too quickly could harm an incipient recovery, however: a St Augustine-esque chastity but not quite yet. These pools of savings provide potential investments in the national infrastructure bank.

Promoting savings and investment will only work if the risk levels of the financial system are reduced. The UK has only partly gone down the road of real reform of its banking system (it is a major shareholder in two of the biggest banks, so it is actually conflicted when it comes to reform). The Independent Commission on Banking (ICB) laid out the case for a fundamental reassessment of the UK's financial sector, but fell somewhat short of that. In certain respects, it is like a flood risk report providing evidence that only a 20-foot-high concrete wall will protect a town from flooding but then actually only recommending the installation of sandbags. The flood risk is ever-present and remains, as the report states: 'There is an inherent uncertainty about the nature of the next financial crisis.'

So we are not dealing with 'if' here; we are dealing with 'when'. This statement, buried in section 4.173 of the ICB interim report, follows a long section on the need to protect the competitiveness of the UK's financial sector. It provides jobs and £50 billion of tax revenues, after all (though £10 billion or so are from the retail operation, which presumably is not going to be off-shored any time soon). That is not insignificant. As we have discovered, it is not a cost- and risk-free income; in fact, it is highly risky and costly. At the time of writing, the UK has domestic banking assets of more than four times its GDP – only Sweden, Switzerland and the Netherlands are similarly exposed. As the ICB has warned: 'Had the asset quality of UK banks turned out to be as bad as that in Ireland, the hit to the UK's fiscal position would have been significantly worse than it was.'

This is the real issue regarding the position of the UK on the re-regulation of its financial system – the traditional defence of the UK financial sector's competitive position as an unarguable good is still given too much weight. The ICB was criticised for not doing enough to promote further competition (and the UK's banking sector *is* mono-cultured and uncompetitive), a fair accusation. More can also be done to separate casino from utility banking. Such measures as there were in this regard were watered down even more by the Chancellor of the Exchequer. The worry is an even greater one: the UK economy and UK taxpayers may not be able to sustain the risk of a financial sector this large at all – even with better regulation. Actually, 'competitiveness' might be economically calamitous.

Despite the reforms to the structure of banking, its regulation and the regime that is responsible for it, that cannot be the end of the story. Once the current banking reforms are in place and the current crisis has passed, it will be necessary to revisit these questions repeatedly. Financial risk is currently assessed by the Bank of England's Financial Policy Committee in a financial stability report produced twice a year. In addition, the ICB's report should be revisited periodically by an external panel of experts so that a comprehensive assessment of systemic risk, structure and competition is undertaken. The financial system contains terrifying levels of risk from the perspective of UK plc. Monitoring that and the entire regulatory framework is necessary.

With a safer banking system, the encouragement of greater levels of saving, a new way of accounting for government investment based on its actual economic impact, and a national infrastructure bank for low-risk, long-term investments in place, some of the foundational institutional changes will be complete. These are national-level innovations next to new institutions that increase wages and move the UK towards a wages- and investment-led economy.

Ultimately, though, the purpose of these interventions is not dry economics. They are about enabling people to live enriched lives with more control over their own destiny. These changes are simply the means to that end. Umair Haque argues forcefully in *Betterness: Economics for Humans* that we should seek a commercial environment that is 'rich with relationships, ideas, emotion, health and vigor, recognition and contribution, passion and fulfillment, and great accomplishment and enduring achievement, exactly what 'business', 'output', and 'product' seem so achingly deficient at producing'.

Future prosperity relies on 'getting out of business and in to betterness'. What we now need is a new political economy that reaches beyond utility, profit, efficiency, output and productivity, and becomes a vehicle – through better institutions – to enhance both people's capabilities and their freedom. A more local institutional and business reform agenda to achieve these ambitious ends will be discussed in Chapter 7. It has been important to establish the economic case first. Higher wages will lead to a stronger and more sustainable economy, as we have seen – as long as they are supported by pro-saving, pro-investment institutions, and competition.

There is a big argument that needs to be made prior to these interventions. Value in a service-based economy needs to be better understood. The purpose of this would be to move away from industrial-age calculations of productivity. A parallel set of national accounts is needed to outline the reality of public-sector productivity and increases in value in the service sector. These accounts would assess the long-term asset investments made in human capital. It is clearly absurd that an orchestra playing Beethoven at double pace, a teacher having a class size doubled, or our barista being replaced by a self-service machine would all be productivity increases. In reality, they would mean lower quality and less enjoyment, less personalised learning, and the loss of the human enjoyment of going to a coffee shop.

Having developed this parallel set of accounts, a real national discussion could be had. Businesses would be able to think about their dealings in a different way and reward those who were generating real value. The government would be able to invest in public services in a way that improved outcomes even if it did not seem to increase outputs proportionately. Our gregarious barista might get a decent living wage; and her colleague might be encouraged to shape up. For the economy, it will mean greater efficiency – the right skills and people will be invested in – and more stability as a result of higher wages, savings and therefore investment. Over time we would move away from the neo-liberal orthodoxy of low wages, instability, under-valued people and ever greater inequality. The result would be a political economy that worked with people rather than treating them as disposable commodities.

Back in the intellectual fount of neo-liberal economics, the University of Chicago, it has clearly been a humbling time for the traditional elements of the Department of Economics. Those converted on the road to Damascus include Richard Posner, who has re-discovered – or more accurately, discovered – *The General Theory of Employment, Interest and Money* by John Maynard Keynes, as many economists have done. From a committed belief in neo-liberalism, Posner now sees the global financial crash as 'a failure of capitalism'. He now suggests that the term 'Chicago school' should be 'retired' (as reported by John Cassidy in the *New Yorker*).

Another Chicago University economist (though based in the University's Booth School of Business), Raghuram Rajan, economic adviser to the prime minister of India, Manmohan Singh, and former chief economist of the IMF, argues that inequality and imbalance were at the heart of the crisis. As Rajan puts it: 'The US financial sector thus bridged the gap between an overconsuming and overstimulated United States and an underconsuming, understimulated rest of the world.'

Neo-liberalism was supposed to make the market more 'efficient' but in fact exposed it to calamitous breakdown. This came in the form of the credit crunch and subsequent recession. In both the UK and the US, as wages stagnated, there was a need not only for individuals to borrow more but also a macro-economic incentive to over-stimulate. Governments cannot help holding on to the good times a little longer – there is an electoral premium to be siphoned. Rajan sees the crash as an almighty confluence of politically perverse incentives and neo-liberalism. Political and financial moral hazard became an explosive gas, and a fuse was lit in 2008.

Both the left and the right are culpable. The right, with as little serious intervention as possible, will be happy to see a return to business as usual. With a minor change here and there, they basically accept the neo-liberal argument. The left will be tempted once again to tolerate excess as it justifies ever more spending on public services and redistribution. Neither is sustainable.

The institutional logic of the economy needs reform. We have to respond to the economic crisis with a sound economic strategy – beyond neo-liberalism and 'vulgar Keynesianism'. The left's political challenges, however, are not simply economic. There is also social change to consider, as we saw in the previous chapter. Moreover, there is the rise of cultural identity as a political force. Economics and culture intersect, clash and combine. As people are buffeted on the waves of economic change they are left disorientated and disconcerted. Class incoherence has made this more acute. Where class once stood almost alone, cultural identity now stands alongside it, and as people feel a sense of culture and economic threat this can mutate in many different ways – some terrifying but all of political consequence. Fear and anxiety replace hope and security. We are engaged in both an economic and a cultural struggle. The question is whether and how we will build a common future out of this struggle. Cultural identity and anxiety add extra urgency to this moment of economic crisis.

CHAPTER 4

The Force of Cultural Identity

The Black Watch was an Infantry regiment until 2006. It had helped to expand the British Empire and fought in the Crimean, Boer and the two world wars. Gregory Burke's 2006 eponymous play set in Iraq explores how a group of squaddies fighting for the Regiment in Iraq are deprived of their self-worth. All they want is their moment of greatness. The Black Watchers could not be more different from the characters in the Scottish cult hit film *Trainspotting*, directed by Danny Boyle and based on a novel by Irvine Walsh. These soldiers do not abandon the galleon of society, they man its cannons. But while Renton and Sickboy, *Trainspotting*'s central figures, fly off in precisely the opposite direction from Cammy and his fellow squaddies, they are flung from the same waltzer. The Black Watchers do not 'choose life'. They choose glory. When this is not forthcoming, they are left with nothing but the raging emptiness of hope denied and pride betrayed.

Set at the time of the debate surrounding the future status of the Black Watch, the play is themed around a golden thread that connects one generation of Black Watchers to the next: ancestor, grandfather, father and son. It is a military covenant. More important, it is a cultural covenant. The stability of regimental history interplays with the decline of the mines, of shipbuilding, of manufacturing – of community history, in other words. Stack shelves in Tesco or angle for military glory? No competition for the squaddies.

Ultimately, the regiment's golden thread was broken when the Black Watch became the 3rd Battalion of the Royal Regiment of Scotland. It kept its name and its signature red hackle on the soldiers' bonnets – so its heritage lives on even as its status is slightly diminished. The real message of Burke's play is of the profundity of culture and pride – and the intensity of loss when they are shattered. These are deeply resonant human needs and motivations. Culture is not simply something that emerges from the state of social or economic relations. It is real and has meaning. There is something persistent in the human species regarding the intensity of its devotion to the group. Human groups come in all manner of forms: national, local, tribal, or based around religion, politics, race or ethnicity, trade or workplace, or club, team or hobby.

When change is rapid, people may feel a sense of cultural threat, which can become corrosive. Their sense of identity is challenged. Where there is a sense of security – economic, community, national and cultural – it can be a force that pulls individuals together. Too often the left ignores the power of cultural identity and meaning, focusing instead exclusively on social and economic identities. For the right, it is often the reverse – and that can lead it to rely on some pretty crude stereotyping, as we shall see. As culture steps in to the space vacated by class, it is becoming more relevant rather than less. Class and culture intermingle, separate and conflict. Change can be exciting and energising if you have the power, skills and resources to bend it to your advantage or use it as a buffer against the unexpected, but most people are not endowed with these. So change can be bewildering and anxiety-inducing, and provoke some hostile responses.

As novelty became a creed, so cultural commitments came under threat. The free market, the state and social change have all played their part. When the human need for security is not fulfilled, and when, through adverse personal experience, hope is extinguished, there is often a hostile reaction to social and political life. This can simply be a hatred of others, of elites, or a lack of trust and a sense of resentment. In a small minority of cases it can become something more terrifying: a violent or nihilistic impulse that can do real harm. When cultural suspicion and fear enter that sort of territory, the response required tends to be some law-enforcement intervention: monitoring at the very least. There are a whole host of responses – personal, familial, community and economic – that can prevent such attitudes from becoming dangerous.

Cultural identities cut across class, party affiliation and attitude. People are defined by their relationship with the world around them: their needs, their values, their degree of security, and their trust of others. This influences their social, economic and political outlook.

It is also self-reinforcing: positive experiences tend towards further positive ones, and negative experiences towards more negative ones. This is why there are localities where crime, worklessness, lack of opportunity, addiction or lack of care for one another seem to gather. It is also a reason why prosperity, social capital and opportunity are reinforcing. Once a sense of security, fellowship and trust has broken down, it is incredibly hard to rebuild it. The left has too often seen these things in purely material terms, just as the right has viewed it predominantly through an individual moral prism. It is both, in fact: culture interacts with economic opportunity and deprivation.

Just imagine that, tomorrow, Canterbury Cathedral vanished. What would be the consequence of that? As a nation we would feel a sense of bewilderment and severance. A piece of who we are, our history, would vanish. The loss would be cultural. For the people of Canterbury, their very understanding of their place in the world, their stability of identity and local pride would be gone. The local economy would suffer considerably as tourism to the town dried up. Such things have happened in communities such as Longbridge in Birmingham, Stoke in Staffordshire, Glasgow, Dagenham and Burnley. Their industrial prowess was their cathedral: their loss is both economic and cultural. Both the right and the left have a point.

Change both empowers and disempowers. A recent ethnography, *British Voices* by Joe Hayman, tracks the scars of change up and down the land: the upwardly mobile – the wired-up millennials, entrepreneurial immigrant communities, and the formerly downtrodden Catholic population of Northern Ireland. And he tracks the losers from change – the white working class of Glasgow with almost a despair of life manifested in a life-decaying diet of saturated fat and alcohol; loyalist working-class communities in Belfast; and those for whom the 1960s was a moral nightmare despite their relative affluence. What resonates is that people are trying to make sense of a rapidly changing world – one that human beings are not normally well-prepared for unless they are the instigators.

In a piece in *Newsweek* in February 2012, the US-based Canadian 'compassionate conservative' David Frum upbraided the conservative social theorist Charles Murray, who had argued that a 'cultural change' that occurred in the 1960s was responsible for the declining incomes and prospects of working-class white America. In response to Murray's *Coming Apart*, Frum points out that real wages have fallen, as have the prospects of most working-class Americans. Real wages have stagnated in the US since 1970 for the lowest 75 per cent of US workers. So far, it has been less severe in the UK. Nonetheless, the process is the same, as we have seen – low wages are corroding the lives of many.

As de-industrialisation has taken place, people have lost both income and opportunity: the service economy in the context of globalisation is now even threatening the middle classes, because many professional jobs such as IT services are being offshored, and technology is making some jobs obsolete. Perceived, and real, cultural and social changes have also taken place simultaneously. Both the liberal and conservative arguments have a point: lack of opportunity breeds despair, and cultural loss sustains it. People need to have a sense of hope and belonging: to work, to family, to friends and social support. Despondency increases as that sense of belonging is diminished in one sphere; it then spreads across a person's life and becomes a reinforcing negative. It is not just in one direction: reversing deep alienation is both a cultural and economic task, and they feed off one another. It is important to understand that this process has heavily influenced people's outlook on politics – and in some very negative ways.

We saw in Chapter 2 how experience influences people's needs, and how social class is no longer a strong determinant of political outlook. This chapter takes this one step further and reviews how issues of identity – defined as a person's perceived relationship to (or against) others – create a further political, economic and cultural challenge. Culture arises from the associations that people make with others on the basis of their identity. It is a shared set of outlooks, relations, practices and behaviours. Where there is a reference to 'cultural identity', it means the cultural tendencies of particular associations: whether they are based on ethnicity, nationality, locality, cultural history or some other strong notion of belonging. These are the 'tribes' referred to in the discussion on social change. Once a sense of security and identity is threatened, there can be a sense of loss and despair, and these feelings can induce either angry reaction or social withdrawal.

Welfare, immigration, economic hope, optimism and a sense of belonging are all sucked into this dynamic of culture and identity. When the reporter in *Black Watch* meets the characters on which the play is based, they are whiling away their days playing pool and drinking pints in a local club. In one scene set in the war zone, one of the squaddies despairs: 'There will be no victory parade for us.' And that encapsulates the pathos of loss. Economics alone cannot resolve this. We must also understand how culture and the sense of identity have changed, why they have changed, and begin to consider what we need to do to ensure we can continue to get along together on these islands. That may at times be easier said than done; we need to be prepared for that.

The 'Liberal Moment' and Identity 'Tribes'

The *Guardian* famously backed the Liberal Democrats in the 2010 General Election, declaring that we were at a 'liberal moment'. It could not have been more wrong, as no set of ideas or allegiances are dominant. Instead, we are at a deeply pluralistic moment where common action between incompatible outlooks is the norm. We have a static politics but a diverse society. There is an even greater tension between the two, as a majoritarian constitution with strong party discipline is incapable of coping with real pluralism.

Politics is always a tension between two powerful forces – identity and political economy. For almost all of the latter half of the twentieth century it was political economy that dominated, and identity flared up only occasionally in street battles, racist beatings, or vicious by-election campaigns, notably in the Midlands. The two forces still co-exist, but the political resonance of culture has strengthened. Manuel Castells forecast this very clearly in his monumental 1990s work *The Power of Identity*:

> Along with the technological revolution, the transformation of capitalism, and the demise of statism, we have experienced … the widespread surge of powerful expressions of collective identity that challenge globalisation … [these expressions] include a whole array of reactive movements that build trenches of resistance on behalf of God, nation, ethnicity, family, locality.

Culture is often seen as a consequence of economic position or as something ephemeral. It is not. It is something real and powerful. It is both independent of economic change and heavily influenced by it, and vice versa. A sense of loss of control and power over one's life and cultural assertion are heavily linked. Economic and cultural issues enmesh. There is a strong reaction to globalisation and economic change, but cultural identity is a powerful force in its own right.

In early 2011, Nick Lowles, of the anti-fascist campaign group, 'HOPE not hate', and I wrote the *Fear and Hope* report based on a large-scale 5,000-representative sample of English respondents conducted by Populus. Using cluster analysis, six main identity groupings were identified. On the 'left' were the 'confident multicul-turals' and 'mainstream liberals', who were largely comfortable with diversity and immigration. Their opposites are the 'latent hostiles' and those in 'active enmity', who are deeply antagonistic to immigra-tion and cultural diversity, with the latter group even being willing to sanction violence in order to protect their culture. In the middle are the 'cultural integrationists', who believe in a strong national culture into which everyone should integrate. The 'identity ambiv-alents' sit just to their left. They are pragmatic about immigration, though anxious, and are more likely to face economic concerns than the 'cultural integrationists'. Reflecting on the *Fear and Hope* report, David Miliband wrote an article in the *Guardian* which argued: 'A convincing economic response is necessary but not sufficient. An authentic sense of identity is just as important. Labour's politics must be suffused with both cultural understanding and meaning and a pragmatic economic mission.'

Figure 1 shows the breakdown of the six groups by percentages. The first thing you will notice about the left–right scale of identity politics is that the groups on the left are those normally seen in the centre of the media-political discourse that drives the political agenda. The groups consisting of more professionals in the main, educated to a higher level, and liberal, but rather than being in the centre-ground of English politics, they are at its left-hand edge and together consti-tute 24 per cent of the population. This is why the Liberal Democrats find it difficult to get beyond 25 per cent or so of the vote – they find it

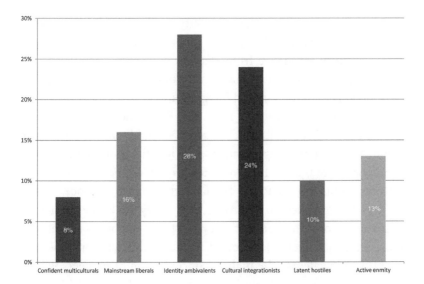

FIGURE 1   Identity groupings of English respondents to the Populus survey (percentages)
Source: Lowles and Painter, *Fear and Hope* report, 2011.

difficult to reach beyond this section of society. Their minority status here demonstrates that the 2010 election was not a 'liberal moment'.

Latent hostiles and active enmity lie where you'd expect to find them – on the right fringe, and they constitute 23 per cent of the vote. The BNP takes its support mainly from the group on the far right. UKIP takes support from both of these groups. But the real centre-ground of English politics is the 'cultural integrationists', who comprise 24 per cent of the population, and the 'identity ambiva-lents' who are the remaining 28 per cent. The difference between these two groups is that the former are more concerned with author-ity, national culture, and conformity – and are more likely to vote Conservative. They are relatively well-off and are likely to be subur-ban, non-urban and rural dwellers. Cultural concern drives their outlook. The 'identity ambivalents' are more economically insecure and their cultural concern tends to rise as their level of insecurity increases (many of those in 'latent hostility' and 'active enmity' will be former 'identity ambivalents', having moved over in response to personal circumstances). These 'identity ambivalents' bear a striking similarity to the *squeezed middle* – economically insecure voters who switch political allegiance from election to election. They also care about culture, immigration and identity, but they are more economically anxious than the 'cultural integrationists'.

Going back to value sets from the Pat Dade and Chris Rose research considered in Chapter 2, settlers would tend to congregate within the 'cultural integrationists' and 'identity ambivalents', and a good portion of the two hostile groups would also be settlers. In fact, activists within the BNP and the far-right English Defence League (EDL) are more likely to be prospectors – they are in the parties for status and a contorted sense of glory, but their supporters are settlers. Prospectors are likely to be found within 'mainstream liberals' and 'identity ambivalents'. The highest concentration of pioneers will be found in 'mainstream liberals' and 'confident multiculturals'. Because the Dade/Rose value surveys and the *Fear and Hope* survey measure different things, they do not map exactly but there is some degree of correlation. In general, the more settler-like someone is, the more likely he or she is to gravitate towards the groups on the right of the identity axis above. The more pioneer-like they are, the more likely they are to be found in the groups on the left.

Through whichever prism we view the English population, it is clear that there is no 'progressive majority' in English politics – despite claims among liberal leftist politicians and the media that there is. They just spend a lot of time with fellow 'mainstream liberals' or 'confident multiculturals' and presume a deeper legitimacy than they have: they themselves are a group like any other, but one with media and political power. The real 'swing' voters of British politics are the 'identity ambivalents' – even though they make up the largest block of Labour identifiers (37 per cent) they also make up the largest block of people who don't identify with a party (46 per cent). It is this group that has fallen out of love with Labour over the last decade. In fact, they are falling out of love with every party, and if they are ever in any relationship, it's often only one of convenience.

Each party is holding together an unstable coalition of quite incompatible views. This demonstrates a degree of success for parties in reaching beyond their core. The Conservative 'core' is the 'cultural integrationists', who make up 42 per cent of their vote, but their identification comprises 17 per cent from the groups on the left, 17 per cent 'identity ambivalents' and 24 per cent hostiles and active enmity. Labour, by contrast, has a split 'core' between the 'identity ambivalents' that are 37 per cent of its identifiers and 30 per cent the 'multiculturalist' and 'mainstream liberals'. For both main parties these are uneasy coalitions. The Conservatives have a little more coherence – 54 per cent of its vote are 'cultural integrationist' or 'latent hostile'. To a certain extent this explains David Cameron's rhetoric around 'muscular liberalism', 'Christian country' and against 'state multiculturalism'. He is reaching for his base and keeping it intact, just as Michael Howard did in 2005 and William Hague before him in 2001.

These splits and incoherent coalitions of support explain the diffi-culties that social democrats are having across Europe. They find themselves impaled on the politics of identity as their traditional (usually white) working-class-based support makes an increasingly uncomfortable political bedfellow with new professionals and others with a more liberal outlook. This is exactly what we have seen happen in Sweden, Germany, Spain and elsewhere. So traditional social democracy is not up to the task. What about a progressive alliance of liberals, social democrats and greens? Could Labour try that? In doing so it can only go deeper into the two groups to the left of the identity axis while potentially antagonising those in the centre. It is 'narrowcasting'. If Labour follows the 'progressive alliance' strategy, it is limited in the politics of identity. Only a minority of the electorate are actually what can be termed 'progressive': that is social democratic *and* socially liberal, not one or the other, as 'progressive' is sometimes asserted to cover. A 'progressive majority' strategy is thereby limited.

A major risk is that neither party reaches the 'identity ambivalents': Conservatives miss them to the right and Labour misses them to the left. A recent Japanese poll reported in the *Washington Post* showed that 50 per cent of Japanese voters supported no party at all. That could be the fate of British politics as traditional party and class alle-giances rapidly loosen. Labour's support is broad but shallow. The fate of 'identity ambivalents' will heavily influence the fate of our politics. If there is a political argument to which they feel an attachment, they will almost all remain in the mainstream. If they develop a deep sense of insecurity and anxiety, and lose optimism for the future, then they could leap-frog into hostility. With austerity all around us, the risks are great. This is the link between the argument for economic change and cultural awareness. The left will need a convincing and credible argument for economic change; the economic institutions to increase investment and wage levels while reducing volatility, outlined in the previous chapter, are the sorts of interventions that are desperately needed.

In addition, the left will also need to demonstrate clearly that it understands the cultural attachments that people hold for themselves, their country and their history. The fact that almost half of this group do not identify with any party demonstrates the degree to which this attachment is not there currently. This does not mean that the left – Labour more particularly – has to ditch its values. It means that it has to acknowledge a sense of loss and anxiety as a first step to engaging in a different conversation about culture and identity. There will then be substantial policy, local, legal and constitutional responses that flow from that acknowledgement. We have more in common than we think: as a population we have just become too separated to realise it and we need to respond before that separation becomes even more embedded in a sense of cultural angst.

Ronald Inglehart and Pippa Norris have begun to investigate the impact of feelings of insecurity on a range of attitudes. Their most recent paper (2011) has the slightly ominous title of *The Four Horsemen of the Apocalypse: Understanding Human Security.* They find that people distinguish between three types of security risk: national, community and personal. The degree to which humans feel secure or insecure has a major impact on their values and behaviour. As feelings of happiness decline, personal and community insecurity increase, and the same is observed with life satisfaction. The higher the level of personal and community insecurity, the lower the level of trust. Inglehart and Norris predict that these levels of security drive human behaviour, 'affecting psychological feelings of well-being, and happiness, as well as social and political values, with important societal consequences'. Security matters – without it there is a greater chance of identity angst and conflict.

Robert Putnam conducted some research on the impact of rapid cultural change on trust and happiness titled 'E pluribus unum'. He argues that social change creates a 'turtle effect'. People withdraw into themselves in reaction to major economic and social upheaval. There could be a short-term aspect to this, and much of Putnam's analysis is about the possibility of reversing this 'turtle effect' – a question on which he is very positive. It is important not to simply accept what fate throws our way.

As resources such as jobs or housing become scarcer, this conflict intensifies. Putnam's argument is that, rather than diversity (and he was principally writing about ethnic diversity) increasing in-group solidarity it actually leads to reduced in-group solidarity and social isolation. He summarises his argument: 'Diversity seems to trigger not in-group/out-group division, but anomie or social isolation.' Some argue this means that diversity and community cohesion are incompatible. This is too despairing. In fact, recent research in the UK context shows that it is socio-economic stress that explains more of a lack of community cohesion than increasing diversity. Shamit Saggar and Will Somerville challenge the bleaker aspects of Putnam's work in *Building a British Model of Integration in an Era of Immigration*. These findings match closely the coincidence of social and political distress within areas that have faced large-scale deindustrialisation.

Inglehart and Norris's research should caution us to understand the real impact of social and economic change, which leaves certain people dispossessed. By acting to lessen this impact – by, for example, looking to the type of economic institutions that provide people with a decent wage and opportunity, or through encouraging a more active community life – we can reduce the negative impact of change. The problem for the left is that it has been too change-neutral for too long. Change can empower some people but disconcert others. This has social, economic and political consequences that we cannot ignore.

The experiences of working-class Britain have been extremely varied in recent decades. Some people in former mining villages, major manufacturing towns and cities, and former mill towns have experienced loss and dislocation. Others have benefited from industrial change as new industries have established themselves in new locations, such as Honda in Swindon. However, many families now require two incomes, where previously one would have sufficed, or they may exit the labour market altogether. In some respects – for example, from a gender equality perspective – this may be welcome. However, the paucity of well-paid, working-class jobs creates an insecurity and anxiety all of its own. People are running fast to stand still – or even to journey backwards. This changes their relationship with those around them.

There are still romantic notions of working-class solidarity in the face of this economic change. The *Fear and Hope* report data found that working-class communities are the least likely to go to a local pub, be involved in sport, do charity or community work, have dinner or drinks with neighbours, attend a place of worship or be involved in political activity. The thriving working-class communities of folklore are becoming a thing of the past. For all its rhetoric, the Big Society is actually a more natural fit for communities that already have, to use the term of Robert Putnam, social capital. Unless there is some form of community intervention and activism in poorer communities the Big Society will either mean even more focus on the comfortable, or on those who are comfortable 'saving' the poor. In many ways, it could constitute – in ethos at least – a return to Victorian customs and attitudes, where the bourgeoisie save the damned.

It is no surprise that many of the areas where the BNP made its most substantial gains in the 2000s are in the very communities and localities that have experienced the most economic and social change – particularly those built up around one or two key industries. These include Barking and Dagenham (car industry), Stoke-on-Trent (steel, potteries and coal), Nuneaton (coal and car industry) and Barnsley (coal). Economic upheaval has both led to social upheaval and, in some places, it has been compounded by a sense of perceived cultural change. It is as though the social, institutional and cultural glue that bound the community together melted away in the heat of economic change and left behind a disconnected, dislocated and increasingly disorientated population.

The London Borough of Barking and Dagenham is worth considering as an extreme case. The Borough Council's own figures show that between 2001 and 2011 the White British category declined from 82.5 per cent of the total population to 56.4 per cent. Meanwhile, the Black African population increased from 4.4 per cent to 15.4 per cent and 'White Other' (likely to be predominantly Eastern Europeans) increased from 2.6 per cent to 10.8 per cent. Asian ethnic groups are now estimated at 14.4 per cent, compared with 5 per cent in 2001. The Ford plant in Dagenham has produced engines rather than complete cars since the early part of the twenty-first century and employs 4,000 people (in its heyday in 1953, it was employing around 40,000). Further job cuts were announced at the end of 2012 and the workforce now looks set to be in the region of 2,000. This is rapid economic cultural change by any measure, and the BNP were the beneficiaries until they were beaten back by a very well organised 'Hope not hate' campaign in the General Election of 2010. This case demonstrates quite clearly how economic and cultural change can interact; one feeds off the other. Which of the forces – economic and cultural – is more powerful depends critically on context.

There isn't a simple economic answer to questions that are about both culture and opportunity. The left has to ask itself whether it wants to engage properly with identity ambivalence and meet people where they are. A top-down response alone will not be sufficient. A willingness to engage with thorny issues that are easier to ignore is required. If political voices do not understand and respond to both the cultural and economic dimensions of people's anxiety then they will not be heard. Yet the left has been reluctant to engage in that way – its leaders and spokespeople are more likely to be 'liberal multiculturalists' and so are either blind or unsympathetic to cultural anxieties. Few issues challenge the notion that we are in a 'liberal moment' than attitudes to immigration. The left avoided the topic for as long as possible and when it finally addressed the concerns it too often adopted abrasive language that lacked nuance. It has reached for socio-economic explanations alone when there is also a cultural dimension to the issue. It looked at the macro picture rather than at the neighbourhood level where the lived experience of cultural suspicion is felt. For all these reasons it failed to sound either relevant or sincere.

Immigration

'The centre cannot hold,' wrote William Butler Yeats; 'the best lack all conviction, while the worst are full of passionate intensity.' Anyone observing or participating in discussions surrounding immigration will feel that Yeats had it about right. However, there is a quiet majority in the debate. They are the pragmatists. In the immigration numbers game, the level of net migration has become the be all and end all – damagingly. The problem with simply debating overall net numbers is that it can cause economic and social damage, as there is a focus on that to the exclusion of everything else. It makes no sense not to allow people to come into the UK if they can help to plug skills shortages or purchase the country's services, such as university or further education tuition. Besides, the pragmatic majority wish to see immigration reduced and managed, not stopped completely or erratically.

Failure to fill skills shortages can be socially as well as economically harmful – think health care workers, scientific researchers or engineers. The economic harm itself is bad enough. What sense does it make to bar students who buy one of our leading exports, namely higher education? Very little, is the blunt answer. Yet, with the obsession about numbers rather than the type of immigration and proper border management is where policies such as the government's immigration cap end up. What is more, because of the impossibility of controlling intra-EU migration, the policy will fail.

The media and politicians seem to be determined to outbid each other on where to head next in a rhetorical Dutch auction. It is often asserted that there is a disjuncture between the realities of immigration and people's fears. In fact, the real disparity is between the panicked response of a detached media-political nexus and the pragmatism of the majority. There has been no real attempt to conduct a less emotive and simplistic conversation on immigration. Yes, people are concerned – immigration is still second on people's 'issues of national concern'. However, when the question is posed in relation to an individual and their family it is in sixth place – 14 per cent put it in their top three issues of personal concern according to YouGov. And evidence has shown time and again that people are far more pragmatic when it comes to immigration than politicians and the media give them credit for.

While the Populus survey in the *Fear and Hope* report found that 60 per cent of respondents thought that past immigration was 'bad for the country', that does not translate into a closed-door mentality. A temporary freeze was supported by 16 per cent. A further 18 per cent were in favour of a permanent end to immigration. That leaves 61 per cent of people who favour a managed immigration policy and 5 per cent who favour the open-door approach.

Research from The Migration Observatory at the University of Oxford backs up these findings. They commissioned Ipsos Mori to conduct a poll on their behalf, looking at public attitudes to immigration. This found that 69 per cent do think that immigration should be reduced a little (24 per cent) or a lot (45 per cent). However, of those who think it should be reduced, less than half – 42 per cent – think legal immigration should be reduced. But when questions were asked about specific types of immigration the results showed a much more nuanced and pragmatic picture: 31 per cent thought the number of university students coming to Britain should be reduced; 33 per cent thought the same of English language students; 41 per cent thought that the number of non-British immediate family members entering should be reduced; but this rises to 57 per cent for non-British extended family members and 56 per cent for asylum seekers.

When it comes to skill levels, 31 per cent considered that there should be a reduction of 'most high-skilled' workers but 64 per cent thought the same with regard to the 'most low-skilled' workers. In fact, 21 per cent thought we should allow *more* of the most highly skilled workers to enter the country. So there is a net minus 10 per cent support for more over less numbers of high-skilled workers. The corresponding number for low-skilled workers is minus 57 per cent.

This is a huge difference which, while being reflected in the immigration points system, is not reflected in public discussion, which is dominated by pure net immigration numbers.

These attitudes in part reflect the reality of different types of workers on jobs and wages. The empirical data (see a collation of some of this data in Ruhs' *The Labour Market Effects of Immigration* from The Migration Observatory) show that immigration has a minimal effect on averages but increases the wages of those at the top and has a small negative impact on those at the bottom. A strong impact on employment levels has not been found. The notion that it would have a strong impact on employment levels is to misunderstand the way that labour markets work: in a complex economy they are dynamic rather than static, so the more people that are in work, the more work there is (economists call the opposing view the 'lump of labour fallacy'). Looking at this data, it is easy to say, given the small average impact, why allow immigration at all? The answer is that these calculations only look at things quantitatively and the data is incomplete. It ignores the entrepreneurship, job creation, investment, productivity and public service contributions that migrants make. This is a big omission. Also, a diverse society, with a high degree of interaction and exchange, has access to new ideas, skills and innovation, which a static society does not. Would Apple Inc. now exist had Steve Jobs' biological father, Abdul Fattah Jandali, who was born in Syria, not migrated to the US?

Without immigration we forgo access to skilled health care practitioners, engineers, researchers, chefs, and, yes, plumbers and baristas. Try to imagine a day in London, Birmingham or Glasgow without migrant workers – these cities would come to a shuddering halt, as would their economies and public services. One might ask, 'Can't we train British people to do these things?' Yes, we should to a far greater extent – it's not either/or – but that still will not be enough as there will always be skills shortages and a need for unique talent and creativity that cannot necessarily be taught.

It is important to note, however, that while the overall impact is small on the jobs and wages of the lower paid, the effects can be concentrated in certain places. Many of those affected will, of course, be migrants themselves. Nonetheless, there is a need for a swifter response in areas of rapid change where there is competition for resources, such as housing and jobs – in the short-term at least. Britain doesn't have restrictions on the internal movement of people, and nor should any free society, but we do need to ensure that interventions take place to help communities that are going through a transition. As we have seen, this can be very disconcerting for the existing population. Real time responses at the local level through education institutions and local authorities are critical to ensure successful rather than conflict-provoking change. However, the strain of change should not ever be underestimated.

If the left misreads the politics of immigration, it will end up in a vicious downward spiral of political rhetoric in a damaging auction with the right about who can be the toughest. This will lead in the direction of a more damaging public policy. It also misreads the more pragmatic and nuanced national mood, and will also alienate the growing non-British-born population. The only way of taking this situation further is to pretty well discontinue non-EU migration and potentially also leave the EU – which will take the possible economic damage to a whole new level. Like it or not, we are part of a European economy and our economic future depends on it. Whatever the short-term difficulties, 50 per cent of our trade is still with the EU. Remember, just because we might have left the EU does not mean we will not have to apply EU regulations and pay for the pleasure (Norway pays more per capita than the UK does despite not being a member of the EU). We shall just no longer have any say over EU regulations.

There is another path: honesty and pragmatism. In this view, Labour would re-assert that the UK should revert to the points-based immigration system, which issues visas to non-EU migrants in accordance with skills needs rather than using the destructive immigration cap. Not only that, we should welcome with open arms highly qualified people who add economic value and contribute to our society. The UK Border Agency should be reformed and, successful or unsuccessful, visa applications should be processed rapidly. The UK should encourage highly qualified people to stay and make music, do research, set up businesses and trade from our shores. Labour would have to demonstrate that this system is clear, transparent and fair.

The left in general and Labour in particular need to acknowledge the potential downsides from immigration. The type of labour-market institutions recommended in the previous chapter, with localised living wages, should be introduced gradually, to reassure people about the wage-impact of immigration. Further action should be taken to prevent the worst employers out-competing the best through inferior conditions of work and casualisation. Temporary work must be a particular focus. Ed Balls has made some sensible suggestions about reforms to the Free Movement Directive, to prevent benefits and tax credits received in the UK being repatriated to other European countries.

Politically, Labour would then need to find a language to articulate the message that the economy is not static. There is not just a set amount of jobs to go round. When someone is employed he or she becomes a consumer as well. In the main, unemployment comes from insufficient demand, technological change, international competition, lack of skills or lack of mobility. The two regions with the highest net inward migration – London and the South-East, with a third of the total – has had the lowest increase in unemployment during the course of the recession. Net immigration to an area is a sign of economic buoyancy rather than the reverse. Nonetheless, there are real strains that do need to be acknowledged.

Many of these pressures are on social need. When a local population changes rapidly – more quickly than the ten-year timeframes of the census, as we have seen occurring in Barking and Dagenham – there is a time lag in response and pressure on resources. We need smarter population-change estimates that instantly trigger more investment in local services where rapid inflows have occurred. Furthermore, in acute situations, we need community-level responses. These will be different in each area but will require resourcing from central government budgets. Community responses – common activities that can be quite basic, such as sharing food, helping to keep the streets clean or even, as we shall see, setting up choirs – can make an enormous difference.

Finally, there is the urgent issue of housing. It is frankly irresponsible for us as a nation not to have increased our stock of affordable housing. This is not just related to immigration, and housing need should never be reduced to a conversation simply about immigration.

If it is, then the necessary houses are even less likely to be built. Between 1981 and 2008, the number of single-person households in Britain increased by 73 per cent, from 4.3 million to 7.5 million. The drivers of increased demand are demographic and economic changes of a variety of different forms.

These actions constitute a more honest and pragmatic way of approaching concerns about immigration: honesty about the benefits, costs and consequences of immigration and of stopping it; sensibly managed migration; legal changes at both domestic and European level to ensure fairness and a level playing field; responsive national and local government; and a major house-building programme. A priority consideration for local people in new social and council housing is sensible and fair. There is an expectation that benefits should come from contributions made over time. Access to services and welfare should reflect that expectation.

Putnam's findings that diversity and common citizenship are inversely related are a potential warning to us rather than fatalistic determinism. The same applies to the decline of trust that communities faced with negative economic change experience. We have more in common than we have things that separate us, though it is the latter that have become exaggerated in our distorted public discourse. Perhaps we should start to talk about the things we have in common – family, aspirations, anxiety, hope, love of Britain, a desire for freedom and the need to belong – rather than always over-emphasising the differences. In the 2009–10 Citizenship Survey published by the Department for Communities and Local Government (DCLG), the two ethnic groups with the strongest attachment to Great Britain were Pakistanis and Bangladeshis.

In the late nineteenth century, and throughout much of the twentieth century, the Labour movement was one means by which people were brought together. Churches were another. Large workplaces were also fundamental. None of these things can realistically fulfil that role in the twenty-first century. We need to consider seriously what our binding institutions are for the twenty-first century. They have a cultural purpose – they bring us together – as well as an economic one.

Open-door immigration is a non-starter, not only for political reasons but also for economic and social reasons too. Closed-door immigration is politically toxic, economically insane and socially divisive. Luckily, the pragmatic majority have a great deal more sense. They deserve better than the dishonest politics and policy that they are offered. The centre can hold; but only if it is more determined and passionate than the extremes. Unfortunately, politicians and the media cannot resist picking at the sore of culture and identity, and that has even included the current prime minister. It is a dangerous game.

Politics, Media and Identity

In July 2011, an extreme right-winger, Anders Behring Breivik, bombed a government building in Oslo before heading to the island of Utøya, where he massacred 69 young people who were there for a camp of the Workers' Youth League of the Norwegian Labour Party. He killed political activists of a party that he held responsible for the 'Islamification' of Norwegian society. The guilty parties in the Oslo attack and Utøya massacre were Anders Behring Breivik and whoever might have directly assisted and motivated him in the attacks. Nonetheless, it is important to examine public discourse in the light of Breivik's atrocities without shifting any focus from the deeper issues of violent extremism. How we discuss cultural difference needs great care. This becomes even more important once terrorism and violence are among us.

Breivik latched on to a number of arguments that are freely articulated – hence legitimised – in the mainstream media, which focus on Islam. He wrote a 1,500-page manifesto of hate that referenced many of these arguments to be found in the Norwegian and British mainstream. He also had contact with extremist groups such as the EDL in the UK. There is no one making any subtle arguments in favour of 'Islamic' cultural resistance to secularism or 'crusaders' on the pages of national newspapers. There are people who call for a cultural resistance to Islam in the mainstream media, however. That is one of the major differences between Al Qaeda and far-right terrorism.

This is absolutely not to argue that Al Qaeda or other extremist Islamic organisations and networks who peddle hate and seek to murder and maim should not concern us. They absolutely should – the threat is very real. It should concern us intensely, as they kill and destroy lives. It is possible to worry about and respond to *extremisms* and not just to one form of *extremism* or another. In fact, the two extremisms are feeding off one another in quite frightening ways: a plague on both their houses.

The first means of combating the far right is to cut off its feeding supply, which involves a greater degree of responsibility in the main-stream media. Again, this is not to say that the people making the arguments are responsible for the violence. There is a very great distance between casual, politically or journalistically motivated misinformation, misunderstanding, sensationalism or wrongful analysis about Islam, and violent action. But there is a funnel and a feeding tube. These should be cut.

In 2008, in an article headed, 'This country to so [*sic*] pro-Muslim that it is giving succour to the extremists who would destroy us', Melanie Phillips argued:

> They [the British elite] are simply blind to the ruthless way in which the Islamists are exploiting our chronic muddle of well-meaning tolerance and political correctness (backed up by the threat of more violence) to put Islam on a special – indeed, unique – footing within Britain.

It is classic elite perfidy as political narrative, and it is the narrative that is definitive on the hard right. It is often combined with 'othering'. The following sentence from that piece is a classic case: 'Believing that Islamic terrorism is motivated by an ideology which has 'hijacked' and distorted Islam, [the last government] will not acknowledge the extremism within mainstream Islam itself.'

According to this argument, Islam *by definition* contains the seed, if not the sapling, of extremism. It is clear that Phillips strongly articu-lates that there are Islamic moderates:

> The reason so many older British Muslims are traditionally moderate is that they were brought up in the Asian subcontinent under a tamed form

of Islam, deriving from centuries of colonial rule, which glossed over much of the teaching of the religion.'

Unfortunately, this does not sufficiently weaken the categorisation. The implication is that Islam, left to its own devices and without the moderating influence of another culture, in this case British colonialism, would inevitably tend towards extremism. Once this 'colonial' generation has died out, then all that is left is unfettered extremism.

There is a real concern with extremism linked with Islam and, it should be noted that Al Qaeda-related/inspired terrorism has brought far more death and violence to Europe and the US than their far-right equivalents. In March 2012, Mohamed Merah shot dead a rabbi, two of his children and a third child outside a Jewish school in Toulouse in France. There can be no hesitation in confronting terrorism, extremism, hatred and violence in every possible lawful way.

However, the sort of 'othering' and religious determinism based on selective reading of religious texts that Phillips exhibits in the piece quoted above has the potential to harm the anti-extremist cause. It helps to contribute to a sense of injustice that can be one element of the process by which people are pushed further towards political (and religious) extremes.

So while there is no direct link at all between articles in, say, the *Daily Mail* on one hand and extremism and violence on the other, there is an environment in which extremism finds an easier anchor, and a certain type of culturally divisive, over-general argument is often part of that. Mainstream media can contribute to a climate of suspicion and difference, which, inadvertently, has a role in legitimising more extreme expressions of antipathy to certain groups. If your culture is under threat, you may resort to violent means to defend it. This is precisely what occurred in the case of Breivik. The same goes for the right-wing militiaman Michael Wade Page, who killed six people in a Sikh temple in Oak Creek, Wisconsin, in the US. His conspiracy theories about a country stolen from its original people and such ideas can easily be found within the right-wing media and the Tea Party organisation – touching the US mainstream, in other words.

Islam is a culture, an identity, a spirituality, a set of beliefs and values, a faith, a belief-set, an expression of belonging to a people and of a community. In this regard, it is rather like Christianity and is just as varied and plural. Phillips does not accuse all Muslims of subscribing to the 'extremism within mainstream Islam', but some readers will inevitably make that association or will feel that such an association is justified – especially if they are already politically and psychologically primed in that way. None of this may be intended, but that is the problem with such culturally charged analysis. Islamic extremism absolutely is a problem and a threat. That makes it even more important to handle the issue and dialogue surrounding it very carefully.

We have to be concerned with more than just violence, though. We need an awareness of the political, psychological and cultural processes by which certain groups within British society are turned into the 'other'. At a very basic level, this process begins with defining individuals via their group membership rather than as with the complex set of identities we all hold. These groups are then assigned (usually negative) characteristics. The individual in the group then acquires this characteristic regardless of his or her own character: think of such stereotypes as the angry Muslim, the rich Jew or the lazy Afro-Caribbean. These stereotypes are corrosive, offensive and dangerous. By 'othering' we contribute to radicalisation – the 'other' responds to their alienation with retaliation.

Furthermore, both extremists – self-defined 'Jihadi' and 'counter-Jihadi' – feed off one another. The environment in which they operate is influenced by the mainstream political and cultural conversation. This applies to those in party politics who play the politics of racial and ethnic division: the Respect party on the left, and the BNP, British Freedom Party (BFP) and others on the right. There are some in mainstream politics who also do so. If we are not careful people may be forced towards hardened mono-cultural identities rather than the plural identities that we are able, and need, to hold. A sense of threat can precipitate this process. Breivik, Page and Merah are warnings of what we might have to deal with if we do not discipline ourselves in both the political and media space to ensure that sustenance is not given to those who peddle hate.

The hostility and enmity picked up in the *Fear and Hope* report warn us about the radioactivity of identity politics. There is a real security threat. It comes both from radicalised Muslims and the far right. Great care must be taken that in confronting one we do not create a supply of nourishment to the other. That responsibility applies above all to leading politicians. Unfortunately, the Prime Minister himself has fallen short on occasion. Giving a speech on 'multicultur-alism' in Munich on the day of an EDL rally did not demonstrate the best planning. The rally was designed to terrify minority citizens in Luton. It didn't help that his speech erected such straw men as 'state multiculturalism' – in other words, a deliberate state approach of seeing people through the prism of their ethnicity or group and then responding with resources and policies to these groups. It is difficult to find much, if any, actual contemporary evidence of 'state multicul-turalism' despite some inadvertently divisive state policies that have appeared to serve some communities over others through clumsy application and targeting. Unforeseen consequences are not the same as a deliberate ideology.

In a follow-up speech in April 2011, David Cameron made the following reference to forced marriages:

> For a start, there are forced marriages taking place in our country and over-seas as a means of gaining entry to the UK. This is the practice where some young British girls are bullied and threatened into marrying someone they don't want to. I've got no time for those who say this is a culturally relative issue – it is wrong, full stop, and we've got to stamp it out.

Who are these people who favour forced marriages on the basis of 'cultural relativism'? There may be some out of ignorance or a false sense of political correctness who do, but they are few in number. Of course, forced marriages are wrong – they are outlawed in the Universal Declaration of Human Rights, and legislation was intro-duced in 2007 to strengthen the hand of the courts in dealing with forced marriage. Of course coercion, including threatening behaviour – violent or not – is criminal.

Cameron then went on in his speech to bemoan the lack of integration of new arrivals to Britain. He is right to be concerned. But then his government has reduced the availability of English-language lessons that will enable people to integrate more quickly. It is not responsible to identify problems without proposing solutions. The Prime Minister then went into political attack mode:

> On the one hand, there were Labour ministers who closed down discussion, giving the impression that if you raised concerns about immigration that was somehow racist. On the other, there were ministers hell-bent on sort of burnishing their hard-line credentials by talking tough, but not actually doing anything to bring the numbers down.

There is no doubt that Labour lost control of the politics of immigration in the early 2000s (a different thing from losing control of immigration, it should be noted). Its legislative programme put in place a perfectly rational set of policies to introduce a points-based immigration system, new citizenship rules and tighter controls. Numerous bills, EU treaty reforms, administrative decisions and targets throughout its period of office served to implement changes that made immigration more transparent and managed. But yet again we see the obsession with the numbers game. Cameron was right that Labour politicians too often panicked in response to the fraught politics of immigration and culture. Labour has to share responsibility for that, but the Coalition has set itself up to fail on the numbers – Cameron will find out that net immigration is beyond the government's absolute control and depends just as much on the state of the economy or the desire of British citizens to move elsewhere as it does on government policy.

Security, culture and identity have a close and incendiary relationship with one another. Diminished security makes cultural difference and antagonistic identity more assertive. Ensuring that the dependencies remain as inert as possible requires a responsible media and political leadership. Too often, both elements are lacking. Irresponsibility is one thing; there are also groups that exist to peddle hatred and division. Where cultural difference and insecurity start to become accentuated, these groups prosper. Without the right response, communities will suffer. It requires challenging extremism of all types, with equal readiness and volume but also displaying a cultural sensitivity.

The Extremist Threat and Response

The stunning success of the Military Wives Choir – who had the 2011 Christmas No. 1 single – is a wonderful story. Their tale is one of resolve, of finding meaning in one's own locality and among the people with whom we rub shoulders day to day, of combating our fears, giving voice to a voiceless group, and of brilliant amateurism.

The story of the military wives was the fourth in the TV series *The Choir*. The third series took place on a council estate in South Oxhey, Hertfordshire. When the BNP tried to give this choir a cheque for £1,000 it was rejected, with one committee member saying: 'We've worked really hard as a group to be inclusive of everybody and promote an ethnically diverse choir. We don't feel the BNP shares those values so, as a group, we decided to turn the money down.'

One of the tragedies of recent years has been the way in which extremists, including the BNP, the EDL and the BFP (which is linked to the EDL) have been able to latch on to anger and alienation and give expression to them through a corrupted notion of Englishness. The response from mainstream politicians has been weak – a St George's flag waved here, a bulldog image there, faux attempts to make St George's Day a real national celebration, mixed with the odd over-enthusiastic expression of support for a national football side full of under-achieving prima donnas.

The BNP, which has captured the most attention in recent years, has over-reached itself. In an attempt to make the political big time, it stretched its resources and organisational capability beyond the point of elasticity. Triumph for the forces of hope over the forces of hate? Yes. But, as Matthew J. Goodwin argues in *New British Fascism*, the extreme right is a more permanent phenomenon capable of reinventing itself than we might care to admit. This has deeper consequences for our politics than we seem to want to accept.

The rise of the BNP has been a result of a different way of communicating hate – focused more on culture and nation than on race per se – and it was also dependent on community-based organisation, hence its interest in the community choir. Community activities such as clearing front gardens for people proved to be a powerful motivating force in environments where community had thinned to the point of translucence.

Matthew Collins' personal account, *Hate: My Life in the British Far Right*, covers the decline of the National Front, the rise of the BNP, mainland unionist paramilitarism, the appearance of Combat 18, the terrorist attacks of David Copeland and the fight-back led by Searchlight and 'Hope not hate', who responded in different ways to different threats and groups. It is a gripping yet discomforting read. For anyone wishing to know what we are contending with – including those who naively want the police and security forces to treat the EDL as a protest movement instead of an extremist organisation – Collins' account is an essential text.

Hate makes the violent, Holocaust-denying, Nazi and racist foundations of the BNP absolutely clear. Holocaust denial has served an important function historically for the far right. If you can deny the Holocaust, you can deny anything. That then gives enormous room for political manoeuvre. Violence follows, as night follows day. So denial is not just harmless political posturing.

The BNP started life as a modern version of the British Union of Fascists, with John Tyndall as a preposterous reincarnation of Oswald Mosley. His right-hand man was Richard Edmonds, who recently walked out on Nick Griffin (the leader of the BNP) and his disintegrating party following a failed leadership bid. One by one, Collins lays bare the deeply disturbing organisms one finds in the fetid waters of the British far right. The lucky thing is that political unity on the far right is no more enduring than that on the far left. Their pasts, with their enduring enmities, always catch up with them in the end.

Beyond the damage and harm he caused, Collins' biggest regret seems to have been missing out on more female company. But it raises the question about what we can do with unloved, angry, lost, hurt and vengeful young men. Their existence is miserable unless they are offered sanctuary in a bottle, a pill, a wrap or a gang, a cause or an organisation. Extremism – of all types – is at once political and personal, ideological and social, criminal and cultural. How much more violence will it take?

Collins recounts a particularly vicious attack by the far right on a community meeting in Welling Library in south-east London which resulted in 17 people – including many women – being taken to hospital. A pregnant woman was locked in the toilet, in fear of her life and that of her unborn baby. Around this time Collins started leaking snippets of information to *Searchlight* magazine. The role of *Searchlight* – and their 'HOPE not hate' campaign more recently – in bringing down several far right individuals and organisations is clear from Collins' account.

So far, no political movement has found an effective way to tap into latent nationalism in a mainstream fashion. It's no longer purely about race, but about immigration, nation, Islam or corrupted accounts of Englishness. It amounts to the same thing. An 'other' is defined and used to mobilise hate. A fault-line is exposed and people are driven apart. If the right mix of charisma, organisation and outside events occur, who knows what the result could be? This process is terrifying in the context of economic hardship. These elements have never been combined in the UK context. We have been lucky with our far right-ists in a political sense: they have been pretty unpleasant, poorly led, off-putting, disorganised, fractious, and just plain weird or threatening. The poor victims of their actions in targeted communities are anything but lucky, living their lives in fear and meeting with physical and psychological harm from time to time.

Whether the BNP is still with us at the next election or not, it will have a successor. Its supporter exodus is latching on to other groups and parties – the English Democrats, the BFP and the EDL seem obvious places for disillusioned BNP activists to head. Many may desert the ballot box and go for 'direct action' instead. Their own personal outlooks will decide in which direction they go. Indeed, ex-BNP London Assembly member Richard Barnbrook has been in talks to join the English Democrats. It remains to be seen whether the English Democrats can survive their transformation into the successors to the BNP, as their existing membership base may revolt.

Two substantive factors have changed since the late 1990s. Racially driven extremism has been rejected. The parties are still racist, but the BNP and others have evolved their argument into a more sophisticated critique of cultural and religious threat, political betrayal and economic desolation. With this in mind, the BNP has claimed, falsely, that they are the 'Labour Party that your father voted for'.

The second factor that transformed the far right was historically high net immigration. Quite simply, mainstream politics was blindsided. Immigration tied together cultural angst, economic anxiety and political distrust. As an issue, it moved from the fringe to the mainstream. The BNP's successes were both a symptom and a catalyst of that.

So, who is attracted to the BNP? Members are generally aged over 35, C2 or DE social classes, not in full-time work but they do own their own houses. Are we talking the National Front grown up? Yes and no. The activist base – especially at senior level – often has roots in the National Front, but its supporter base is strikingly different in many ways. BNP supporters are more northern (41 per cent are in the north), whereas National Front support was based more in urban London and the West Midlands. We may be talking about a similar socio-political phenomenon, but its geography is strikingly different. What is notable from Matthew Goodwin's interviews with BNP activists is their Labour background – they feel let down by Labour, but live in traditional Labour, single-industry or highly concentrated industry towns. The BNP's voters, on the other hand, are more mixed, with a quarter coming from Conservative backgrounds.

In terms of the 'identity tribes' that were analysed earlier, BNP voters are in a state of 'active enmity' – the furthest group on the right. Many of them will once have been 'identity ambivalents' and they share a number of socio-demographic characteristics with that group. They are not economically comfortable and they have been disorientated by change. The major difference for those in 'active enmity' is that they have lost a sense of optimism for the future. They are also more likely to condone violence as a defence against what they see as threats to their identity. Their value set is 'settler', though the activists are more likely to be prospectors, unfulfilled and on the border between the two groups.

In previous times, working-class solidarity and the labour movement guarded against fascism. Now the working classes are fragmented, politically pluralistic and do not feel anywhere near the same degree of class solidarity. Labour can try a nostalgic political strategy but it will fall on deaf ears. When Labour came into office in 1997, there was a thin and defensive (mainly northern) class solidarity in reaction to 18 years of Conservative government. The Labour Party no longer exists solely as the political wing of the English working class. Nor will it be so ever again, if it remains a serious contender for office as the working class fractures and declines.

Goodwin is right in his contention that the far right are not like bees, described by the American historian Richard Hofstadter – 'once they have stung, they die'. Rather, they are more like moths: they come out in the dark and metamorphose from one form to another. The BNP may only be the pupal stage of the British far right. From National Front to BNP to who knows what? At each stage they have tried to shed their previous form. Luckily, they have failed – and that may be intrinsic to the psycho-political type we are talking about.

The EDL is a reversion to the National Front type – violent street thuggery and physical, verbal and psychological threats – and this limits it, terrifying and dangerous though it is. Already, they are seeking a partner in electoral politics as a result and the BFP seems to be their current partner of choice. To what the extreme right will evolve next is unpredictable: violent extremism, fragmentation, street protest and violence, a credible French Front National-style protest party, or perhaps towards a populist stance like the Danish People's Party, say. It will depend on leadership, organisation and opportunity. What is to say that a culturally nationalist yet rhetorically moderate and populist form of fascism won't emerge? Neither of the major parties in the UK are trusted. In the context of austerity, it is not inconceivable that such an alternative could thrive. It happens very quickly in a situation of weakening links between parties and their traditional bases of support, backed by the networked media. There are examples across Europe of this happening – Geert Wilders's

Dutch PVV, despite its setbacks in the 2012 election, is one such example.

We have seen how the paradox of class, a growing sense of identity, especially in an environment of economic change, and the rise of networks over institutions are changing the nature of politics. The future of extreme-right organisations is as varied as the social and political world in which they operate. One likely model will be networked extremism. It has been deployed effectively by the 'movement for a better Hungary', Jobbik, who are now the third most important party in the Hungarian parliament, having won 17 per cent of the vote in 2010. Writing in *Der Spiegel*, Keno Verseck quotes political scientist József Jeskó:

> [This right-wing extremist network is an] almost completely self-contained virtual system that gives its users an unbelievably strong identity and a comprehensive worldview, their own complete way of living that only allows means or information to penetrate from outside with extreme difficulty.

This network contains a multitude of sites, social media, community action and its own broadcast capability. Like the Tea Party in the US, it does not need the mainstream media (though Fox News helps!). In fact, the more antipathy shown towards it in the mainstream media and politics, the stronger it seems to have become. When we add into the mix the economic situation with lower middle-class wage stagnation and increasing job insecurity it becomes even more potentially combustive. The threat to security and discomfort that can result from change creates an environment in which populism, and even extremism, can prosper. Loss aversion is a well-established psychological proclivity. These are dangerous and corrosive political movements built on this aversion as well as economic destruction, social fragmentation and the power of networks over established civic, political and media institutions.

In what sense is the constant assertion of traditional social democracy powerful in the face of this deep structural change? Where are the foundations of solidarity and the institutions on which social democracy relied in its golden age just after World War II? Where is the togetherness of spirit at the local, or even national, level on which social democracy depends? The reality is that these have all weakened. *The Choir* TV series brought the South Oxhey community together, and people found that they had more in common than they imagined. More focus on local life and relationships, with national support, resourcing and investment can help to manage change. A responsible political and media culture that does not indulge in 'othering' and ambiguous insinuation would also be welcome.

All of this requires a profound rethink about how the left sees the world. It needs a careful politics of local engagement and trust-building rather than off-the-shelf big national schemes of redistribution. People need to be brought into politics rather than just stacked in blocks of support to secure electoral success. That trick is facing diminishing returns – and is being replaced by a more networked interest and community-based politics. The politics of the left should instead seek to empower people in their everyday lives. This will not be something it does on their behalf. It will need the inclusive economic institutions we discussed in the previous chapter. New and more inclusive democratic institutions are needed alongside these; they should be founded on the principle of self-determination.

Identity, culture, the need for institutions and democratic self-determination are all converging slowly but surely on a big national dialogue that concerns the notion of nationhood itself. A civic nationalist conversation has been taking place in Scotland, Wales and Northern Ireland for some time. A similar process is now only just getting under way in England. This will have consequences beyond culture alone. It will change Britain's politics and constitution too, as the country is in a state of unrest and political instability. The left now has a choice: engage fully in that discussion or leave the decision about England's national future to others. The latter course will be a losing strategy. The left fears national identity; that fear could provoke major strategic defeat.

CHAPTER 5

England and Scotland

W e have long associated regional pride with secessionist regions in the north of Spain. FC Barcelona, anti-Francoism and fierce independence is what spring to mind when we think about Catalonia. It is easy to see Scotland in the same sort of independent light. But could England have an independence urge – albeit a milder one – of its own? *The Dog That Finally Barked*, published by the IPPR, assembled a stack of evidence suggesting that after many years of a predicted rise of 'Englishness', this is now actually happening. Not only that, but this rising Englishness has a political expression that may become irresistible. This has profound implications for the future of the centre-left.

In a selection of European 'regions' (or 'nations' – cross-national definitions are tricky, but bear with me), the IPPR survey showed that 45 per cent of Catalans feel more Catalan than Spanish. Scotland is top of the 'regional' pride league in Britain, with 60 per cent saying they are more Scottish than British (only 11 per cent say they are more British than Scottish).

Yet it is the English results that are the most interesting. Forty per cent feel more English than British, with only 16 per cent the other way round. That is more 'national' pride than the other 12 in the select group of 15 Austrian, Spanish, French, German and UK regions included in the report. Indeed, results from the 2011 census support these findings: 57.7 per cent of English and Welsh residents reported themselves to be *only* English, while 29.1 per cent chose British as their national identity (alone or in conjunction with another identity).

Labour's traditional favoured solution to asymmetric federalism is for regional assemblies to be introduced. This is a complete non-starter. Even in the north it is the preferred constitutional solution for only 10 per cent of the population. The majority have a desire to locate greater power in English political institutions, though this has different expressions: 17 per cent want the greatest influence for local councils; 12 per cent overall for regional assemblies; and 36 per cent for an English Parliament (when 'English votes for English laws' – that is, where only English MPs are allowed to vote on laws related to England alone – was not included as an option). Fifty-four per cent prefer to have either an English Parliament or English votes for English laws. In other words, only a quarter of the English want to keep things pretty much as they are now.

These data are just a snapshot. It is difficult to discern how these attitudes are changing and the intensity with which they are felt. The political establishment has been cautious up to this point. If this was a stable environment, then these data would be interesting, but should not induce a panicked reaction. The problem is that the situation is changing – Scotland's constitutional settlement may shift, Englishness denied is being used as a mobilising force for antagonistic nationalism, and a cultural conversation about Englishness has begun to blossom. What has not happened to a great degree – yet – is for these shifts to become reflected in mainstream political conversation. If it is only a matter of time before there is a politicisation of Englishness, which seems possible and perhaps even likely, then it is better to get ahead of the discussion rather than to leave it to be defined by some negative or self-interested voices. The left in general, and the Labour Party more specifically, cannot afford to ignore this issue for too long, as happened with the immigration debate. It may become too late for the left to influence the direction of political Englishness should it fail to engage at an early stage.

A sound principle to uphold in these conversations is the notion of 'self-determination'. This should be the core principle of the UK's constitutional future. It should apply to Scotland, Wales, Northern Ireland, Cornwall (Kernow), Birmingham and the Falkland Islands alike. If communities want certain powers, and the basic human rights of particular groups do not suffer as a result, then they should be granted. It would not be neat, but it would be democratic.

A response to the asymmetry of power in the UK will come, and perhaps sooner than we think. The English dog is now barking. In its stand on English constitutional reform, and in its fierce defence of the status quo in Scotland, Labour is letting the tail wag the very same dog.

Time for an Optimistic Englishness

National communities tend to be imagined or re-imagined at times of convulsive change and crisis. Yet though such change – social, economic, technological and constitutional – is currently undermining the status quo, the political conversation around Englishness continues to be largely avoided, treated as academic or seen as superficial. This is a serious error.

There are three potential sources that could force a more serious dialogue about the political (as opposed to the cultural) consequences of Englishness: an increasingly assertive and antagonistic English nationalism; a resurgent and forceful Scottish nationalism; and the changing contours of the international economy and financial crisis, which are likely to lead to constitutional change, especially within the EU and the Eurozone.

Evasion of the issue comes in two main forms. The first seeks to avoid rekindling any nationalism in a globalised, post-national world, but this liberal universalism has found it hard going in a post-9/11 world, where security concerns and economic anxiety mesh: cultural antagonism has blended with economic insecurity to create nationally based resistance to the changes wrought by globalisation. Increasing political demands for labour mobility protectionism – immigration control – is just one example of this reactive impulse. But the stronger force for resisting a politics of Englishness is the status quo that wants to keep Pandora's Box closed. The fear in this mindset is that to open the dialogue is to take undue risk. In its conservative guise, the concern is the risk to the constitutional order: the argument seems to be that Englishness is a dormant identity that should not be disturbed. But as we have seen, this is changing.

Liberals and multiculturalists do have a voice in this risk-averse perspective. The fear is that antagonistic forces will take control of the dialogue, resulting in social and political disturbance. This fear is entirely understandable, given the historical connectedness of nationalism, antagonism, racism and violence. As Paul Gilroy wrote in *There Ain't No Black in the Union Jack*: 'The politics of "race" in this country is fired by conceptions of national belonging and homogeneity which

not only blur the distinction between "race" and nation, but rely
on that ambiguity for their effect.' Gilroy also notes that the Union
Jack has now been replaced by the cross of St George as a threatening emblem of the far right. Englishness is replacing Britishness as
the favoured form of exclusive identity among the culturally antagonistic. Only 14 per cent of British Asians considered themselves
English or 'hyphenated-English' rather than British in the Searchlight
Educational Trust's *Fear and Hope* survey. Gilroy's concerns, shared
by many minorities living in England, are not trivial.

The nub of the issue is whether a nation in mourning over its relative economic and geopolitical decline has the capacity for a generous
dialogue about its English ethos: one that can find broad, inclusive and
legitimate political expression. If the risks of initiating an Englishness
dialogue are so great, why gamble? The answer is that there may be
few other options.

Antagonism and Englishness

England currently faces threats to its economic, cultural and constitutional order, from both within and beyond its borders. The degree
to which it is able to confront these threats will depend on a new
political settlement. As outlined in the previous chapter, the internal threat comes partly from an increasingly menacing expression
of assertive and antagonistic monocultural nationalism. These forces
take a number of forms: from violent street confrontation to nationalist populism.

They mobilise around forms of English symbolic expression in
a context of anxiety induced by economic change and dislocation,
nostalgic loss of national pride, and significant cultural shifts. It is
easy to dismiss the EDL simply as thuggery, or the BNP as a rabble
in respectable dress. But they represent something more sinister: a
mutated nationalism in the absence of serious mainstream engagement with the desire for national belonging and meaning.

In-group loyalty is hard-wired into our moral sense, as the
psychologist Jonathan Haidt showed in his 'moral foundations
theory'. What is more, biological research is looking more closely at

group selection in human evolution. The socio-biologists Edward O. Wilson and David Sloan Wilson have argued that group dynamics can play a role in evolutionary selection. Humans can develop a group mentality and commitment that goes beyond narrowly defined self-interest. Individual interest remains the more powerful force, but selection is 'multi-level'. Anthropology and biology both hint at the enduring power of group identity, and in the modern era national identity is certainly one of the strongest existing identities. People have been willing to sacrifice their lives for it. So nationalism is real, and the group dynamics and competition that underline it are completely explicable. However, group formation and culture are entirely contingent. Sometimes group loyalty mutates into something atrocious.

In 2010, the first person to be convicted in relation to the production of ricin under the Chemical Weapons Act 1996 was a white supremacist working with three other men. Ian Davison prepared ten ricin doses and it appeared that he may have been planning to use them in a pipe bomb. Crown Prosecution Service lawyer Stuart Laidlaw described Davison and his son, Nicky, as: 'Nazi zealots who believed in white supremacy and revered Adolf Hitler. They hated minority ethnic groups, be they black, Asian, Muslim or Jewish.'

This case was largely ignored in the mainstream media. So the violent threat is real, but there is also a populist English nationalism that has yet to find mainstream political expression in the way that national identity has done in France, Sweden, Denmark, Hungary, Finland or the Netherlands. Yet a similar widespread notion of cultural threat exists in England as in its European partners. The German research institute Friedrich Ebert Stiftung published a cross-national comparison of attitudes to immigration and race in 2011, authored by A. Zick *et al.* and entitled *Intolerance, Prejudice and Discrimination*. The UK shows high levels of antipathy towards immigrants: 45.8 per cent of British respondents agreed that 'because of the number of immigrants, I sometimes feel like a stranger in [my home country]'. The comparable figures for the Netherlands was 37.7 per cent, and Hungary 44.6 per cent. These are two countries that have had successful right-wing parties – Geert Wilders's PVV in the Netherlands and Jobbik in Hungary.

The point about the likes of Jobbik and PVV is that they can appear and expand very quickly as they adopt networked rather than institutional forms of organisation. The PVV, which motivated a network around anti-Islamic sentiment, loss and economic frustration, were in a co-operative parliamentary arrangement with the Dutch Liberal Party (VVD) until they left government, precipitating an election in September 2012. Successful political parties would previously have taken decades to build, but it can now be done in a few months. We saw in the previous chapter that there is a potential pool of supporters for such antagonistic parties. There is certainly an opportunity for a populist alternative on the right (in fact, in one question in the *Fear and Hope* survey, almost half of the respondents said they would consider supporting such a party).

Mainstream political forces – particularly on the left – shied away from issues with an identity element, such as immigration, in the early 2000s, only to find that by the time they entered the discussion the terms had already been set by the fearful tone of the right in the media, and in popular and political discourse. Essentially, the emphasis of the mainstream left has been on the more pluralist notion of Britishness – the good nationalism, while a political focus on Englishness has been largely avoided, leaving it as a cipher for more antagonistic political forces. It should be noted that Britishness and Englishness are not mutually exclusive at all. But what happens if Englishness is thrust centre-stage by external developments? There is enormous risk of mainstream political discourse trailing behind on this terrain. Indeed, it is already doing so.

Proceeding hand in hand and in intimate communion with antagonistic nationalism is the external threat of global economic change and crisis. The shift of the international division of labour towards emerging nations, and the economic muscle of those nations who enjoy a financial surplus, has had an impact on perceptions of identity. This has concentrated both the winners and the losers from global economic change within the UK. It is in the localities of loss, where economic change is most visible, that this process of identity reaction has been greatest. There is also a constitutional ramification of global economic change that will impact increasingly on the UK's ability to maintain a flourishing economy amid change.

The future of the Eurozone is unclear, as its survival will depend on a new constitutional settlement between members, including a form of fiscal union and a new political union. However, if it is successful, the Eurozone will increasingly become an even more co-ordinated and co-operative political and economic bloc. This will return the UK to a fringe position, with the main economic show being elsewhere – as it was prior to its signing of the Treaty of Rome in 1973. The concern is the degree to which this economic (self-)exclusion will start to place the UK in an unfavourable position *vis-à-vis* neighbouring Eurozone members, as they collude to stack the rules of the game in their favour.

Over time, Eurozone membership could become a more attractive proposition for Scotland if insider status becomes critical – though it is definitely unattractive at present. This is one of the longer-term sources of threat to the continuance of the United Kingdom. England is very unlikely to enter the Eurozone in the foreseeable future. While a majority of Scots are currently against membership, will the centripetal pull be too great in the future? If British economic and political union breaks, England could be left alone in its untended garden of antagonistic Englishness, facing unfavourable global economic change and constitutional change within the EU/Eurozone. Even if independence and the Eurozone do not prove to be sufficiently enticing political and economic alternatives to the UK for Scotland, any further devolution will place the politics of Englishness front and centre. Such a desire for greater devolution, including fiscal independence, is a real possibility and, perhaps, even within the next decade, whatever the result of the independence referendum to be held in 2014 (it is likely to be 'no', but not certainly so).

Scotland's Optimistic Nationalism

Reformulations of national identity and major constitutional change have usually tended to be a response to some serious threat: security, cultural or economic. The Act of Union itself in the early eighteenth century was such a response, as England sought to nullify ecclesiastical, dynastic and security threats from France and Catholicism, while Scotland sought to extricate itself from an economic and financial black hole. A similar period of political, civil and constitutional change occurred in the aftermath of the French Revolution and the Napoleonic Wars. Krishan Kumar noted in *The Making of English National Identity* that the first successful attempt at the formation of an English nationalism – though more cultural than political in form – was in the context of demands for Irish Home Rule and nationalist fervour on the Continent at the end of the nineteenth and beginning of the twentieth centuries.

It is less clear what threat motivates the current increasing success of Scottish nationalism as a political movement: Scottish nationalism is, it would appear, a nationalism of choice rather than necessity. Yet it has been remarkably successful, and this has significant consequences for England. John Curtice of Strathclyde University reports polling that shows 60 per cent of Scots in favour of either full independence (28 per cent) or so-called 'devo max' (32 per cent), whereby all powers are devolved to the Scottish Parliament other than those related to foreign policy, defence and monetary policy. 'Devo max' is now a mainstream argument, and even received the backing of former UK prime minister John Major in a speech to the Ditchley Foundation:

> Why not devolve all responsibilities except foreign policy, defence and management of the economy? Why not let Scotland have wider tax-raising powers to pay for their policies and, in return, abolish the present block grant settlement, reduce Scottish representation in the Commons, and cut the legislative burden at Westminster?

In the straight choice between separation and maintaining the status quo, it still seems likely, though far from certain, that the status quo would be maintained. It will come down to who wins the economic and emotional debate, and that is anything but clear-cut. Once 'devo max' is in the mix, things become significantly more complex, with the status quo becoming the second most favoured option after 'devo max'. Furthermore, things may change over time – and rapidly.

Another recent poll, this time from TNS-BMRB, showed that support for independence was very strong among 18–34 year olds and evenly split among 35–44 year olds; only those aged 44 and over are against it. Whatever happens in the referendum, the current constitutional settlement seems an unstable one: a change of some sort is likely in time.

Scottish National Party leader Alex Salmond and his party have been able to construct a pluralistic and optimistic nationalism that fits Scottish society as it is, not as a tartan utopia of the imagination. At the 2011 opening of the newly elected Scottish Parliament, Salmond evoked Robert the Bruce and William Wallace, but as voices of the past rather than of an Anglophobic present. Instead, he reached for Scotland's twenty-first-century voices: members of the Scottish Parliament (MSPs) whose first language was Italian, Urdu and Arabic, alongside English, Gaelic, Scots and the Scottish Doric dialect. Scotland was to emerge from the 'glaur of self-doubt and negativity', no longer the junior partner but standing as an equal with England. This optimistic nationalism is about being better, whether it is a question of defeating alcohol abuse, building a new renewable-energy economy or confronting sectarianism.

If optimistic nationalism results in 'devo max', it would create new English political institutions by default. New constitutional arrangements, a new economic challenge and the sudden re-emergence of political Englishness would surely then focus the English political conversation. The internal threat of distorted Englishness, the global economic changes and constitutional reforms within a newly federal United Kingdom would combine to make the question of Englishness a mainstream and urgent political concern. It is not unimaginable that a strong Englishness could emerge with the Conservative Party – as long as that did not contradict the continuation of the Union. There is a political advantage to it doing so, as Labour relies more heavily on support north of the border: one of the aspects of its structural advantage.

Paradoxically, Scottish nationalism is both a catalyst for a dialogue about Englishness and English political institutions, as well as a guide to how it can be managed while avoiding toxic overflow. Scottish nationalism's recent rise has been achieved without English people being beaten up in the streets and without political vandalism or violence. Though it challenges the constitutional order aggressively and consistently, it does so through democratic and civic channels; it presents a vision of the future rather than nostalgia or melancholy for the past. It is about a choice rather than a need. It is proactive and positive. Scottish nationalism is not only a challenge to political Englishness; it could also chart its salvation.

Cultural Liberty and National Identity

There are, of course, limitations in adapting the optimistic nationalism pursued in Scotland to the conditions in England. Englishness and Britishness are proximate, and there is still an enormous commitment to the latter – the successes of Team GB at the Olympics have emphasised that further. The two terms are so close that they have often been used interchangeably – and this is perhaps one reason why the constitutional absurdities thrown up by devolution have largely been ignored.

Scotland has always been differentiated in some sense as a nation within the UK, even when this did not have political expression. As Arthur Herman showed in *The Scottish Enlightenment*, Scotland was deliberately transformed intellectually, economically and culturally after the Act of Union. This was a point of historical rupture. For England, there was no similar point of rupture after the Union. There isn't a similar sense of an alternative view of national destiny that can be reached for; and nor do many English people contemplate the removal of the Stuarts from the throne in the Glorious Revolution (the most recent point of rupture in English history) with a sense of bittersweet regret. In contrast to this, many Scots mourn the end of independence in the context of national failure.

Nonetheless there are clear elements of the Scottish approach that suggest a workable politics of national identity. It is not culturally or ethnically exclusive, which enables it to respond to a pluralistic society. It is defined on its own terms, which avoids the pitfalls of creating a cultural 'other', to be differentiated or demonised. It is forward-looking and so contains promise while avoiding a debilitating politics of loss.

Cultural liberty in the form of a life free of cultural and national identity would seem to pull in opposite directions, but Scottish optimistic nationalism suggests that this need not necessarily be the case. It is possible to achieve an accommodation between the two. In many ways, this approach to Scottish nationalism is compatible with the thinking of Amartya Sen, who rejected the notion of a singular and compulsory identity as he wrote in *Identity and Violence: The Illusion of Destiny*: 'The insistence, if only implicitly, on a choiceless singularity of human identity not only diminishes us all, it also makes the world much more flammable.' For Sen, the issue is choice: he is concerned about both communitarian monoculturalism (the strong and integrationist national culture view we met in the last chapter) and separatist multiculturalism (where different communities live separately but with equal status). He quotes Gandhi's objection to groupist separatism – the separatist multiculturalist view – as being the 'vivisection' of the Indian nation. It is possible for national identity to accommodate self-expression, as long as it does not take an acute form in which a sense of national coherence and togetherness can be lost.

In this context, a plural yet grounded national identity is just one aspect of an individual's identity, albeit one that has political consequences in a nation state – which is why political Englishness arouses such apprehension. Two major strands, both of them unhelpful, have previously dominated the political discourse of Englishness – idealism and instrumentalism – and this is one reason why the conversation is viewed so anxiously both on the left and the right.

Englishness – Ideal and Instrument

For Stanley Baldwin, the Worcestershire-born Conservative prime minister of the 1920s and 1930s, Englishness was a sensibility:

> The sounds of England, the tinkle of the hammer on the anvil in the country smithy, the corncrake on a dewy morning, the sound of the scythe against the whetstone, and the sight of a plough team coming over the brow of a hill, the sight that has been in England since England was a land ... the one eternal sight of England.

Unfortunately, this describes an England that no longer exists: the tinkle of the hammer on the anvil is no more; we don't hear the scythe on the whetstone; the corncrake is on the Royal Society for the Protection of Birds' red alert list, occasionally glimpsed, ironically, only in western Scotland and in Ireland; and the plough team is now mechanised – not so eternal after all. As evocative as Baldwin's words are, they describe an England that we can only now access through the words and art of the past.

When Englishness assumes a monocultural form, when it is idealised and amplified, tightly defined and dissected, it quickly slips from one's grasp. Soon after, there is little option but to pursue an elegiac course and inevitably declare its death. Thus Conservative philosopher Roger Scruton has declared England dead – what else is there to do? His England includes parlour songs, the Saturday-night dance, the bandstand and so on – those cultural forms and institutions have gone almost entirely. His *England: An Elegy* is a mournful song for his own childhood and the childhood experience of the English today is so very different; yet it is still English culture that they experience. Much more of their cultural experience is now imported, but cultures are ultimately about deep human contact. And they are still local and personal.

Sir Roy Strong, in *Visions of England*, an iconographic account of England written in 2011, locates Englishness – as an ideal – in rural traditions exemplified by the landscape and social order. With breathtaking and unsubstantiated boldness, he argues that this is the England that British soldiers fought for: 'They [soldiers] did not fight for Manchester or Birmingham but for the likes of Chipping Camden and Lavenham.' Sir Roy Strong's England is an idyll. He asks us to choose an England of pastoral tranquillity. Constructed around the iconography of artists, writers, monarchs and religious thought, Strong would have us revelling as modern-day John of Gaunts in Shakespeare's *Richard II*. This is a blessed plot and it should be revered.

There are not many actual people in Strong's England. There's the odd aristocratic landowner, such as Mr and Mrs Andrews in Thomas Gainsborough's eponymous painting. There's the occasional monarch, and Strong has a particular, though hardly original, soft spot for Elizabeth I. Now and again a peasant drifts into view, as in Constable's *The Hay Wain*. Cities and towns are an embarrassing secret to be hidden in this England. Orwell, Dickens, Canaletto, Lowry, D. H. Lawrence, Greene, Ballard and Betjeman and their depiction of England are either omitted completely or given a cursory mention. It seems that the response to English cultural angst is to indulge in fantasies.

Simon Heffer also sees England as 'monocultural' – though 'tolerant of other cultures'. No wonder there is such suspicion of Englishness among the many who do not feel that they fit into this monocultural straitjacket. A national identity with such an unbending attitude cannot hope to survive. So England is repeatedly declared dead. And yet – Lazarus-like – it returns to life, time and again. Perhaps it is the universalising, idealised monoculturalism of this – admittedly intoxicating – view of Englishness that needs to be rejected, rather than Englishness itself?

Though often deploying similar techniques of belonging and loss, radical instrumental Englishness is usually framed as an alternative to this idealised monoculturalism. Alastair Bonnett has pointed to important sources of nostalgia in radicalism; there is a recurring theme of returning home to a lost and uprooted existence. His *Left in the Past*, which was one of the inspirations for the title of this book, studies this sense of uprootedness powerfully. Perhaps George Orwell's description of England as 'a family with the wrong members in control' encapsulates this perspective best, tied as it is to notions of 'home' that are intrinsic to nostalgia. Orwell was determined to separate patriotism from conservatism in his revolutionary Englishness.

But this form of patriotism can quite quickly become instrumental, put to the service of a wider revolutionary mindset. For Hobsbawm, patriotism must be fused with working-class interests. E. P. Thompson also, while rescuing Englishness for the English people, sees it as benign when put to the service of class interests. However, both of these versions of Englishness – idealised and instrumental – fail to provide a viable pathway for an English political conversation. The first has little regard for the actual lives of English people as they are lived; and the second is put to the service of some class interest and can only be justified in those terms. Both are unsatisfactory, anachronistic and potentially dangerous if placed in the wrong hands.

The work of Benedict Anderson always arises in discussions of national identity, particularly his formulation of nations as *imagined communities*. But Anderson's theory points to the historical development of nations as embedded in specific convergences of economy, culture and technology. If technological and economic change are key factors in creating the context for new ideological forms, then what of our current technological and economic context? What impact do the social and technological changes analysed in previous chapters have on our sense of Englishness and belonging?

Technological and economic changes are fragmenting and pluralising culture. These include the rise of the internet, the social media, and cable and satellite television; the growth of the service sector; the expansion of consumerism; and the decline of the large-scale employer and single-industry town. Social change is also contributing to this fragmentation: the increasing privatisation of our lives as we centre them ever more on our own family and friends; changes in family structure and power relations between men and women; historically significant migration flows; the diversity of popular culture; and the secularisation/religious diversification of spiritual life. The notion of the existence of a homogeneous working class – or any other historical agent, for that matter – ready to be mobilised for revolution, seems fanciful in this technological and socio-economic world. Mass events that have near-universal national appeal, such as the royal wedding, are notable because of their rarity.

So the question then becomes: are there any fixed points of commonality? Because without fixed points Englishness is likely to become a weak and divided plurality of monocultures. It is not at all clear that any national identity, other than a thin one of passport, flag and sports allegiance, could hold the country together without more solid points of reference. There are notions of Englishness that have a fixed form, including the primacy of the English language, the rule of law and common law, supplemented by democratic statutes. There also exists an affinity for the land – both rural and urban landscapes – and an aversion to extremes, which some argue can be seen in the

Book of Common Prayer, and in English political history. But beyond these fixed notions there is a constant antagonism between different aspects of our national sensibility that is never resolved: little England versus global citizen; north versus south; radical versus conservative; rural versus urban versus suburban; scientific versus humanistic; and modern versus traditional.

Englishness has elements that are sturdy, but also those that are in perpetual tension. However, some English cultural forms combine inflexibility and fluidity. There is a body of literature and art that is seen as a repository of commonly valued works of English iconography, and there is also an ever-changing and diverse body of new and newly discovered work. A set of historical stories meshes with a global history of nations, and economic and intellectual development. Collective senses of memory and loss also include the migrant experience.

Fixed and contested – and beyond this, fluid, plural and individual – notions of identity form a complex web of modern Englishness. The collective challenge is to shape all these components of national identity into something both real and imagined that can support a nation state amid internal and external change. It need not be defined in opposition or reaction. It can be positive: England's cultural, historical and political resources are an embarrassment of riches. Nonetheless, to gather these abundant qualities in a way that is meaningful and workable needs more than imagination; it requires political dialogue.

An English Political Dialogue

Scottish devolution was the outcome (but not the end point) of an inclusive civic process. By the time of the 1997 referendum, Scottish civil society was reconciled and positive about devolution. In other words, in contrast to referendums that have been defeated, such as that on the Alternative Vote (AV) and on the north-east assembly, civic dialogue led to constitutional change rather than vice versa. This dialogue took place over the course of two decades and more. The lesson is not to impose institutions from the top down but to allow them to bubble up from an inclusive, national and civic dialogue.

If the English question – how to reflect notions of Englishness politically – is to assert itself in a time of internal threat and external change, it is crucial to begin a serious dialogue immediately and to allow it plenty of time. But before such a dialogue can take place it is important to identify as dead ends both idealistic and instrumental Englishness. Neither permits a meaningful debate to take place, since their conclusions are predetermined. Equally, this exercise is not about rejuvenating an imperialistic missionary nationalism. That is another dead end that wants to drag England back to a romanticised past. Instead, the dialogue needs to be non-deterministic, non-exclusive, pluralistic and democratic. It will be grounded distinctly in the present and therefore inclusive, non-oppositional and antagonistic. It will have a cultural element that will give voice to Englishness as it is actually experienced and felt, as both everyday practice and high art (and the past is part of this story). It will have a civic element, as institutions of congregation and association on a local level, and new communities of interest will be expressed as a relational Englishness.

While Englishness is not exclusive – the commitment to Britishness is deep – it will also be expressed in constitutional forms. Already there is an informal English legislative process: English laws, policies and regulations are passed in the Westminster Parliament; it is just that non-English representatives vote on them too. If Scotland moves to 'devo max', this constitutional anomaly will be unsustainable and, indeed, it may already be so. English parliamentary arrangements are likely to be necessary should devolution proceed any further – though they cannot simply take the form of existing British institutions (of which many still remain) made English by sleight of hand. Instead, new institutions must fit the reality of English pluralism – an English Parliament for the English people as they are not as we feel they should be, or once were.

To simply evolve an English parliamentary model from the British parliamentary model completely ignores the reality of English pluralism. Majoritarian politics has been increasingly inadequate for the task of expressing British democratic opinion. The same applies to England. We cannot simply allow Conservative majorities centred around the south and south-east of the country to dominate national life to an even greater extent, given wider pluralism. A new English political pluralism – with a voting system and institutions to match – is the only sensible and democratic option.

Self-determination matters beyond the national level too. A symmetric British federalism is neat but unrealistic. Instead, we need a bottom-up democratic restructuring. If the north-east or Kernow want new powers then they should have them. The north-east and north-west, in particular, could lose out through greater Scottish self-rule as business and enterprise is attracted north of the border. If these areas demand the political tools to respond, they should be given them – as long as a set of nationally identified basic economic and social needs are met.

The mistake in the past has been to try to impose a regional system of government on England that is poorly suited to the emotional attachments that people have. In some places, regional government may be suitable. In others it will be city or city-region. For some it will be at county or local level. Clusters of political authority may also come together in as yet unimagined ways. Once again, the core principle is self-determination – responding to bottom-up demands for devolved power. That in itself would provoke an English democratic revival. New democratic institutions are part of the new settlement.

Commitment to a national identity can move beyond cultural, civic and constitutional. There is also the promise of national identity – the 'American dream', Bismarck's corporate state, the extension and universalisation of the British welfare state after World War II. These were all, in Oakeshottian terms (see, for example, *Rationalism in Politics and Other Essays*), 'enterprise' projects designed to underpin a sense of common citizenship. This substantive offer cannot be side-lined in any discussion about English political expression. And, in fact, nationhood is also intrinsic to social justice. As the political theorist Margaret Canovan has noted in *Nationhood and Political Theory*: 'Most contemporary theories of social justice carry with them a tension between universalist moral principles and particularist political commitments, a tension that has been concealed from many participants in the discourse by the tacit agreement to take nation-states as given.' The advance of social justice requires an anchor in nationhood.

So it is not just about democratic reform, it is about a radical shift of economic and social power too: everyone should have a real stake and a real say. That means taking power from some who have a surplus and giving it to others who have too little.

The demise of the corncrake, parlour games and the forward march of the English working class may be regrettable, but Englishness lives on. It appears to die and yet is continually reborn. This death and rebirth is traumatic. In the face of an alternative that is corrosive, antagonistic and includes a threatening undercurrent of aggressive monocultural Englishness, there can be no waiting for others to decide the English national fate. A constitutional, cultural, civic and citizenship-centred dialogue about Englishness becomes necessary. Paradoxically, such a dialogue could lead to a more settled and balanced federal United Kingdom – albeit, in true English style, with a degree of asymmetry. At the very least it should prise Englishness away from those who wish to use it to exclude and harm.

This new English dialogue will need to be infused with new ideas. Luckily, this is a fertile time for political thought. Carried through channels of distribution and engagement opened up by new and social media, old philosophy combines with modern psychology in the vacuum created since the global financial crash. It is a time of opportunity when it comes to new thinking. The academic, journalistic and political worlds are beginning to cross-pollinate in new ways; even the commercial world occasionally gets involved. England's future and beyond will be profoundly influenced by these ideas, and the sense that the left is able to make of them will determine its bearing on that future.

CHAPTER 6

Imagining the Future

Two golfers walk up to the first tee. The first pulls out a shiny, new, technologically engineered driver and pings a 250-yard shot straight down the centre of the fairway. He strokes his designer cap and steps back, so that the second player can settle into her stance. She lifts her single club – a six iron – and swings at the ball, just clipping it as she loses her balance with the effort of it all. The ball bounces a few yards forward, coming to an embarrassing stop 65 yards and 45 degrees off to the right. She daren't take another shot, such is her shame.

How can these golfers compete? What should be done to enable them to compete?

The answer to this question sits beneath the modern political conversation about what is just. Four ideas dominate the recent political discussion in seeking to answer this question: anti-state neo-Hayekians; pro-equality and pro-state Croslandite social democrats; new fraternalists who emphasise human relationships; and the new moralists who seek 'virtue' – for example, Blue Labourites and Red Tories. Socialism has weakened considerably, but sits on the fringes alongside these perspectives. Ultimately, though, none of these approaches by themselves satisfactorily resolve the golfing dilemma. Elements of all of them have a contribution to make. A new set of ideas based on empowering the individual without determining his or her fate is required. These ideas would understand both the co-operative and competitive nature of humanity. They would acknowledge humanity's moral capability. Yet the philosophy would be freedom-loving without assuming naively that this freedom can thrive in the absence of the correct practical institutions. Elements (but by no means the entirety) of democratic republicanism – which emphasises the power of voice and ownership – mixed with the pragmatic institutionalism of Amartya Sen's 'capability theory', which emphasises realisable opportunity, offers a good way forward.

Going back to our golfers, the neo-Hayekian view would be that to interfere in the golfing contest would mean interfering in free exchange. It would argue that it is a slippery slope to the destruction of the liberty of both players, and ultimately the game itself. By allowing the best to thrive, others can also acquire opportunities – all gain, but some gain more than others, is the argument. If you determine outcomes in advance, what is the point of even playing, no matter how much of a mismatch there is between two players? Certainly, the advantaged player would lose interest and find something else to do. We encountered the economic ideas of many who would be neo-Hayekian in outlook in Chapter 3. Such liberalism is creative but also volatile and destructive. All too often it leaves a path of devastation in its wake.

A 'Fabian' – as Jesse Norman caricatures the left in his well-argued handbook for Cameronism, *The Big Society* – would reach for the handicap system right away. Croslandite social democracy, so-named after Anthony Crosland, author of the seminal revisionist left book, *The Future of Socialism,* is a better way of explaining this outlook. Equality is the end, and the means are carried out by the state. The two players could play together for a time using the handicap system, but really it wouldn't be a competition. The first player surges ahead and wins but the scores would be narrowed at the end and both players would be left angry, frustrated, or both. The advantaged player would feel unfairly restricted, and the less able and under-resourced player would not improve much. We can compensate the less well-off player but it will not change the fundamental disadvantage: it looks more equal but in reality it is not.

This explains the problem we have identified with traditional redistributive social democracy – and why it is becoming less sustainable. The redistributive approach, which is seen by those on the left as 'fairness', is interpreted by many as encouraging a lack of responsibility and reciprocity. Think again about those voters we encountered in Chapters 1 and 2, who left Labour in 2010, concerned at the party's failure to deal with welfare dependency among other such concerns typical of reciprocal fairness. Jesse Norman and proponents of the Big Society respond to this in reference to the conservative philosophy of Michael Oakeshott and his typology of societies.

The first of the Oakeshottian ideal types is 'civil society' where equal citizens associate freely under the rule of law – they have much in common but no common cause. Then there is the 'connected society' which is Norman's own construction. This is the Big Society of individuals with an affinity for one another, who are co-operating, empathising and institution-building. Norman proposes a 'civil society' with a 'connected society' layered on top. There is much crossover in this argument with Norman's fellow centre-right fraternalist, Danny Kruger.

Kruger argued, in an article for *Prospect* magazine, 'The Right Dialectic', that both the left and right of British politics have been trying to free themselves from their historical positions in politics – the left grounded in 'equality' and the right in 'liberty'. Modern conservatism is based on a liberty-loving fraternity. Kruger defines 'fraternity' eloquently as 'the sphere of some': concerned with small groups, co-operatives, communities, families and so on. In other words, it is the spontaneity, accessibility and proximity of civil society that provides security and prosperity. Edmund Burke's 'little platoons' share this context. Essentially, small is beautiful, but this is not the same as Conservatives pursuing a Hayekian or Randian (after the popular American writer, Ayn Rand) individualist 'society'.

Jesse Norman and Danny Kruger are seeking to find a more coherent conservatism that links liberal individualism to something more socially realistic and stable. Thatcherism has been described as 'liberal conservatism'. It is a good term because it demonstrates the crisis of conservatism quite clearly: liberalism is chaotic, radical and subversive, whereas conservatism is about stability, continuity and certainty. Thatcherism unleashed market forces and in doing so tore apart the very type of society that conservatives hold dear – there is no such thing as society, remember. That societal damage was the wellspring of New Labour's intellectual and political opportunity. New fraternalists see fellowship as the glue between liberty and security.

But what does fraternalism do for the golfer whose talents are less developed? She might be lucky and someone might devote time and attention to improving her game – perhaps even the first golfer – but, more likely, she will be another lost talent. Fraternalism will work most effectively where there is already a strong base of, in the terminology of Robert Putnam, 'social capital'. Where there is not, it will be more difficult. It is not that fraternalism has no role to play. It's just that it may be insufficient. While bringing people together can lead to exchange, fraternalism does not necessarily do enough to alter the power between them. And under what circumstances will a golfer in an exclusive private club come together with the golfer on the municipal golf course? Power disparity has a geography.

Connected in spirit to new fraternalism is a new moralism. It takes the fraternal ethos – there is much crossover between the new fraternalism and new moralism – and charges it with a moral perspective constructed through some notion of public 'virtue'. The interesting thing about the new moralism is that it cuts across left and right. It is seen in both 'Red Toryism' and 'Blue Labourism'. While the moral tone is much milder in the latter, it is still discernable. New moralism emphasises traditional values, family, responsibility, community, security, right and wrong, good and bad. It is concerned primarily with the 'common good' over the rights of the individual. In fact, it has an alternative name – 'post liberal'. It is distinctively and definitively anti-liberal. A Judeo-Christian thread runs through it.

A characteristic argument of the new moralists is that Britain has faced two liberal revolutions in the last fifty years: social liberalism in the 1960s and economic liberalism in the 1980s. Both were disastrous and explain why our society faces its current travails. They are the reason why people are rioting. New moralism sees liberal elitism in many forms as the enemy of society and a betrayal of the vulnerable as it weakens their economic and cultural resource-base. As we saw in Chapter 2, this analysis misses the important reality of the nature of social change in developed societies. The left new moralists (Blue Labour) tend to emphasise economic liberalism over social liberalism in the challenges that society faces, and the right new moralists (Red Tories) the reverse.

At its best, the new moralism confronts the injustices of the market and the dangerous disintegration of social bonds that leave many adrift. It defends important social institutions, such as family and marriage, and insists that we all have responsibilities to each other.

At its worst, it constructs grand historical narratives of betrayal – mainly by liberal elites – and obsesses on catastrophic turning points. These have included the Reformation, the Enclosure Acts, the creation of the industrial economy, the 1960s social revolution, and the neo-liberal revolution. Rather than simply challenging the powerful, the moralisation argument can become both a Canute-like desire to turn back the ocean and deeply counter-productive.

Phillip Blond, founder of 'Red Toryism', responded to the 2011 riots by calling them 'liberal riots' and arguing for a 're-moralisation' of society. While it is true that people who believe that rioting, looting, perpetrating acts of vandalism and violence are wrong do not tend to engage in such activity themselves, quite what a process of 're-moralisation' could achieve, even if it were possible to any significant degree, is ambiguous. Immediately we are drawn to the question of whose morality should we follow? 'Common good' ideas either simply describe their own moral perspective as a common good or are evasive about the notion of 'virtue'.

New moralists are influential in both main parties. Ed Miliband alludes to a 'moral economy' and 'responsible capitalism'. The global financial crisis is not simply seen as an economic, institutional, network or governance failure, but also as a moral failure. So a new morality or set of virtues is needed to step into the void. In this, we can see the influence of 'Blue Labour', which combines traditional values with a sense of radicalism. There is also a hint of the type of 'good society' narrative pursued by campaign groups such as Compass or think-tanks such as the New Economics Foundation. On the right, David Cameron is more inclined towards the personal moral code aspects of the new moralism. He described parts of British society as 'sick' after the riots of 2011, and asserted that Britain is a 'Christian country' in a speech on the 400th anniversary of the King James Bible. Theology is never far below the new moralism if you scratch the surface.

In terms of our golfers, the new moralists might well pursue a similar path to the fraternalists. A difference might be that the interaction could carry with it a punitive edge or tone – it wouldn't be a voluntary arrangement so much as a dutiful one. For all its rhetorical clarity and academic pyrotechnics, the new moralism falls short.

We are now rather used to ignoring moral lessons, especially if we are powerful companies, governments or individuals, and so the new moralists may well end up relying on the very statism that they abhor. Moreover, there is not just one 'virtue'. The nature of 'virtue' is itself contested as, indeed, is the question of whether political life should be based on 'virtue' at all. How do we adjudicate? If we are to build a new moral framework, how are we to decide whose morality it is based on? Political and civic life are not devoid of morality – human beings are deeply moral and could co-exist peacefully without moral underpinnings. It is just that in a pluralistic nation – the 'bubbles society', discussed earlier – there are numerous, valid 'moral' perspectives which can sometimes disguise conflicting interests. A project of 're-moralisation' misses this diversity and has the potential itself to be a source of conflict – a morally charged politics raises the stakes considerably.

As old ways of thinking are being re-established in a current setting, both the new fraternalists and new moralists have added to our political discourse. They have both had a positively disruptive influence in the field of ideas. They both have their shortcomings too, though, and suffer from enormous over-optimism about their potential impact. We have already analysed the weaknesses in the traditional social democratic case in this economic, social and political environment. Nonetheless, the ideas which animate the left in future will borrow from all these schools of thought.

Elements of democratic republicanism and the pragmatic theories of justice offered by Amartya Sen and others offer a different way. Its general approach is to ensure that the second golfer is given *power* to pursue her talent and improve her ability. It is a broad philosophical church which often rests on a concept of the 'common good'. This element of democratic republicanism is not useful here, however, for the same reasons that it creates problems for the new moralism. The 'common good' either creates an unnecessary moral overlay to practical institutions and interventions, or it opens the door to all sorts of top-down moralisation – it becomes a new elite project in itself. The risks associated with the politics of 'common good' are that very quickly all kinds of things can be sucked into it and very quickly a theory resting on non-domination becomes influential. Republicanism sits between and overlaps with liberalism (freedom from domination) and communitarianism (the common good). It is in its former guise that it provides a more plausible way forward in a diverse and pluralistic society.

'Freedom from domination' is just one desirable element of modern democratic life. People also need to be able to build a life for themselves among others. In philosophical terms, this is the 'capabilities approach' associated with Amartya Sen and Martha Nussbaum, in contrast to the outcomes-oriented and utopian philosophies of, say, John Rawls or Anthony Crosland. This approach is shy of abstractions such as idealistic 'equality', and seeks only to make practical interventions to advance the power that people have over their own lives – knowing they are capable of deploying that power in ways that can meet their own needs and the needs of the wider community. It avoids both the idealism of Rawls and the Croslandite sleight of hand which pretends that means and ends can be separated. If you define the ends, then implicitly you will also have started to define the means. If equality of outcome is the ultimate aim, then large-scale central state intervention becomes the inevitable means, even if the approach is distinct from democratic socialism. It is better instead to focus on the means and empower people, working together, to define their own ends. Given that people are intrinsically social and moral as well as individualistic, they can be trusted, within the context of beneficial power-balancing collective institutions, to pursue their notion of 'a good life'. It does not require a communitarian notion of 'common good' beyond the basic instruments of democracy and freedom for this to be the case.

In Oakeshottian terms, as considered earlier in this chapter, an 'enterprise' society is one where people pursue collective goals by sometimes deploying the state to build new institutions. These institutions are not based on what inevitably becomes a top-down notion of 'virtue'. They are there to meet people's needs and enhance their ability to control their lives. They will, in a democratic republican sense, free them from domination by investing in institutions that enhance both their political and economic power.

Our female golfer has to work long hours at a minimum wage; she has a family to feed. She lacks time, resources and support, and consequently self-esteem. Quite simply, she does not have the opportunity to nurture her talents so that she can at least compete and gain some form of parity of esteem. What if some lessons were organised for her and she practiced intensely for a few years? Someone might enable her to buy a new set of clubs – that would make her more able. The more fortunate golfer might even be her teacher, so that when they met again they would be able to have a balanced, competitive game. They might even get on rather well – and learn from one another. The conversation might reach out into other aspects of life where they might be able to help one another.

The Big Society – and its 'new moralist' and fraternalist ethos – has the potential to make a number of fascinating and often valuable local changes. Ultimately, though, it will not make real and lasting change until its proponents accept that there must be something of the 'enterprise society' alongside it. Traditional social democratic utopianism struggles to stay the course, collapsing under the weight of its own over-ambition and impatience. The leftist version of new moralism, Blue Labour, is possibly more benign in that it is more about civic engagement and local institution-building. But its language of 'virtue' and the 'common good' will fit uneasily in a world of 'bubbles' and 'tribes'. If you are calling for a 'common good', what argument is there against 'virtues' of which you do not approve? Politics is, in part, a moral conversation, but is also far more than that. We have a pluralistic society. Such a society does not lend itself to absolutes. To seek absolutes beyond those without which UK society and democracy could not function courts reaction and polarisation, if indeed these absolutes are not simply ignored.

Instead, the democratic left will have to find a more practical set of ideas. These will inevitably be eclectic but they do need to be radical and non-utopian in seeking to secure change. Deep and practical thought is needed to create a real and lasting change to the circumstances of those who have too little control over their lives and access to opportunity. That is the ultimate concern of the left. How these ideas relate to the past, present, morality and human needs will determine their success. The mistakes of ideas such as nostalgic moralism, convulsive Hayekianism and utopian social democracy are key to assessing how a viable future for the left can be captured. It is through understanding these shortcomings in the context of the type of society discussed in earlier chapters that a different future may be imagined.

Red and Blue Country

Japan has a Big Society and Blue-Labour-style solidarity. At the end of the 1980s and in the early 1990s Japan was seen as the main economic competitor to the US. Its ability to eschew individualism and embrace collectivism in pursuit of the long-term common good exemplified everything the Anglo-Saxon West was not. This all disappeared when its asset bubble burst and little has been heard from the country since – other than as a warning of what can go wrong. Japan has endured two decades of low growth as a consequence of a financial crisis that continued to have aftershocks throughout the 1990s and 2000s. But it largely adjusted to the situation – despite a rapidly ageing society, which, in part, contributes to ongoing low growth.

If Blue Labourism is termed 'flag, faith and family', then Japan's watchwords could be 'flag, firm and family'. The country has a deep commitment to enduring institutions and values: ancestor worship, reverence for the emperor as the symbol of nation and continuity, corporate allegiance, family strength, pride in one's neighbourhood, and festivals are a common part of local Japanese life. Japan's history can be summarised as a quest to maintain national independence and cultural continuity.

That was Japan's motivation behind closing its borders for two and a half centuries, until Commodore Perry's gunboats sailed into Edo Bay in 1853. After that date, Japan industrialised and militarised rapidly along Prussian lines, its feudal system having failed. Its objective of maintaining its independence was still in sharp focus. With a brief interlude in the 1920s, this is why Japan continued on an imperialist course until its total and catastrophic defeat in World War II. And why the *kaisha* (the company) took the place of the military in preserving Japanese pride. There is a famous Japanese saying that encapsulates the process of creating a sense of common purpose over individual freedom: 'The nail that sticks up must be hammered down.'

Japan has had at least three revolutions since the mid-nineteenth century – though they would never call them that (they tend to call them things like 'restorations' instead). Yet, the country still paradoxically retains enduring core values alongside hyper-modern consumerism. The Japanese people maintain a deep connection to their past and their land; and they have built one of the world's most impressive megalopolises – Tokyo. They save cautiously for the future; and yet they have one of the most materialistic, consumerist cultures on the planet. Their education system promotes mind-numbing homogeneity; yet they have a mind-blowing level of artistic, architectural and design-focused creativity. The reciprocal commitment of individuals to firms and vice versa has its corollary within an in-firm gender exclusion, only possible because the wives run the family homes. Communities are strong, brought together both in neighbourhoods and the workplace.

Some of this social and economic organisation is beginning to fracture, however, under the weight of relative economic decline and social change. It has become sclerotic as new entrants are prevented from competing against corporate giants, and its economic dynamism has suffered as a result. However, Japan has remained truer to its traditions than most advanced economies. Social stability has held. The Red Tory and Blue Labour new moralist critique is that our own social bonds have not held. Japan's institutions have withstood the spread of network society with some change, but nothing major. This creates both positives and significant negatives.

So what can be learnt from this 'big Japanese society'? There are a number of lessons – most of which are too late for us, however. We have become consumerists like the Japanese, but our collectivism has already waned to a degree theirs has not. They have built freedom on top of traditionalism through economic success. We have chosen freedom over traditionalism. While it is easy to see how a more traditional society can become more liberal as it ceases to go to war and becomes more prosperous, it is more difficult to see the reverse happening in the same context. Liberty and traditional solidarity are in tension and contradiction. It is easier to unpick a rigid social order than it is to construct one on a bed of liberty. Any reversal of social change, while not impossible, is extremely unlikely.

Even if it could be replicated, this type of society, admirable in many ways though it is, has significant downsides (which are not coincidental): deep gender inequality and notions of Japanese racial supremacy – certainly over other Asians – is pervasive; the subsuming of personal independence into that of the group can suppress individuality; and a rigid system of rule-imposition that is constantly reinforced within the home, the classroom, in the street, in the meeting room and through popular culture. The other side of the high trust society is corruption, as the dismissed British chief executive of Olympus, Michael Woodford, discovered when he alerted the board to multi-million-dollar gaps in the firm's accounts. This elitism drifts into the country's politics – where elites only deal with each other, and hierarchy triumphs, as it does in the corporate world.

Jonathan Haidt's 'moral foundations theory' helps us to understand the appeal of both Japan as a nation, and Blue Labour and Red Tory ideas. Haidt describes morality as a '[graphic] equaliser with five [vertical] slider switches'. The two slider switches furthest to the left are marked 'harm' and 'fairness'. 'Harm' is about not doing harm to others, and 'fairness' is about reciprocity and justice: I will give to you if you give back to me. These are the two foundational principles of the modern welfare state and these values tend to be slightly more strongly expressed among the left. The three remaining slider switches are marked 'in-group loyalty', 'authority' and 'purity'. While the first two of these are self-explanatory, 'purity' is linked with religious ceremony, moral behaviour, hygiene and so on. We all have a mix of moral impulses, but people on the left will value the avoidance of harm and 'fairness' morality over 'in-group', 'authority', and 'purity'. Those on the right seem to have more of a relative skew to the latter three settings than those on the left. It is our individual mix of moral beliefs set at different levels that makes the graphic equaliser analogy so apt.

Japan is a nation that values the 'virtues' of the right over the left. The key thing about moral foundations theory is that it is derived from anthropological, biological and psychological research. It is about the human moral sense or, to put it more accurately, senses. Of course, where those slider switches are placed for any individual depends in part on their experiences and needs – this is the process of generational and some individual change observed in the values data from Inglehart and Dade that we looked at in Chapter 2. A person's politics are a complex interplay of experience, history, culture and psychology. each person's moral sense is communicated by political actors through the practice of 'framing', as the psychologist George Lakoff has argued. Different words 'work', as the pollster Frank Luntz would put it, and the moral baseline helps to determine what these words will be.

Both Blue Labourism and Red Toryism were attempts to break out of this right versus left framing. Red Toryism was an attempt to appeal to the 'fairness' virtue of reciprocity while keeping the moral commitments to the right. Blue Labourism was about seeking an appeal to the conservative 'virtues' of 'in-group' and 'authority'. Both eventually reach a similar place. Red Toryism never really manages to appeal convincingly to the left, as its language of 're-moralisation' feels very authority-heavy. The nostalgic labourism of Blue Labour similarly limits its appeal to those on the political right, to the post-industrial working-class and those of a liberal disposition.

The primary source of morality in both Red Toryism and Blue Labourism is the community (and this is why, despite valiant efforts to distinguish these ideas from communitarianism, there is more than a tinge of resemblance – communitarian philosopher Amitai Etzioni's books are called things like *The Common Good* and *New Common Ground*). The individual is brought to life by the community, through their vocation and through civic interaction. It is on the basis of these associations that the 'common good' is crafted. There is, in this sense, an idealistic element in this thinking. Market and state liberalism not only coincide but they also threaten the 'common good', and hence the flourishing well-being of individuals. Rights, equality and fairness are just abstractions in this worldview. What counts are the interrelationships that enable people to thrive.

In a 2009 essay entitled 'The politics of paradox' – and it should be noted that the collected volume on Blue Labour thinking referred to in Chapter 2 had a strikingly similar title, *Labour and the Politics of Paradox* – the theologian John Milbank outlines his own 'blue socialism', which he relates to the Compass campaign group. He also credits Phillip Blond, founder of Red Toryism, as a thinker from the right who appeals to the 'Radical Orthodoxy' of Christian thought. Milbank is deeply influenced by Catholic social thought and practice. He describes blue socialism as 'socialism with a Burkean tinge'. Milbank's political theology is about building a layer of institutions between the state and the market on the one hand and the individual on the other. The critical passage of his essay is the following:

> These debates concern the role of nuclear and extended families, of cooperatives, of trade guilds, of mutual banks, housing associations and credit unions, and of the law in setting firewalls between business practices, defining the acceptable limit of usury and interest and the principles that must govern the fair setting of prices. Above all perhaps they concern how we can turn all people into owners and joint-owners, abolishing the chasm between the mass who only earn or receive welfare and so are dependent and the minority who own in excess.

A little outdated, but so far, so good in practical terms. Who will lead us to this promised land? Worryingly, it is to be a 'noble outlaw-guardian'. This figure is part Batman (and Milbank references the moral vigilantism of the US comic-book series *Batman: The Dark Knight*, approvingly), part outlaw, part pastor, who must 'pursue virtue in uncorrupted secrecy'. The community organiser is also cast in a similar light by Saul Alinsky:

> The organizer, the revolutionist, the activist or call him what you will, who is committed to a free and open society is in that commitment anchored to a complex of high values. These values include the basic morals of all organized religions; their base is the preciousness of human life.

The community organiser has played a strong role in the Blue Labour argument and appears in both Big Society thinking and policy. In fact, the government has been recruiting hundreds of community organisers as part of its Big Society action. John Milbank ends *The Politics of Paradox* by arguing for a 'Catholic centre' that can 'think and act its way out of our current heretical, immoral and neo-pagan political morass'. It becomes quite dramatically apocalyptic.

There is a web of interrelationships here between Red Tories, Blue Labour, blue socialism (Blue Labour's more cosmopolitan brother, as represented by Compass), the Big Society, community organising, Radical Orthodoxy, and Catholic social thought. Along the way we find Karl Polanyi, Pope Leo XIII, Hilaire Belloc, G. K. Chesterton and Saul Alinsky. If we consider Milbank's list of intermediary institutions, there is clear common ground with the argument of this book when it comes to building the new institutions for a more just nation. It is in the other aspects that the problems begin. Why would that be the case?

We live in times of great uncertainty – financial crises, riots, unemployment and declining standards of living. For the left, it is also a time of political uncertainty and that is why we reach for new ideas and fixed points of certainty. The moral conversation is a hubbub that is becoming deafening. British society is socially divided: values are plural, needs diverse and attitudes varied. Judgement is cast on both the weak and the strong. Cultural battles are beginning to emerge, as they did in the 1960s and 1970s in the US. Take as one example the furore over the question 'Is the UK a Christian country?' and the battle over the right of same-sex couples to marry. Debates about the right to privacy (which is what the US Supreme Court case that sanctioned abortion, *Roe* v. *Wade*, was about) when it comes to abortion are resurfacing. Radical atheists and religious defenders speak a different language on different terms. Most of us are just left bewildered as the argument rages around us. The problem is not the absence of moral certainty; it is the presence of clashing moral certainties.

Politics as the progenitor of morality is, in some ways, a faintly disturbing notion, beyond a certain number of moral universals to which pretty much all right-minded people subscribe (such as 'Thou shalt not kill'). The purpose of democracy is a genuine dialogue between moral viewpoints, as well as interests, values and needs. Your morality cannot be left in the temple when you step into the public square – or the marketplace. But a top-down moral politics in a pluralistic nation is bound to result in anger and resentment. So, no matter how mild the notion of 'virtue', the dangers are clear. When you reach for notions of 'the common good' or assert the virtue of community, then immediately it provokes questions of 'Whose good?' and 'Whose notion of virtue?' Quite quickly, it becomes the virtue of either the committed – the self-appointed organiser or 'outlaw-guardian' – or the powerful, no matter what checks are put in place. Each of us has a different configuration of Haidt's five-slide equaliser, and we shall need to find a way of living a democratic life which acknowledges that and seeks to find a workable common ground.

However, Haidt's moral universe extends far too widely. In his *The Righteous Mind*, he defines moral systems as: 'Interlocking sets of values, virtues, norms, practices, identities, institutions, technologies and evolved psychological mechanisms that work together to suppress or regulate self-interest and make co-operative societies possible.' This is society rather than morality. Morality could be defined far more tightly as a set of regulating norms, rules and behaviours defined by good and bad which, when violated, create an intuitive objection and attract some form of sanction. It is the latter half of this definition that matters: if the moral universe is drawn too widely then politics becomes a long admonition between warring moralities. Do you want to know what that is like? Just watch cable news or wade on to Twitter from time to time. It gets us nowhere.

So 'moralities' are often simply perspectives or outlooks rather than universal truths. David Cameron's affection for the Big Society comes from his 'Shire Toryism' – paternal, patriotic, law-abiding, ordered, culturally integrated, but nonetheless retaining a complex relationship with capitalism and liberal markets. It is grounded in a set of established local social relations that the free market can tear up, which is profoundly disconcerting for the Shire Tory. However, for this outlook, market discipline is a deeply moralising force. Markets ensure that each individual makes a contribution; indeed, they have to. It is localist and suspicious of disruptive change. Together these values can come together to resist the free market – just take the town of Lymington in Hampshire, where both Argos and Wetherspoon's became corporate barbarians and were turned away at the gates. So it tends towards a 'free market for others, established social relations for our town' mentality. The 'red' of Red Toryism is thus subtly sidelined.

Blue Labour shares some traditionalist conservative elements with Shire Toryism. It has a more fundamental critique of the commodification of labour that results from global capitalism. Shire Toryism despairs of the harm that capitalism does to the social order while applauding it as a moralising force. Blue Labourism sees global capital as being destructive of horizontal ties of mutual respect and reciprocity, while Shire Toryism sees capitalism as destructive of vertical ties of mutual obligation (lord–squire–peasant).

The 'good society' creed of Compass shares the moralistic flavour but rejects the more conservative elements of the 'new moralism'. At the Compass conference in 2011, LSE academic Professor Francesca Klug asserted in a challenge to Blue Labour that the left's case for 'liberty, equality and solidarity' must be reasserted. Neal Lawson, founder of Compass, said that while he did do 'family', he did not do 'faith or flag'.

However, both Blue Labour and Compass share a love of 'virtue' while disagreeing about what this means in practice. Francesca Klug asserted, 'We must turn *our* values into policies which build a good society.' What if people do not care much for 'our' values or 'our' policies and find talk of 'a good society' just plain bossy? To put it another way, when do the people have a say? This is the fundamental issue with the new moralism. It misses the mainstream, substituting a notion of 'virtue' that is theirs rather than one that is shared meaningfully. If we were to plot Red Tory, Blue Labour and Compass on the *Fear and Hope* report 'tribes' it would conceivably appear as shown in Figure 2.

Blue Labour grazes the non-Tory mainstream to the right. Compass is anchored in the liberal left – almost exactly where the 'yes to AV' campaign (remember them?) was to be found. Ethical concern instantly turns to political reform: the 'common good' encompasses economic, social, environmental and political reform as 'virtue'.

Of course, Blue Labour, Compass and Red Toryism are not sold on the basis of their mass appeal. They are designed to shift the centre of political gravity. Could some sort of amalgam of these ideas provide a way forward, though? There is crossover in the language of

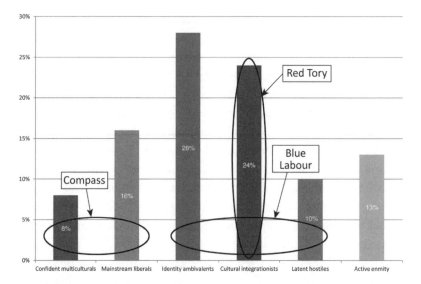

FIGURE 2   Figure 1 amended to show positions of Compass, Red Tory and Blue Labour

'relationships' and responsibility. However, there are mutual exclusivities between them. It is not possible to be a metropolitan progressive, urban labourite and Shire Tory at the same time (other than on single issues). They have very different views on culture.

A political vacuum will still exist. The 'identity ambivalents' – economically anxious, politically distrustful and with a degree of cultural angst – will be left without a voice. Their political concerns are not predominantly in high-minded ethics or with moral purpose. They think something has gone wrong and they are suffering, but they are not interested in utopian solutions – they want to get on with their lives. They want a helping hand and a voice, not a lecture. So, despite the merits of each of these elements of the new moralism, they miss the plural realities and political necessities in building a dialogue for change. So this diverts the left and Labour from the real focus: how can they meet people where they are rather than where they assume them to be, in order to initiate permanent change and greater justice?

Where new moralists and new fraternalists overlap – in promoting civic and economic relationships that can help to develop social capital – there is a powerful case for listening to what they have to say.

In the case of the new moralists, there are deep flaws, as we have seen. In the case of the new fraternalists, the risk is that change is weak other than where there are already strong community ties.

This word 'community' comes rather too easily, and it is seldom considered seriously. It is rarely defined. It is a word rather like the abstractions that new moralists despair of: equality, fairness, liberty and so on. Is it about locality? The reality is that some feel part of the local 'community' but many do not. Is it about 'group'? People have a complex interaction with various 'groups'. Their feelings of association with particular groups can be exceedingly weak despite their relationship to them. Is it about workplace? We saw how workplaces have become cellular and fragmented. Does it mean 'interest'? 'Communities' of interest may be densely formed or globally spread.

All these things can be described as 'communities' of some kind or another. The reality is that they are all collections of individuals with a range of commitments and depth of attachment. They are all voluntary. We can normally move neighbourhoods, leave our job or drop certain interests and take up new ones. Even if we see 'community' as something real it has changed massively in nature and form since the 1970s; the new moralists tend to overlook this basic fact. Community is often just another abstraction and a neat way of describing human interaction, relationships and commitment. It is individuals themselves who are the 'moral agents'.

By imbuing a collective or 'community' with 'virtue', some quite shocking things can start to happen. What if you are a young girl who finds yourself pregnant, decides that you don't want to continue with the pregnancy but you happen to be in a 'community' that thinks that abortion is shameful? What if you are homosexual in a 'community' that thinks same-sex relationships are morally wrong? What if you have ambitions to be an artist but live in a 'community' that only values manual work? What if you are a woman who wants to use her talents in the world of work but that is frowned on in your 'community'? These are not the views of the new moralists, but it is the logic of their position that ascribes the community's moral agency. The added irony, of course, is that by transferring moral choices to the community, or even the state, the capacity of the individual to make his or her own moral choices is diminished. Notions of community good might not go into any of this territory. But they *could* and that is the point: new moralism does not necessarily limit itself by, say, an aversion to domination. Human freedom is seen as a subset of a wider 'common good' rather than prior to it.

Is this an individualist liberal objection, as new moralists would claim? New moralists always see 'liberals' as their adversaries. But theirs is a caricatured 'liberalism' in the way that their notion of 'community' or 'society' is idealised. 'Liberals' believe only in the individual, the market and the state in this worldview. If you adopt that view then this is not the motivation behind this critique. In fact, the need for more and better social institutions that sit between the individual, the market and the state are at the core of the argument of this book. It also expresses a more humanistic notion of the individual.

Human beings are innately social, and moral in a variety of ways, as Jonathan Haidt and others have shown, and they thrive when the right institutions, cultures and enlightened state action enables them to do so. To look for *a* moral or *a* virtuous path is to brush over what is actually fiercely contested – and this applies even if the 'virtue' is civic life itself in a kind of oppressive democratic activism. At its most severe, the 'new moralism' or communitarianism has the potential to be a denial of human uniqueness. Humans are capable moral agents and it is to humans rather than abstract 'communities' that politics is targeted most sensibly. To do otherwise is to create a space for domination. This is only made worse if it is done at the behest of self-anointed community leaders, organisers or 'outlaw-guardians', despite the short-term good they might do. Some would argue that all political perspectives have an underlying moral agenda. To an extent, this is true. The difference with new moralism is that its starting point is not a case for change but a definitive good, thereby aiming to sit above the pluralistic reality we face. It will achieve clarity at the expense of engagement with complexity.

Where new moralism and new fraternalism do have value is in reminding us that there are things of value we can lose. Much of Japan's resilience is based on some deep and positive fraternal institutions, as we saw earlier in this chapter. It is not an oppressive moral state, as in countries such as Iran, for example. It is a deeply fraternal nation. This has value, but the downsides are significant too – it is a closed society. Japan has deployed fraternalism and philosophic conservatism to enhance the well-being of its people – and built institutions on that basis – and that is a strength.

Despite its radical mission, the left retains a degree of conservatism and fraternalism. This philosophic conservatism is something that is rich and important for any political movement that wishes to embark on radical but effective transformative change. It forces the left to reclaim some of what has been lost while protecting things that people hold dear. The question is whether it can achieve this without being manacled by the past. Can the left make a case for a different type of change without becoming stuck in the past or swallowed by the future? A considered relationship with change and loss is necessary for the left if it is to offer a different and resilient future.

Change and Loss

There is a tragic oscillation that occurs cyclically on the left between over-confidence and capitulation. It is summarised by a Christopher Lasch quote in Alastair Bonnett's study of the complex relationship between nostalgia and radicalism, *Left in the Past: Radicalism and the Politics of Nostalgia*: 'Their confidence in being on the winning side of history made progressive people unbearably smug and superior but they felt isolated and beleaguered in their own country since it was so much less progressive than they were.' As Labour enters office, it is certain in its knowledge of how progressive the country is, but leaves office in despair at how reactionary the country is. Having tried to buy the British public off with reactionary and authoritarian language and policies, Labour is still perplexed at this. Neither perspective is quite true, however. Britain is neither predominantly 'progressive' nor 'reactionary'; it is both. It is both radical and conservative, as we have seen. It is not a case of either/or. Yet precisely this dynamic of over-confidence followed by overdone despair has been seen in the last few years.

'Progressives' look to the future with gleeful zeal. Philosophical conservatives warily eye the past, in part longing and part warning, and step into the future only tentatively. In that sense, they are more attuned to the default human condition – people place a high value on security. We are a species that is disconcerted by convulsive change. How strange, then, that we have built an economy and society around such change. How predictable that there has been a social and psychological reaction to such change was seen in Chapter 4. As Ian Dyck writes of farm labourers in the early nineteenth century: 'They remembered a better life and they wanted it back.'

For agricultural labour in the early nineteenth century, read miners, car-workers, telephone operators, shipbuilders, and anyone else who has been cast aside by economic, administrative, technological and political change. In fact, we all look at the landscape of our world, with its atomised geography and anti-social organisation, and feel a sense of loss and regret. Because that is what humans do. Like everyone else, the left shares this nostalgia, but often pretends not to.

Alastair Bonnett's argument is that nostalgia – 'a yearning for the past, a sense of loss in the face of change' – is a core part of the radical left's instinct and worldview. This yearning seeks to return to a better, more humane and more social world – no matter how much a progressive instinct may deny nostalgia. The problem is that, while change can be slow, it can rarely be stopped and much less reversed – Humpty Dumpty can't be put back together again, not even by all the king's horses and all the king's men. The question then becomes one of how change can take better account of security and how it can be coaxed in a more worthwhile direction.

The opposite view – the white heat of change – has dominated the Labour perspective since the 1980s on both the party's right and left extremes. New Labour neo-Croslandism and the socialism of the alternative economic strategy are two expressions of this modernism, though each approach it from very different perspectives. Real socialism is against capitalism. It is an alternative economic and social system. It is a replacement. Early social democrats (who were socialists) saw a reformist route to this alternative. Marxists just want to get the job done, and done properly. There are many other variants.

Capitalism and socialism are mutually exclusive. Anthony Crosland realised this and tried to avoid the problem by arguing that real capitalism no longer existed in any meaningful sense.

Tony Benn has contended that the Labour Party was never a socialist party, and he's largely right. Labour's constitution describes it as a 'democratic socialist' party, but in fact the words themselves describe no such thing. Its constitution is concerned with transfers of power, wealth and opportunity (as long as we take democratic power as being implicit in that). It does not suggest the replacement of capitalism – which is intrinsic to socialism (despite Crosland's sleight of hand). In other words, the party has been in a state of constant identity crisis. This has been necessary to enable it to manage its divisions – within the party and beyond.

Where Labour's (new) Clause IV talks about 'power, wealth and opportunity' being spread through the populace, it touches on what can be an animating mission for the post-traditional social democratic left. The party's way forward is buried in a party constitution that few read. This ethos was the animating spirit of much of early New Labour in office: it devolved power, established a minimum wage, invested in health, and established greater powers for workers. In some ways the early years of Labour's period in office from 1997 reached back to the spirit of Labour republicans such as G. D. H. Cole by seeking to put power back into the hands of the people. Democratic public service and institutional reform were part of this; they just did not go nearly far enough.

A few paragraphs into the first chapter of his 1920 book *Guild Socialism* – in a chapter entitled 'The Demand for Freedom' – Cole exhorts: 'The essential social values are human values, and society is to be regarded as a complex of associations held together by the wills of their members, whose well-being is its purpose' and 'Society will be in health only if it is in the full sense democratic and self-governing.' He continues, '[The] conception of democracy involves an active and not merely a passive citizenship on the part of the members.'

In ethos and in philosophy, surely these sentiments are a neat fit for a modern left? There must be something in them that enables people to manage the trauma of change and loss? They do not resort to moralism, communitarianism or romanticism. Cole's complex solutions to the shortcomings of both Leviathan and Mammon are quaint in a post-communist world. Yet the exact form is not the issue. The notion that power and ownership can be devolved, then pooled collectively with the well-being of all paramount is as relevant now as it was then. There are rich seams of democratic republicanism in the works of Cole, of Tawney, and in Labour's constitution. They were just swallowed up by the historical tide. Now is the moment to drill for this democratic republican oil. These ideas and concepts never quite went away: the Co-operative party and movement, J. B. Priestley's Common Wealth Party in the middle of the twentieth century, and the 'new mutualism' of the late 1990s, all kept them alive.

There is value in the past and in institutions that make sense to people. Ideas are not unique to this – a conservative instinct looks back in order to find a path forward. There is deep antipathy on the left towards conservatism. This critique is a misunderstanding and confusion of 'conservatism'. The small 'c' is important. It is a philosophical outlook and an instinct rather than a political ideology, programme or refusal to contemplate change. It is about managing change. It also reminds us that we should understand the past – and the disorienting nature of some change – as a guide to a more tentative future. Beyond socialism and social democracy, old Labour and new, change and stasis, there is a practical and humble argument for a purposeful left that, nonetheless, initiates major institutional change.

What is the Left for?

The left exists to disrupt concentrations of overweening power. Whether it is the slave-owner, a belligerent nation, reservoirs of wealth open to some and drought for the many, political power and authority for an elite and exclusion for the rest, or exploitation of the weak by the politically or economically strong, the left's purpose has been to fight for the excluded and disempowered. At times this has been pro or anti-state, for free trade or against, localist or centralising. Real socialism was largely rejected by the democratic left in the years following 'Operation Whirlwind', when Soviet troops crushed the Hungarian Revolution in 1956.

Social democracy became the sole democratic carrier for the ideal of equality. The pursuit of the social democratic ideal in the context of a society with strong reserves of solidarity meant the cause of the many was advanced through free education, publicly enabled or provided health care, and a safety net at times of strife, in the early years of life and in retirement. Equality was sometimes termed 'justice'. Equality over time became a mixture both of legally sanctioned equal rights and an ever stronger urge to redistribute income: in the open or, increasingly, by stealth. If it had been a sustainable political project, the stealth would not have been necessary.

Despite significant triumphs for social democracy after World War II, twenty-first-century Britain is a society where there are still gross inequalities of power, wealth and opportunity. Instead of confronting imbalances of power, we've compensated those who lose out instead. So a whole section of British society is locked into benefits and cash transfers, while another section settles down comfortably in their gated enclaves. Ever greater numbers have been imprisoned. Yet much of the left's response floats in idealism, utopianism and an imagined onward march. Sometimes, new abstractions and utopias such as the 'common good', the virtuous community and the good society serve the left's need for self-justification, even when they serve little other purpose.

Labour is a practical mission of change or it is nothing. Its greatest successes came when the party was in power and able to create practical institutions that gave people greater freedom in their lives. These institutions included new schools after the war, and again under the Academy programme in the 2000s aimed at the poorest areas. After 1945, the Attlee government built houses: homes fit for heroes. It created the Beveridgean welfare state (though Beveridge himself was a liberal), which matched contributions with insurance underpinned by responsibility. The National Health Service is a monument to practical institution-building that can transform lives. The Wilson governments legally outlawed discrimination on the basis of race and gender in the 1960s and 1970s. The Blair government introduced civil partnerships and legally outlawed wage slavery by legislating for minimum pay.

If Labour is to leave utopianism behind in favour of practical institution-building, then will it lose its direction? To where can an army march without a destination and without orders? In reality, though, utopia is no destination at all. Instead, though the journey will still be long, there are more proximate earthly destinations that can be reached. One of these possible destinations could be to seek greater 'non-domination'. In the words of the republican theorist Philip Pettit, non-domination means that another person, group or the state does not have the *capacity* to 'interfere in one's affairs on an arbitrary basis'. So it is not simply non-interference that matters, but another person not having the ability to interfere, other than in a non-arbitrary fashion.

Self-determination is another aspect of this civic republicanism. This applies to England – locally, regionally and nationally – as much as it does to Scotland, Wales and Northern Ireland. It means that our democratic institutions should no longer manufacture artificial majorities. There has to be a space for civic pluralism. Politics is one of the spaces where we initiate a conversation between different moral viewpoints. Politics is not there to define our morality in an imposing fashion. It is there to make laws and promote a discourse that enables us to find some degree of accommodation. This is done on the bedrock of respect for democratic institutions and dialogue, the rule of law, human rights, a singular source of sovereignty and a common language. Our political institutions no longer embody these principles, if they ever really did.

A civic-focused republicanism is not enough, however. Domination takes place in other spheres too, not least the market-place. The working lives that some people have to lead through no choice of their own – long days, starting early, on low pay and with little time to spend with their families – is one example of the type of domination we see too often. The republicanism of Thomas Jefferson or James Madison did not simply assume that democratic equality would be enough. People need access to assets and knowledge to make democratic society work. Jeff Madrick argues, in his somewhat mistitled (in the European context in any case) *The Case for Big Government*, that Jeffersonian republicanism rested on the abundance and distribution of agricultural land. In fact, it was Jefferson who proposed a 'homesteading' plan for the then colony of Virginia early in his political career. The plan involved gifting 50 acres of land to every Virginian citizen. These principles of ownership of relative small holdings were applied in government in the late eighteenth century to the extent that property ownership was spread among more than 50 per cent of the Virginian (and Massachusetts) population.

That was an agrarian society. But Jefferson's principles still apply: spread the wealth and power. It was one of the motivations for the Louisiana land purchase. The more land distributed, the cheaper it remained, and the more assets were spread. As president, Jefferson also set aside land for educational development. For him, education and democracy were entwined: 'No one more sincerely wishes the spread of information among mankind than I do, and none has greater confidence in its effect towards supporting free and good government.' But, of course, Jefferson devoted his life to fighting the injustice of tyrannical government. If the left is to assume the mantle of 'non-domination' it must also be alert to the potential of state domination. This calls for restraint and humility. However, it does not suggest inaction. Jefferson's land dispersal and educational mission underline that republicanism is useful beyond the civic sphere and into the economic and social spheres too. For this, Amartya Sen's ideas on justice are very important.

To go back to our two golfers from the beginning of the chapter, it is their capability that matters. Sen's *The Idea of Justice* is a complex and comprehensive work and it is very difficult to do it justice. However, a number of his thoughts are useful when considering how domination – of one golfer over another – can be reduced without killing the game altogether. Sen confronts what he describes as John Rawls' 'transcendental institutionalism'. By this, he means idealised institutions that are designed to procedurally achieve universal justice. Instead, he argues that 'justice' or 'freedom' are heavily contested notions. What is more, it is important not simply to construct ideal institutions but to build institutions – democratic, economic, educational, environmental and social – that have a real impact on lives. He argues instead for a comparative justice – less injustice rather than perfect justice (even though such a thing is impossible either to define or achieve, despite the best efforts of many philosophers). We need a better society rather than a perfect one. How do we judge? We compare one set of institutions with another and decide democratically what seems to be a better way. It is messy, but that is the nature of freedom and democracy.

Less injustice means focusing on real improvements in lives. Institutions and practices have merit to the extent that they enhance capabilities – the capacity to actually achieve an outcome, such as earning a living that is compatible with a fulfilling home life. So the idealised end ceases to be of importance. Instead, we have to assess the *nyaya*, a concept from Sanskrit jurisprudence which values the world that actually emerges rather than the ideal. People need real power they can actually use, but once they are in possession of it their lives are their own responsibility: Sen writes that 'Freedom to choose gives us the opportunity to decide what we should do, but with that opportunity comes the responsibility for what we do – to the extent that they are chosen actions.' The philosophy is defensible in the context of a society that intervenes in a manner that broadens capability. Such a society would also value human exchange and relationships as an essence of humanity. A form of democratic republicanism with Sen's notions of comparative justice can succeed in this regard. The old Chinese proverb is the essence of this philosophy: 'Give a man a fish and you feed him for a day. Teach a man to fish and you feed him for a lifetime.' These concepts are applied with regularity to international development, but we've allowed ourselves to become too lazy in the domestic sphere: we try to deal with too many problems with cash or income transfers. It is a short cut, but by taking a longer-term, institutional view, more is ultimately achieved, even if it takes more time. Once someone has the capability of fishing, and somewhere to fish, it is then their responsibility to do so.

This empowering ethos is about practical impact. It does not deny the social and moral characteristics of human beings; nor does it seek a false unity of morality or interest. It accepts that the state is necessary in confronting domination, but that it too can be a dominating force. Democratic life, a bedrock of assets on which to thrive, and education are all critical and valuable. Practical institutions are necessary in support of these. We do not need to replace the market; nor should we ignore the fact that it can be and often is unjust. The relative advantages of our two golfers cannot be eliminated, but with support they can enjoy a proximity in status, and mutual regard. Their destiny becomes about their own aptitudes and application rather than socially manipulated outcomes – in one direction, Hayekian or Croslandite, or another. Perhaps when their children meet they will be much more evenly matched, and it will be a competition on the basis of character and skill rather than advantage and privilege. That would be a triumph for the left.

Our relationships away from the golf course and in the world of work – and the institutions through which they are mediated – are central to this philosophical argument. Nowhere is the conversation more broken than between the democratic civic spheres and the world of business. If that dialogue is re-established then we are more likely to enjoy some victories. Any set of ideas that animate the left must have a convincing argument on how to change the relationship between individuals and business – not just for wider gain but for the benefit of business itself. It is an argument that, with finesse, can be won.

CHAPTER 7

Institutions of Change

A US grocery store chain, Trader Joe's, seems to have cracked the question of building trust with both workers and customers. It inspires stunning levels of loyalty. Its trick? It treats them well. A recent *CNN Money* report showed how workers and customers interact in the stores. Trader Joe's has developed a community feel despite expanding to 344 stores across the US. It sells a smaller range of products than most stores. That's fine, as its customers trust that they are getting the best – often organic – produce.

Store managers, or 'captains' as Trader Joe's calls them, make six-figure salaries and 'crew members' take home $40,000 to $60,000, with a pension contribution of 15.4 per cent of employees' gross income. The pay scales are set to at least match the median household income in the communities the stores serve, as Richard Florida has explained in his look at the growth of the creative economy, *The Great Reset*. All these things serve to reinforce the service culture – people's jobs acquire meaning when their needs are met through an empathetic approach. A sense of just reward is key to fostering this meaning, and that is what Trader Joe's does. Employees are given status and respect. This fosters trust and improves service. Trader Joe's has understood real value in a service economy.

More deeply, Trader Joe's has understood the human dimension to business. Basically, business is really just a series of social networks grounded in trust. To understand value creation, you have to understand how human beings function. Some businesses are starting to realise that they are failing to create new value as a result of looking at people as machines. The old industrial productivity mentality is completely ill-suited to the service economy, as we saw in Chapter 3. There is a mismatch between a rich source of value in the form of human creativity, empathy and interaction, and what is measured as value, such as the number of widgets produced per hour. Productivity is easy to measure, but that is only one source of real value. So business does not measure all the right things. The incentives are skewed. Businesses such as Trader Joe's have realised this – the products on their shelves are top-notch and it wouldn't be profitable without that, but their employees take the offer several steps further.

Businesses are a series of social networks which interact with social institutions. The shifting balance between networks and institutions that we are seeing in almost every domain applies as much to business as it does to society. The challenge is to adapt and create relevant institutions that respond to the shift towards the networked economy and society. Whatever product or service a business provides, it is created on the basis of human beings and their interactions. So if there is an empirical change in how humans are seen and understood, especially in the context of services and creative industries, then that has a huge impact on businesses: they are social entities. This also applies to how public services are dispensed. A shift in our understanding of human needs and behaviours has occurred, and so the consequences have to be worked through. The American management guru Henry Mintzberg had it about right when, in *How Productivity Killed American Enterprise*, in 2007, before the financial crisis began, he wrote: 'Corporations are social institutions – communities. They function best when committed human beings work in cooperative relationships, under conditions of respect and trust. Destroy this and the whole institution of business collapses.'

A central argument of this book has been that a major programme of institution-building and creation is necessary to enable people to have greater control over their own lives. This applies in both the public and private domains. These institutions may or may not be state sponsored and created. Whether they are or not, they must be adaptive and sensitive to their local environment. Understanding business as a set of social networks is critical to this, as new institutions have to be as flexible as the businesses with which they interact. Some of these institutions will fail. They must, however, be built to adapt. In so doing, new and developed institutions will contribute to real value creation. Once business has re-conceived itself more clearly as a social network, then it will understand that access to networks of adaptive institutions providing expertise, enhancement of skills and know-how, finance and a route to market is critical.

Most of these networks will be private in nature, some will be hybrid, and some will have, at least initially, significant state involvement. There is a mutual public and private interest that makes better institutions necessary. At present, too often the state and the market are either isolated from one another or in conflict. Networks of institutions that are nestled between the two, focused on real business needs, will have a heavy influence on our collective ability to respond to both public and private interests. Understanding the nature of those interests is changing, even from some surprising quarters. Take this, for example: 'There is growing concern that if the fundamental issues revealed in the crisis remain unaddressed and the system fails again, the social contract between the capitalist system and the citizenry may truly rupture, with unpredictable but severely damaging results.' Who is this dangerous revolutionary? Well, it is none other than Dominic Barton, global managing director of McKinsey & Company, a prestigious management consulting firm. And what about this:

> At a very basic level, the competitiveness of a company and the health of the communities around it are closely intertwined. A business needs a successful community, not only to create demand for its products but also to provide critical public assets and a supportive environment.

Friends of the Earth? The New Economics Foundation? Actually, it is Michael Porter (with Mark Kramer), high priest of competitiveness theory. In a long essay on 'shared value' – the search for economic value rooted in social and environmental values – which appeared in the *Harvard Business Review* in January 2011, he pretty much washes down the drain Milton Friedman's ideas about social responsibility being about making a profit and nothing more. Friedmanite economics has been a 30-year nightmare from which some are only now just awakening. The point here is not that business should be socially responsible because it is 'good' or 'ethical'. Those are different arguments which actually have less of an impact. The really disruptive aspect of Porter's argument is the notion that there is business *value* in doing the right social or environmental thing. If positive social and environmental behaviour is driven by an enlightened exploration of value, then it will be more enduring. The question becomes which institutions and arguments can cultivate that behaviour, as much as it is about which regulations can outlaw negative actions.

Right on the tail of Barton and Porter is Umair Haque – another *Harvard Business Review* contributor. A business consultant, management theorist and institutional economist, he argues for a different, better capitalism in *The New Capitalist Manifesto*. The case he makes is for constructive capitalism: similar to Barton's long-term capitalism, it also bears a strong resemblance to Porter's 'shared value'.

Haque's core argument is that modern capitalism peaked in 1970 in terms of both wealth creation and well-being. It has been downhill ever since, and the cliff edge was reached in 2008. The institutional structures of capitalism – which, according to Douglas North, are the 'humanly devised constraints that shape interaction' – are geared towards 'thin' rather than 'thick' value. We behave as if we are living on a rich, infinite and bountiful prairie; whereas, in fact, we are on a highly resource-constrained ark. For this reason, our institutions, or 'cornerstones' as Haque terms them, understate the costs of business and overstate the short-term benefits. We are all paying the social, environmental, physical and long-term economic price as a result.

All is not lost. Haque argues that there are constructive capitalist pioneers (though they are often far from perfect or completely ethical) – such as Apple Inc., Nike, Whole Foods (which nonetheless remains shamefully anti-union), Tata, Lego, threadless.com and Nintendo – who are recrafting the institutions that underpin modern business. These companies are not just devising new products, they are changing the whole way they do business, and creating 'thick' or long-term economic, social or environmental value in the process. They enhance people's well-being and create platforms for us to live our lives. Just take Nike Plus or Nike's 'considered index', which makes its latest shoes 83 per cent recyclable, or the Tata Nano, which brings car ownership to the masses – the modern Ford Model T.

The easy retort to these arguments asserts that short-termism is not necessarily bad. There is something in this: if your house is on fire you want to get out rather than start to plan how you are going to re-decorate it. So there is a sensible balance to be struck. If a company is not profitable for a long period then it cannot survive without unimaginably generous creditors. If things get out of kilter and short-term concerns dominate long-term value, then what is wise in the short term undermines long-term value. You can cut back on all sorts of activities that do not have a short-term return – research and development (R&D), health and safety, environmental custodianship, skills development, and building a motivational environment. If you do, though, you could end up with higher short-term profits but no innovative products, a high turnover of demoralised staff, negative publicity and legal action. The argument is not that short-termism is wrong. It is just that too much business has become short-termist, and this is undermining long-term value; a better balance is required.

So there is a profound challenge occurring here. What are we to do as a society to re-gear political and civic institutions towards longer-term 'shared value'? Not all reform is necessarily the right reform. The government's approach to reform of the NHS is definitely in the destructive category. Rather than building institutions that make sense to people, the government has created organisational chaos through unnecessary major top-down reform that makes sense to very few. The lesson here is that reform has to have clear objectives but also needs to engage at the human level. New institutions have to make sense to the people who will be required to make them work. These institutions need a purpose that is clear and, where long-standing insti-tutional structures are in place, an evolutionary approach is necessary.

Ultimately, access to knowledge, skills, networks of opportunity or capital are what has been described by the Nobel-Prize-winning politi-cal economist Elinor Ostrom as *common-pool resources*. In *Governing the Commons*, she argues that such resources can be distributed in a fairer and more efficient way without resorting to heavy regulation (in other words, Hobbes' Leviathan) or through privatisation. As she puts it: 'Communities of individuals have relied on institutions resembling neither the state nor the market to govern some resource systems with a reasonable degree of success over long periods of time.' She goes on to say: 'No market can exist for long without underlying public institutions to support it … public and private institutions frequently are intermeshed and depend on one another, rather than existing in isolated worlds.'

Covering case studies from common agricultural land in Japan to fishing communities in Turkey, Ostrom develops a rich articulation of how institutions that sit between the market and the state can achieve better outcomes and protect the stocks of common resources in the process. Often, smart state intervention can enable these institutions to work, as it can provide resources and conflict resolution, and define a legal framework. In this sense, Ostrom's ideal institutions are polycentric – they should operate at the closest point to the community they serve with support from regional, national or international authorities and institutions. Ostrom focuses on access to natural resources, such as forestry and fishing, but there is no reason why her thinking shouldn't apply to resources of other kinds. At a local level, institutions can be cultivated that are flexible, help to develop individual capabilities and give businesses access to the types of expertise and talent that they need. Access to and nourishment of, for example, skilled workers, becomes the common-pool resource that needs to be safeguarded and developed, with rules defining fair access (such as a decent wage, as discussed in Chapter 3).

For such cultivation of institutions with social and economic value to work, it requires public institutions and political leadership to create the conditions and provide some support. These institutions need to be prepared to step back from trying to control outcomes, norms and behaviour, and leave as much as possible to the participants to define co-operatively. Business will need to appreciate the social and connected nature of creating value. If it softens the edges of its organisation and looks for ways to co-operate and open out, it will benefit. All this requires a serious re-think about the relationship between the individual, the market and the state. The type of political self-determination discussed in Chapter 5 in relation to devolution of power will be a corollary here. Where local leaders demand control over the power and resources that have an impact on their local economy, social, educational and welfare provision, it should be given to them. Central authority should step in only when things go wrong.

A radical restructuring is needed: of education, public institutions, democratic structures, the rules and regulations of the market place, and the rules that govern capital. The long-term nature of public and social value should be understood. Just take the way that welfare, skills, child care, economic development, education and business interface. The welfare system has a certain logic: to get people into work. Yet too often it falls very far short because it is not properly connected to other institutions in the work–skills–economic development system. The skills system delivered through colleges, other institutions and organisations has another logic: to enable people to acquire new, accredited qualifications. Both are national systems, locally delivered. Business interfaces weakly at both the national and local level. It is now being given more control over public skills resources through Employer Ownership Pilot, launched in February 2012, but this is still not a lever to build better relationships with public institutions when it can and should be. Economic development is more regional in scope. Education sits in parallel with most of these systems. At the base of it all should be the needs of the individual and those of business. Yet it is the bureaucratic logic of the programme that prevails – and programmes conflict with one another as different Whitehall departments and layers of government pursue things in slightly different ways. As the OECD put it in its skills strategy: '[Skills] strategies involve not just education and training institutions but ... include firms, employer associations, economic development agencies, employment agencies, trade unions, not-for-profit organisations that can work together to develop skills and training ecosystems.'

The British state is ill-adapted for the type of flexible, local institution-building that makes sense from the perspectives of both the individual and business. These institutions, such as the work associations advocated earlier in the book, or apprenticeship partnerships jointly established between business, skills and welfare providers, are simply absent or only half-formed. As a consequence, different systems aiming to do similar but non-aligned things run in parallel, duplicate one another and conflict. Money is wasted, individuals and businesses do not get the support they need, and reform is destructive rather than adaptive. Adaptation, when it occurs, tends to be at the local level. Yet most of the systems described in this context are driven nationally. At the core of this perversity and inefficiency is the way in which politics operates – with its false divides and short-termist impulses. This chaos occurs within systems of governance as much as it is a feature of inter-party competition.

Both the left and the right are stuck in the tired debates of the 'thin' capitalist age – pro versus anti-business, predator versus producer, responsible versus irresponsible, profits versus wages, business versus the community, the environment versus profit, investment versus consumption, and long-term versus short-term. It is difficult for them to move on. We have a set of institutions that perpetuate these antagonistic dualisms. Business, politics, community, all need a more constructive way of building a society through a set of institutions that enable businesses to build real value, reward employees fairly in a way that encourages real value for the business, helping them in turn to make a more substantial contribution to business. 'Business as usual' just isn't sufficient. And nor is 'politics as usual'.

Businesses, public services and the institutions of the future need to be grounded in our understanding of the way human beings are motivated, make decisions, create and interact. This understanding comes from evolutionary biology, neuroscience, psychology and social network theory. The 'rational man' of the economics models on which we have come to rely is anything but rational.

The economist Mancur Olson, Jr, in his seminal essay on the role of institutions in economic development, 'Big bills left on the sidewalk: Why some nations are rich, and others poor', relays an allegorical tale. Two professors are walking along the street and the more junior of the two sees a $100 bill. He reaches down for it but is held back by the other. The senior colleague sagely cautions him that if the bill were real it would have been picked up already. The moral of the tale is that the free market sorts out its surpluses and rents efficiently – a rational economic actor always steps in to extract them. So if you see a surplus (a $100 bill), it is illusory. In reality, though, $100 bills do sometimes get dropped and are not picked up.

There are all sorts of irrationalities and imperfections that may lead to the bill remaining on the floor – a law may prevent it being picked up, there may be a cultural aversion to picking up $100 bills, or people may feel a sense of empathy for the person who has dropped it and suppose they might come back to find it. Olson's argument was about institutional differences between nations. The efficient thing to do is pick up the $100 note, and it will be picked up if efficient institutions are in place. The irony in this allegory is that it is the rational knowledge of the senior professor which prevents the junior professor from making himself $100 richer. A simple situation surrounding a $100 bill becomes quite constrained.

Good institutions create the right incentives towards desirable outcomes. These outcomes are best when they have meaning for both individuals and business. Such meaning requires something more than simple win or lose, profit or loss. This explains why oblique means are sometimes more successful than direct ones in securing desirable ends. John Kay gives the example of ICI (when it shifted its corporate objectives from 'responsible application of chemistry' to creating 'value for shareholders') in his study on pursuing meaningful ways to achieve better outcomes, *Obliquity*. ICI shifted focus from meaningful value to rational objective. Humans are less motivated in these ways. A great and innovative chemist is motivated by discovery rather than shareholder value. In 2007, ICI ceased to exist as an independent company. Haque's follow-up to *The New Capitalist Manifesto*, entitled *Betterness: Economics for Humans*, argues that to be 'meaningfully rich' is to be

> rich with relationships, ideas, emotion, health and vigour, recognition and contribution, passion and fulfilment, and great accomplishment and enduring achievement, exactly what 'business', 'output', and 'product' seem so achingly deficient at producing.

Future prosperity relies on 'getting out of business and into betterness'. The centrepiece of Haque's argument is that psychology shifted around the time of William James in the late nineteenth century, from a focus on avoiding pathology to creating positive approaches that enable people to achieve their psychological potential. He sees the economics of Adam Smith onwards as being very much about removing pathology (he is no romantic about the pre-commercial economy of guilds and restrictive practices). What we now need is a new economics that reaches beyond utility, profit, efficiency, output and productivity and becomes a vehicle – through the positive impact of mediating social institutions – of human well-being and betterness. We must accept the necessity of Smith in eradicating economic harm but then move on.

The task, therefore, is not to replace one pathology, that of neo-liberalism, with another, centralised statism. It is, instead, to understand how public institutions can work with private actors at the local level to achieve better outcomes. The state's role is to facilitate information flows, participate and encourage creative networks, help to change our understanding about how we can get more out of people and give more back in return, correct market failures using a variety of tools from occasional resources to smart rule-making, and support local decision-makers when they are looking to secure better outcomes in their social and business communities. It will be an adaptive state that, in many respects, will not be particularly state-like.

Ultimately, the aim is partly economic, in that facilitating the right networks and building the right institutions will help business output by, for example, enabling growing businesses to obtain finance at the right moment. There is also a social objective. Creative and innovative businesses can thrive without government intervention, but it may benefit only a narrow few. That is why we may need to link publicly financed education and skills institutions with new economic opportunities.

It is exactly this web of institutions that has been preoccupying Tamara Lothian and Roberto Unger in *Crisis, Slump, Superstition and Recovery*. They put it as follows: 'The favourable institutional setting is one that organises a form of coordination between government and firms that is decentralised, pluralistic, participatory and experimental.' They go on to argue:

> [Institutional innovation] is to empower experimentalism: by establishing arrangements that broaden economic and educational opportunity, by giving small- and medium-size business access to forms of credit, technology, marketing, and knowledge normally reserved to big business, by propagating successful local practice, and, above all, by creating the means and conditions for pluralism and experimentation in the institutional forms of the market economy.

As discussed in Chapter 3, there are necessary national interventions on infrastructure, regulation, value measurement and wages, but it is the local sphere in which the notion of the adaptive state will really come to life. SMEs with high growth potential are the prime movers of Britain's economic future. Businesses are a series of social networks, linked to their local setting and environment. Local institutions such as skills hubs or embedded business support networks, underpinned by national resources where necessary, can facilitate growth and provide social benefit. Financial institutions must be created and placed at the service of local businesses and the community. It is not a moralistic or antagonistic relationship between the politics of the left and business that is required. Swords should remain at the door. Instead, political leaders on the left – locally as well as nationally – must understand what business needs and how to use the power of the state to meet those needs in a way that creates new prospects for more people.

The Adaptive State and Business

For two political generations, and now into a third, we have accepted that, in the economic contest between the market and the state, the market wins. The problem is that the 'market' does not exist in isolation, despite the echoing claims of the neo-liberal right to the contrary. It depends on rules, culture, support and intervention in order to function effectively. The financial crash was not exclusively a 'market' failure; it was also a regulatory one. Regulations are established and enforced through institutions. We got the institutional architecture wrong. The categorical error was seeing large, international financial institutions as dormant volcanoes when, in fact, they were highly active. Where the market fails, it is logical that the state should step in, and sometimes it is necessary for the state to support even seemingly functioning markets. Where it does so effectively, it creates further opportunities for economic development and growth.

There are also deeper issues. An economy such as the UK's is exposed to global competition. Pure market logic concerns itself with *how efficiently* products are made, while a more parochial concern is with *where* they are produced. As a democratic society we cannot afford to be indifferent to these questions. As a result of these global shifts mixed with technological change, whole swathes of middle-ranking employment has been competed away. The middle has not so much been squeezed as sucked away, and replaced by new software or shifted to emerging economies. By the early 2020s, emerging economies will have overtaken the developed world in terms of production – indeed, by some measures, they may have done so already. But the issue is not just in production, it is also in innovation – the two are tied together.

People, their skills and interactions are central to future innovation – especially in a predominantly service-based economy. The expansion of apprenticeships has been welcome and should be continued. But there is far more that needs to be done to ensure that people are being equipped for the economy of the future. The Chartered Institute of Personnel and Development (CIPD) recently reported the concerns of business with regard to the skills levels of school leavers. Fifty-three per cent cited literacy levels as a concern, 42 per cent cited numeracy, 40 per cent customer service, and the same percentage communication skills. These are skills at a fairly basic level: the creativity required in even seemingly mundane jobs in the service economy is beyond this basic level. As an economy and as a society, we are falling short by quite some way.

In Hackney, a University Technical College (UTC) has been established (as its chairman, it is an institution about which I have close knowledge). It has two curriculum streams: digital technology and health technology. Students take courses such as computer science, and health and social care. They learn both in the school and the workplace. Every student will be expected to attain a high level of core academic and skills qualifications, benefit from work-based learning, acquire proficient levels of technical skills, and develop his or her ability to make a significant contribution in the workplace. It is designed to be a high-quality academic and technical school that serves as a social bridge for many in relatively deprived communities into some internationally competitive sectors. These companies are located 'in their own backyard' yet remain too often out of reach. Where there are local career options in sectors that provide opportunities for high-quality employment, institutions such as UTCs can make an enormous contribution to both business needs and individual life chances.

The involvement of higher and further education (FE) institutions and businesses is critical to the success of UTCs. Hackney UTC is supported by BT, Homerton Hospital and the University of East London as well as receiving the support of many of the creative industries in and around Shoreditch's Silicon Roundabout. Hackney Community College has provided the building and is the principal sponsor. What these partnerships mean is that the insights of employers, their skills needs as well as experience of the real working world and an understanding of progression routes into tertiary education are integrated into the curriculum. Project work will foster cross-disciplinary creative opportunities. UTCs will not only transform the life chances of those who attend them, but will spur innovation elsewhere – new ways of delivering the curriculum, fostering creativity, the role of partnerships and work-related education.

In Germany it is common to find institutions that link to each other and connect individuals to the market place through investment in facilities, teaching and building networks between local communities and business. They go into further and higher education. Community colleges and universities are a key component of this network, which must serve those in work as well as those preparing for the world of work. In the UK, there has been status snobbery against these networks of technical institutions on both the right (not academic enough) and the left (not egalitarian enough). Both are mistaken. The capabilities imperative should be stronger than any idealised or utopian set of institutions. Doing something is better than doing nothing, not least if doing nothing is because of a defunct ideological purity.

This could all be supported by new specialist institutions in technical higher education with business involvement, and a new suite of coherent technical qualifications designed with employers to be delivered in UTCs, FE and new specialist technical higher education institutions (some of these could be established within existing colleges or universities). A new TechBac qualification has been proposed by Labour, and the International Baccalaureate Career-Related Certificate (IBCC) has also been discussed. Whatever it is, it should combine high-quality classroom-based instruction, academic and technical skills, good work experience, and broader skills. A-levels are the gold standard for schools, and degrees are the same for universities; there is now similarly a need for a clear and esteemed coherent qualification for students with a technical focus. Then employers, students and institutions can support it.

Welfare reform is critical to getting people into networks of training, work and social capital once they are no longer in education or at school. At present, welfare is too regimented, bureaucratic and fragmented. It is not directed sufficiently towards the needs of the individual. People need better advice both in and outside of work, followed by support tailored to their needs in the context of a local economy. At present, there are two parallel systems: the Work Programme; and secondary and/or further education. Work Programme 'prime' contractors are now doing the sort of work that FE colleges used to do.

One department – the Department for Work and Pensions (DWP) – controls one system through large private providers. Another two departments – the Department for Education (DfE) and the Department for Business, Innovation and Skills (BIS) – each control another. These institutions should be completely localised so that they are properly co-ordinated, networked to local jobs markets, and respond to individual needs rather than bureaucratic direction. This is the institutional structure recommended by the OECD, and it is right. This would be real welfare reform. And it would also be more successful and efficient.

The other major aspect of institutional reform of welfare is in the area of child care – which is actually a key labour market institution (as well as being socially valuable). The Mirrlees Review simulated a change in child tax credit, targeting it at those who had children under the age of five. It would lead to an increase in employment of 52,000 people. The Resolution Foundation found in its report *The Missing Million* that an additional 700,000 women would be in work if the UK performed as well as countries such as Sweden, Norway and Denmark in its female employment rate.

The Resolution Foundation research shows that properly funded child care has a high impact on employment. Almost half of Denmark's spend on families goes on services rather than cash benefits. In the

UK it is a quarter. High-quality service provision – such as Sure Start – seems to be the clincher in freeing women to return to the work-place. At the present, such care tends to be part-time and for no more than 15 hours per week, which would be difficult to build a working life around, as the Resolution Foundation emphasises. This can have a large impact on (usually) the mother's well-being. Also, if the children are in well-managed child care, they are gaining the benefits from learning to play, interact and socialise with other children and adults, which will be beneficial for their development. At their best, these services are linked to the local and personal educational, work advice and social capital networks described above.

But good child care, better educational and training institutions, and welfare reform is not enough. Opportunities also need to be expanded. This is where new institutions that support business through a deeper pool of financial and social capital become necessary. The way the state intervenes is critical. In the past it has been heavy-handed and inefficient, which has led to the false conclusion that intervention doesn't work. It is about the quality of the interventions that are made rather than the quantity. Mariana Mazzucato and colleagues pointed out in a recent paper for the European Commission that actually the US has intervened rather better than European nations when it comes to fostering growth. They have emphasised that the US federal government spends 2.6 per cent of per capita GDP on research compared to a 1.3 per cent average in the EU. The role of defence research in advances in materials science, communications, satellite technology, the internet and computing technology is strong. Mazzucato *et al.*'s paper also points out that the US pharmaceutical industry is reliant on enormous investment by the National Institutes of Health – some $31 billion a year. By way of comparison, the UK government will invest £4.6 billion in science and research in total in 2012/13.

We know who creates jobs. As the independent charity Nesta has shown, 6 per cent of firms – high-growth firms – create 54 per cent of jobs. The vast majority of these firms have been around for longer than five years. These firms need access to capital, skills and networks in a timely fashion. Unfortunately, banks see SME lending as a low-return, higher-risk activity. However, they are willing to engage in the risk-loaded casino-style financial gambles that led to the recent crash.

An additional boost to the UK's domestic capability could be developed by the use of incentives to invest. The Conservatives tend to see this in one-dimensional terms: tax competition. Tax levels are not irrelevant, and Labour should not fall into the trap of pretending that they are. But it is about more than tax. Again, state support is often dismissed as an inefficient subsidy. Sometimes it is. But the evidence is more nuanced. John Van Reenen has shown, in a piece entitled 'Rethinking industrial policy: Size matters', through the analysis of 2.3 million grants given over almost 40 years that the EU's regional selective assistance scheme has been a success, but only for small firms. This scheme supports investment in deprived areas. It is focused on firms serving both national and international markets. Large firms do not tend to increase investment and employment as a result of receiving such support, but small firms do. How many high-growth firms not in deprived areas are missing out? You have to take growth where you can get it.

Financial capital interventions in support of business also require a sophisticated view of social capital. Local Enterprise Partnerships (LEPs) – introduced by the Coalition – are a more localised and networked version of regional development agencies. Social networks of innovation, venture capital and opportunity dissemination grew in the Silicon Valley in California, USA, from the technological innovation of Stanford University. LEPs will have an important part to play in seeking to identify and promote such potential networks in a UK context, where innovation is just as likely to be inter-firm as intra-firm. They can also help to develop international links and networks: emerging economies are potential markets as well as competitors.

Cities will have an even more concentrated place in economic life in the UK, as both lifestyle choices and locations of social capital (face-to-face as well as social media enabled). These could be cutting-edge science and technology cities such as Cambridge, pharma-manufacturing networks such as those in the M25 circle, energy industry centres such as Aberdeen, and creative industry hives such as Shoreditch and Hoxton in London. The governance of cities

– including democratic structures such as elected mayors – will be an important part of the national economic and social architecture.

It is in our cities that the human network will be the most intense – and hence where the major contribution to Britain's prosperity will be made. This is an increasing social, geographical and economic theme picked up most clearly by Ed Glaeser in *Triumph of the City*, and by Richard Florida in his writing on the creative economy and 'creative class'. Cities are better understood as social rather than purely physical landscapes. Glaeser sums it up thus: 'We must free ourselves from our tendency to see cities as their buildings, and remember that the real city is made from flesh, not concrete.'

Just as we must free our concept of business away from purely financial, legal and managerial aspects, we must see cities as the complex social networks that they are. The more dense the human networks, the better; and the more diverse they are, the more successful they become. Even taking into account education, experience and industry of workers, American cities are 50 per cent more prosperous than small metropolitan areas. There is high poverty, but that is often because people who move to cities in search of opportunity are poor when they arrive. Crime, disease and pollution are part of a city's life cycle, but with leadership, investment and management this can be, and has been, overcome. Technology, robust policing and the innovation of community engagement has, for example, cleaned up New York. Simple things like putting more female and ethnic minority police in community-facing roles has improved police intelligence and enabled them to better combat crime.

Once these issues are confronted, Glaeser shows that cities can become happier, on the basis that people are less likely to take their own lives in cities, they tend to be on average wealthier, and are environmentally more sound. People make more connections with others who are different from themselves – technology is a poor substitute in building trust compared with face-to-face engagement. This helps to create fine art (fifteenth-century Florence), a consumer and cultural centre (today's London), extraordinary wealth (New York), and new technological and educational advances (Bangalore). It is about linking people to opportunities to resources. It is in our cities that we can widen and deepen social networks of value, combining political, public service, voluntary, finance and business networks and institutions.

There will be a particular creative and economic opportunity in centres of dense social and economic connection, and specialisation. All these principles must apply beyond our economic centres too. The life of towns is also a vital component of British life. Those who live and are raised in towns need similar opportunities to the people in thriving cities, and the autonomy to attract investment and develop their own unique character – just take Swindon and car-manufacturing, for example, or Totnes's new age and environmental culture, or St Ives in Cornwall and its art- and tourism-led regeneration.

Beyond location-specific policies, a sectoral focus is essential. Particular attention would be given to thickening the supply chain in areas where the UK or particular localities have a comparative advantage, ensuring that more of the production – and the jobs – remained on home turf. Steve Denning, in an article in *Forbes* magazine in August 2011, pointed to the fact that the US couldn't manufacture its Amazon Kindle because of gaps in its supply chain. Thinning supply chains can eventually disappear, and inter-company learning relies on local connections and flexibility. The warning of what happened to the Dell computer company when its outsourcing partner ASUSTeK became its competitor is a salutary metaphor for countries that do not take care to ensure that any supply network is as thick as possible to guard against hollowing out and loss of control and employment. Dell was once worth more than Apple but lost three-quarters of its value in the 2000s. Denning makes the point that if you fail to ensure control over your supply chain, you not only lose the production capacity but also lose the capacity to innovate. Incremental learning is tied in with the production process. Once that is lost, so is the innovation insight. Proximity matters.

Cesar Hidalgo has analysed the proximity of certain products and industries within nations. It is easier to develop strength in one area if you are already strong in a proximate product or service. These insights must be understood, as it has to be said that the historical experience of governments picking winners is poor, with politically influential losers – inefficient but nationally and socially significant industries

– tending to be supported over potential high-growth winners. Companies in the UK, such as British Leyland, were sheltered from tough changes and reforms rather than government money being used to transition their model – as it has been in the case of President Obama's bailout of Detroit. The new state financial institutions must be realistic and give themselves every chance of investing in success that the market cannot support. It is about going beyond the marginal risk that banks and investors are willing to undertake, but not into dead-loss territory. To achieve that requires local as well as sectoral and international knowledge. The difference between the type of institution that is needed for a more networked economy is that it will interface with local networks and strengthen them. LEPs are one such institution that could spawn others. It is not necessary continually to reinvent the wheel; it should, as Tim Harford has identified in *Adapt*, be evolved through learning, local knowledge and practice instead.

High-growth businesses need access to finance of all types with as much flexibility as possible. There is currently a tax preference for debt over equity, as debt interest is tax deductible in a way that returns on equity are not. The Mirrlees Review has recommended introducing a Belgian-style allowance for capital equity. This enables the tax deductibility of the 'normal' part of returns on equity – that is, the element comparable with a 'risk-free' interest rate. This would to some extent even out the bias in favour of debt in the tax system – debt can be more burdensome for a high-growth business. That should create new incentives for venture capital to invest further along the risk curve – where there are still excellent investment opportunities.

There is a case for further careful intervention. State-provided venture capital does not have a brilliant track record, but nor was it a complete disaster in the post-war decades. If there is to be a more networked, more adaptive state model, however, then there may be a role for state involvement in boosting venture capital. The state does not have the expertise to properly assess opportunity and risk. If institutions such as Local Economic Partnerships do become properly embedded there may be some risk weighting that the state can undertake to counter-balance part of the risk taken by venture capitalists. The purpose would be to change the risk profiles of investments at the margin. Such investments would be hybrid in form and co-exist with private capital. Of course, successful investments would mean a return that could then be invested further. The state in its adaptive form becomes one actor among many, knowing its limits and only acting where it has a real contribution to make.

Tim Breedon, former CEO of Legal & General, chaired a task force looking into small-business finance and made some important recommendations. The resulting report, *Boosting Finance Options for Business,* proposed a single delivery agency to increase awareness of the government's existing range of SME finance programmes. Such an agency would need to work proactively with regional and local institutions to ensure the right businesses had access. The Breedon Report also suggested the creation of new platforms for peer-to-peer lending, and encouragement for large businesses to fund smaller ones through their supply chain. Large businesses are sitting on hundreds of billions of pounds – they could effectively become banks themselves and help their suppliers to thrive. Finally, the task force suggested establishing an agency to aggregate small business loans to spread the risk. All of these are sensible institutional innovations.

An innovative form of finance could also be used to link scientific research with commercial exploitation: prizes. It is simply a matter of promising a gift of, say, £1 million to any firm that can make an advance in the application of a particular technology. Awards could be linked to the collaborative use of intellectual capital to be found in universities in a way that brings new ideas to market – especially if the innovation thickens existing supply chains or develops strategically important sectors. These would be one-off awards designed to meet a strategic need: tying innovation or research to economic opportunity.

In addition to this, there may be a requirement to revisit company law, to explicitly enshrine in law the notion that shareholder value is not simply about the highest returns in the short term; it is about supporting sustainable investment in the long term too. As Matthew Bishop and Michael Green point out in *The Road from Ruin,* the Financial Reporting Council's Stewardship Code has been amended to emphasise the responsibility of institutional investors to the firms in which they have a share. This requires more openness about voting in AGMs from the pension funds and others if their members are to be able to intervene. Shareholder or fund member activism may not be enough. A more specific long-term stewardship commitment needs to be incorporated into company law.

However, with average holding times down to just a few months, there is severe doubt that the public limited company (plc) can really be a vehicle for a greater long-term focus at all. It is to other company forms that we shall have to turn: employee-owned companies and co-operatives.

Co-operation as a Means to a Bigger Society

Social democracy had its origins in social movements surrounding industrial labour, religion and collective political action. Increasingly its method has been centralised state-transfers of wealth; its aim has been equality. There has been a deep, abiding question for the left that goes beyond the method: how can freedom be preserved in a complex society? As Lionel Jospin might put it, how can we enjoy the fruits of a market economy without succumbing to the perils of a market society? In other words, we have to return to the challenge laid down for us by Karl Polanyi in *The Great Transformation*: how do we embed the economy – most particularly labour relations, land and access to credit – in society and democracy? European social democracy was simply one answer to this question – in many ways a successful one, though one with limits.

It is not enough to graft a redistributive state on to a catastrophically unequal and unstable global market economy. That only tackles the symptoms and fails to confront the causes. Nor is it enough to endlessly pursue an unsustainable economic and business model, as free marketeers propose – the social and environmental consequences are too great. Instead, a dense core of co-operatively owned and run businesses, financial services, public services, energy providers and community institutions have real potential to shift the individual from a (heavily indebted) consumer, worker and recipient to a provider, owner and partner. They also provide a long-term, focused, value-creating, socially (and environmentally) embedded form of economy.

Co-operation re-embeds the market in ethical, social and democratic relations. It offers a way out of the morass that neither orthodox social democracy nor neo-liberalism are able to do. These ideas are not proposed as short cuts to win votes, but there is certainly nothing within them that would prevent a party of the left – Labour – from offering a coherent and mainstream argument for national leadership.

In the UK and Sweden, that anti-state view has been more subtle, with fraternity, society and civic action positioned as a way of empowering the individual and freeing them from the intrusive and burdensome state. Red Toryism, new fraternalism and public service reform in the UK, and citizen-established public services in Sweden – now copied in the Coalition's Free School model – constitute an intellectually imaginative challenge to the social democratic state. The left has to be careful not to fall into the trap that, because this civic conservatism does not provide all the answers, it provides none of them. In fact, there is much that can be mined, re-crafted and projected in pursuit of the left's desire for greater social justice.

People in the UK have gone from one extreme to another in their working lives. A generation or two ago, the prize was a job for life. We now have multiple employers and even occupations – perhaps this has an echo in our private lives too, which can be chaotic. The sociologist, Richard Sennett, studied the nature of co-operation in his book, *Together*. He argues that we have become used to 'dialectic' communication in the modern era – win or lose, in other words. A more co-operative world would have a greater mastery of 'dialogic' communication: where we find common ground. This common ground comes through participating in joint activity: work, civic engagement, play, hobbies, worship and politics. He looks back at the workshops and guilds of the past. They combined security with flexibility. As Sennett puts it, in a discussion about Robert Owen, the nineteenth-century factory owner and reformer: 'Owen's idea of the workshop is of an institution which combines long-term mutual benefit and loyalty with short-term flexibility and openness.'

The job for life is not coming back, but that does not mean that there aren't human and productive benefits from more long-term commitments. The built-environment engineering firm Arup is owned in a trust for the benefit of its employees. The chairman of the company, Phillip Dilley, sees this model as fundamental to his firm's success:

> If you ask around, most people would say that Arup's ownership model has served the firm well – consistent organic growth over several decades, strong financial independence, and the advantage of being able to take a long-term view that allows us to pursue innovation, creativity and technical excellence, without compromising our principles.

So long-term ownership can promote innovation and business performance. The wider evidence tends to back up these claims. A study by Joseph Lampel, Ajay Bhalla and Pushkar Jha of Cass Business School for the Employee Ownership Association, entitled *Model Growth*, finds a correlation between worker ownership and positive business outcomes. Employee-owned businesses create more jobs than comparable non-employee-owned businesses. They are just as profitable, more resilient and stable, have greater productivity increases and pay higher wages. Yet, the financial industry fails to give them sufficient financial support. The same applies to Her Majesty's Revenue and Customs regulations – the process of gaining approval for employee share plans can be burdensome. These are great businesses but they are not supported sufficiently well. It makes sense in this context to give tax relief to firms who transfer stock to employee-owned trusts.

An obvious place to start is by supporting the spread of employee ownership. It is worth re-emphasising that co-operatives are a high-growth sector. Co-operatives UK reports that the sector grew by 21 per cent in the three years from 2008 to 2010, in which the UK economy was largely in recession. A sound growth strategy channels capital towards its high-growth sectors, and that is likely to include many co-operatives.

State-owned financial institutions are obvious sources of capitalisation for local co-operatively owned financial providers, whether they are credit unions, local authority banks, or building societies. The government should investigate how to make this a reality. The Royal Bank of Scotland is majority owned by the government. It is surely worth exploring how it can better cater for the co-operative sector. As an alternative, an SME co-operative could be established with state support. It would provide normal banking services but would specialise in growing small co-operatives that have potential for growth but lack finance. It would not be limited to that sector but would be mandated to support it where business models are viable. Combined with a Community Reinvestment Act, whereby other banks are surcharged if they fail to lend to viable businesses in deprived communities, this could begin the process of re-capitalising local economies.

There are also some socially (as opposed to purely economically) worthy forms of support, and it is on an explicitly social basis that such backing should be extended. Take the DWP Growth Fund, which subsidises low-cost loans through credit unions for the least advantaged: in just over four years, credit unions who were members of the fund increased their lending by 81 per cent in London. This means that the borrowers' needs are met in a more sustainable way, and they are kept out of the clutches of loan sharks, interfacing more constructively with credit unions, which have the borrowers' interests at heart rather than a focus on corporate or individual profit.

Through the assets the state owns, it can also spur co-operative growth. Two of the most obvious areas are energy and housing. A new electricity generation infrastructure needs to be built. This could be owned by large multinational utility companies. Equally, it could be on a smaller scale. The village of Ashton Hayes in Cheshire is aiming to go carbon neutral by investing in renewable-energy-powered community facilities with a £400,000 grant it received from the previous government. With Danish government support, the island of Samsø went a step further and became carbon negative. The islanders benefit financially as co-owners of surplus energy generation. If local people were stakeholders in wind farms, would their objections to new wind turbines be lessened? It is worth investigating. A new energy infrastructure mixed with a co-operative ethos establishes the link between resources and energy that is rarely emphasised in purely retail markets.

Co-operative housing, common in Scandinavian countries (in fact, the co-operative-owned housing sector comprises 18 per cent of Swedish housing), creates collective wealth and encourages a civic spirit that can create safer communities. Again, this is an area that is controlled by the state, both locally and nationally: it finances social housing, determines planning consent and creates capital-raising opportunities for social housing. It can favour a co-operative appr-oach, which gives residents a wider commitment to their neighbour-hood or estate, as it is collectively owned and managed.

Finally, and crucially, the state controls the tax regime. In the way it taxes corporate entities it could provide further incentives for partnership-based, employee-owned companies. It already promotes employee share-ownership schemes. However, co-operatism provides not only for share ownership. It is about partnership – almost a quarter of workers do not feel engaged at work, according to research by Co-operatives UK. Employees should not only have a stake – impor-tant though that is – but also a say. This is the democratic republican ethos in action. There is not necessarily a direct translation from one thing to the other in practice. Entrepreneurs receive significant support in the taxation system; so should members of co-operatives. There is an economic and social case for doing so. For example, divi-dends received from employee-owned trusts should receive generous tax exemptions (once they are approved as genuine ownership vehi-cles rather than tax-avoidance schemes).

Beyond this, beyond welfare and the Work Programme, there is far too little out there to support workers in a flexible and uncertain economy. Trade unions have not been able to make the shift from an industrial to a service economy in the private sector. Welfare provi-sion is insufficient and inflexible. A modern version of a guild would be too closed and inflexible. Co-operative workers' associations which provide additional unemployment insurance, skills and job brokerage, and support in ensuring workers have a voice in the future of their firms, could fill the gap that has emerged. If these associations offered a genuine service there may be an argument for offering them some financial support.

Arguments for a co-operative economy and state can occasion-ally become utopian. However, with a little imagination, they can provide the left with one of the routes out of an ideological and political impasse. It shifts rhetoric in a softer, organic and human-centred direction and away from hard statism and redistribution. It acknowledges that the state alone is not the solution, but nor is it necessarily an impediment as a means to a bigger society, if its limits are acknowledged. In doing so, it becomes a pragmatic proposition, as the examples discussed above demonstrate.

Co-operation also provides one way of leaning away from the failed neo-liberal, shareholder-obsessed firm model. It questions the predominant models of both the state and the market. Both have failed in different ways, and yet we need an adaptive state matched with a dynamic networked economy. We just need the state to be more strategic, and the market to achieve a better balance of the long and short term. The journey may be slow, but with political determination it will advance over time.

The left cannot afford to be neutral about the way in which people interact in the market place and through the provision of collective services. Power matters, and the growth of co-operation will be a means to empower. Co-operatism is also a national economic success story – growing in a time of recession. As in 1945, the challenge is to re-embed the market in democracy and society. This process will happen through institution-building at the local level. It is fraternal and will widen capabilities. The right's approach will lead to a shrunken state and barely expanded society. Ironically, while the social democrats' reflexive faith in the state should be unpicked, smart state intervention could actually be its trump card. Co-operatism provides one vehicle through which we can secure freedom in a dizzyingly complex society. It is one of the key elements of a new and practical politics of freedom.

As Trader Joe's discovered, there is value in treating people with respect, empathy and decency. It aligns with the reality of human needs. Matched with the adaptive state, which enhances the ability of businesses to grow, this knowledge of who we are and how we are motivated is a rationale for and foundation of a new political economy. Businesses that fail to realise this, even if they remain profitable, will always be missing out on potential value. If they do not become employee-owned, they can still seek to understand why that model is so successful and adaptive. This approach is well suited to the left if it chooses to pursue it in a spirit of co-operation rather than antagonism. To make that argument effectively, the left will have to look at its own institutions – most particularly the Labour Party itself. And that is our final stop: to consider how Labour and the centre-left can make this powerful argument for change.

CHAPTER 8

The Left: Caught Between Populism and Leadership?

In George Bernard Shaw's satire on Christian social action and amoral capitalism, *Major Barbara*, the eponymous heroine leaves the Salvation Army in despair after it accepts a donation from a notoriously unscrupulous arms manufacturer. In her opinion, her good works in London's East End are sullied by this sordid deal. The donor, Andrew Undershaft, is well known to Barbara. He's her father.

This world of religion, labour, temperance, community good works and social action is the cauldron from which the Labour Party emerged. It was originally a community-oriented party. Never underestimate the moral foundations of Labour; they are in its very roots. That is one of the reasons why the New Labour years became so sour for many.

In a sense, there is a little of Major Barbara in us all. The Salvation Army exists to save people's souls, while the Labour Party exists to secure social justice. Labour is divided between romantics and pragmatists. It's not about new versus old Labour. It's not about trade unions versus the party, or socialists versus social democrats. There are romantics, who emphasise the ideal, the human, the ethical, the relational and the communitarian; while pragmatists emphasise power, policy, practicality and process. There is both an emotional amygdala and a rational pre-frontal cortex to Labour politics.

As a party, romance has dominated Labour's emotions; but pragmatism has normally driven the leadership. As William Morris once said to that arch-technocrat Sidney Webb, 'The world is going your way at present, Webb, but it's not the right way in the end.' That single quote sums up the elegiac history of Labour's romantic disposition. The historian H. M. Drucker put it in the following way in his seminal *Doctrine and Ethos in the Labour Party*:

The Labour Party has and needs a strong sense of its own past and of the past of the Labour movement which produced and sustains it. This sense of its past is so central to its ethos that it plays a crucial role in defining what the party is about to those in it. Labour's sense of her past is, of course, an expression of the past experience of the various parts of the British working class.

This was written in 1979 but doesn't feel too far from today's Labour Party – in the hearts of its members and activists. Given that its leaders tend to be driven more by pragmatism, it is fortunate for them that one aspect of this traditional ethos is loyalty to the leadership.

Clement Attlee, perhaps better than other leaders of the Labour Party, was able to combine romanticism and pragmatism. This made him the party's greatest leader and one of the great British prime ministers. He was involved in community action in the East End of London. He eschewed privilege in order to pursue social justice – like Major Barbara in many ways. He was originally a Conservative but responded to the poverty and injustice that he saw by becoming a member of the Independent Labour Party. For Attlee, like Obama decades later, community organising was a formative experience but ultimately an unsuitable vehicle to produce the outcomes he sought.

David Mendell, Obama's biographer, chronicled the President's loss of faith in community organising by his third year on the south side of Chicago. He had come to the conclusion that, without hard political power, his time was being wasted. After the untimely death of his political hero, Harold Washington, Obama 'felt shackled by the limited power of a small non-profit group to create expansive change', wrote Mendell. So it was with Attlee: if he thought local societies and charities could have eliminated misery and poverty he would have pursued that. Instead, he sought first to be the local representative, then chose the parliamentary route, and acquired state power, which he used to remove poverty on a grand scale.

There is a small book, published by the Left Book Club in 1937 and written by Attlee, called *The Labour Party in Perspective*. In it, there is a chapter entitled 'The social objective', which describes the Labour Party's core aims. What is the first aim? Freedom. Attlee wrote: 'The wealth of a society is in its variety, not its uniformity. Progress is not towards but away from the herd.' In this, Attlee echoes the sentiment of R. H. Tawney, who saw the Labour Party as an ally of the working class in securing an 'equality of regard' in which 'money and position count for less, and the quality of human personalities for more'. The key was to grant as much power as necessary to prevent oppression: the very essence of the democratic republican ethos.

Labour reveres its romantics: Aneurin (Nye) Bevan, Tony Benn and Michael Foot. Romanticism is Labour's secret code. But in truth, if it had been those three, or men like them, in charge in the 1930s, would there have even been a 1945 government? Attlee, an Abraham Lincoln for these shores, held together a cabinet of egotists and delivered emancipatory change. His inner flame was his drive, but he was ultimately a man of practical delivery. Romanticism is 'the why'; while pragmatism is 'the how'. Both inform 'the what'. The centre-left is at its best when both combine.

With Attlee, one man embodied both. The problems arise when we have shallow pragmatism with no soul, which becomes meaningless; or when we have romanticism, which delivers nothing without a pragmatic anchor. There is an economy to run, security to be protected, public services to be provided effectively, and, yes, elections to be won. Without this grounding, romanticism tends towards sentimentality. Another figure from the Attlee era, Michael Young, got this about right in his Labour Party pamphlet, *Small Man, Big World*:

> There is no salvation in going back to some misty past in which the small man lived in a small world, no salvation in putting multi-coloured maypoles in every city square or even substituting William Morris for the Morris car.

The pamphlet is a discussion paper for Labour Party members to consider how democracy, which requires smallness, can be combined with efficiency, which often requires bigness. It is about how to democratise the new institutions of the state as it was expanded in the Attlee years. This sums up the dilemmas faced by that generation. They had come through a great depression and a world war. The socialist ideals of William Morris had to remain a spirit rather than a programme of government.

Michael Young was contending with these issues and thinking about how Labour could once again become a participatory movement. Anthony Crosland took a very different approach. In his 1970 Fabian Society pamphlet *A Social Democratic Britain*, he rejects the republican approach (albeit caveated, it should be said):

> Participation, I suppose, should mean that the general public participates directly in decision making, and not just indirectly through its elected representatives ... I repeat what I have often said – the majority prefer to lead a full family life and cultivate their gardens. And a good thing too. For if we believe in socialism as a means of increasing personal freedom and the range of choice, we do not necessarily want a busy bustling society in which everyone is politically active.

Socialism was something done for you, not something you did for yourself. While, of course, he is right about the default desire to have a good private life, this still presents a profoundly pessimistic view. Part of the problem politics has in connecting is the very distance and paternalism that Crosland advocates. Democracy is about the central state and control of it rather than about the citizen. Should the left not have an offer for those who want greater control and to be active, other forces – pressure groups, campaign groups, civic groups, new parties and movements – will harness that energy. What is more, that energy has the potential to build local communities and economies. It can't be simply ignored or patronised.

Labour is just one aspect of the broader left, however. Its function is actually quite specific. Clause 1.2 of its rulebook states: '[The Labour Party's] purpose is to organise and maintain in Parliament and in the country a political Labour Party.' So there has always been a tension between the Labour Party as an organisation, with electoral and political objectives – albeit infused with values and ethos – and the left as a social understanding grounded in the history of working-class angst and powerlessness. This reflects the difference between labourism as an experience and Labour as a means to a political end. This battle consumed the party for the whole of the 1980s and for some of the time since then.

In *Together*, Richard Sennett contrasts the 'political left' and the 'social left'. In the case of the British Labour Party, the 'social left' was mainly seen in its early years – the Major Barbara years. The 'social left' exists as an aspect of civil society. The 'political left' is driven by objectives – such as winning seats in Parliament. The trade union movement sits somewhere between the 'social' and 'political' left (though Sennett tends to see it in the latter category). The Labour Party is the more 'political' left – though, again, the categories are not perfectly aligned. So there is an uneasy relationship between these different sensibilities of the left. As Sennett puts it: 'The social bonds forged from the ground up can be strong, but their political force is often weak and fragmented.'

In fact, Labour voted in 2011 to amend its Clause 1 to include an objective of making 'communities stronger through collective action and support'. While the community-organising experiment in Labour is sensible – especially in communities where Labour is strong electorally but has become aloof from the people it serves – the tension between 'social left' and 'political left' needs to be thought through seriously. There is a reason why both Obama and Attlee moved on from their community-organising years. This is not to disparage it as a pursuit in any way. It is simply important to draw a distinction.

There are now new forces of networked protest on the left, both beyond and overlapping with the Labour Party. Direct action groups such as UK Uncut and Occupy have emerged in response to the economic crisis. The Occupy protest in the City of London was part of a wider global anti-inequality movement. UK Uncut is a protest movement against real cuts in public spending and against Coalition public service reforms. The student protests were another aspect of this networked activism. Trade unions have sometimes touched, co-operated with and resourced these new forms of protest. Across Europe, these new groups, along with environmental concerns and the free data and privacy pirate parties, also challenge the traditional institutions of the left. The tension between populist protest and mainstream political strategy is becoming more acute and is in increasingly sharp focus.

What we are seeing on the left in Europe is, in some ways, a mirror image of what has been occurring on the right in the US in the form of the Tea Party. This emotional movement based around values is dragging the Republicans away from the place where they can both win support and govern effectively. There is a risk that the same could occur with the centre-left in terms of building viable governing coalitions. Labour's challenge in recent decades has been to bring its history and ethos together with its pragmatic necessity to reach beyond its own culture and instincts to appeal to a mass audience. The party is a means of providing long-term leadership whatever the short-term emotive pull. The pluralistic social change discussed earlier has echoes in a less coherent political culture. Labour was previously able to narrow the gap between sectional emotion and national leadership through appeals to solidarity.

That is no longer effective. A central argument of this book has been the need for new institutions to be built or adapted to a different society, economy and politics. That change imperative is just as applicable to the Labour Party itself. Labour's problem echoes that of the worst aspects of the state: too closed, too narrow and too inward-looking. It has a set of institutions that are failing and, as a consequence, the party is finding it more and more difficult to function effectively. At times, it seems completely dysfunctional. This chapter explores the environment in which it will have to make a convincing argument to take up national leadership once again. One hopes that the *Major Barbara* generation will be the Attlees and Obamas of the future.

In the meantime, the party risks falling between the stools of pragmatism and idealism rather than achieving a balance. The question is, from where it can draw sustainable energy for change – and what type of leadership will it take to get there?

The Tea Party Left?

'Republicans seized on a strategy of relentless opposition to Obama, which proved politically effective in 2010 but left the party as bereft of new ideas, a constructive agenda, or a coherent governing philosophy as before.' This is John Heilemann writing in *New York Magazine* about a Republican party torn apart by ideological conflict and political division during the 2012 primary season. He could have been writing about any number of European social democratic parties. It is almost as though the Atlantic Ocean is a political mirror: what afflicts the right in the US afflicts the left in Europe. Heilemann goes on to discuss the missed opportunity of defeat in 2008 to fundamentally reassess the Republicans' political direction. European social democrats, including the British Labour Party, now risk being caught between populism and pragmatism, in the way that the Republicans are caught between the Tea Party and the Republican establishment. One side lacks sanity and the other lacks authenticity.

The left's 'Tea Party' in Britain – supporting direct action and populism – has not gathered under a banner in the way that the rag-tag of anti-government, libertarian, socially conservative, ethnically anxious and low-to-moderate-income Americans, backed by wealthy individuals and Fox News, have gathered under the Tea Party banner in the US. In that sense, the left's version is as yet underdeveloped. It is driven by some of the same impulses as the US Tea Party – a rejection of business and political elites, and a search for a radical alternative – albeit with very different sociological roots.

Left-wing populism is not a movement only of the dispossessed white working class. It is a mix of aggressively defensive trade unionism, and young idealism in a climate of youth unemployment and networked protest. The impulses and origins are different from those of the Tea Party, but many of the methods are similar. They are worlds apart; yet in many ways they are the same. The Tea Party is driving the Republicans away from the support of 'independent' voters. The populist left is beckoning mainstream left parties away from a national towards a more sectional political conversation. It has neither been resisted completely nor has it been embraced emphatically by the political establishment. Populism neither wins the argument nor disappears, but it refuses to accept trade-offs. It's like an anti-social teenage son or daughter: you love your child, but you are worried how his or her behaviour might damage you in the eyes of your neighbours. This has been the case most particularly with the Occupy movement.

It is worth taking a look at the inspirational source for Occupy Wall Street, Occupy LSX and all the rest. A rally of somewhere in the region of 20,000–50,000 gathered in Madrid on 15 May 2011 to protest against the country's political leaders and their incompetent economic management. The date became the signature of the movement – 15-M. Hundreds of thousands participated in 15-M one way or another – in protest, through social media or through direct action. It felt like a genuine movement for change. 15-M was one of the inspirations for Occupy.

Yet, on 20 May 2011, in the middle of the initial wave of protests, there were local and regional elections in Spain. Mariano Rajoy's rightist People's Party surged to victory, beating the Spanish Socialists – PSOE – in every region. The protests continued. A general election followed six months later. PSOE lost 15 per cent of the vote and 59 seats. The party had been forced to embrace fiscal consolidation in the face of bond market pressure and it paid the price despite the fact that there was little alternative. Populism does not do economic reality very well. Mariano Rajoy and his People's Party rose by just under 5 per cent and secured a majority of seats. The leftist 'United Left' and the moderate social liberal party union, Progress and Democracy, saw their support increase by 3 per cent and 3.5 per cent, respectively. This has been a feature of the global financial crisis in Europe: a splintered left and solid right. Turnout fell by almost 5 per cent – the energy of the 15-M movement had not translated into democratic participation.

The Spanish people did want change. They wanted a fiscally conservative right-wing government. There is a noticeable pattern to all this. Networked action seems to be very good at getting people out on the streets – to protest, to riot or to occupy – but seems to be very bad at securing positive change within democratic societies. This is the difference between what we have seen in North Africa since 2010, and what we are now seeing in Spain, the US, the UK and elsewhere.

Occupy's slogan was that they were 'the 99 per cent'. Election results across the democratic world challenge that view. There is a presumptiveness to this that is not reflected in the social reality we saw in earlier chapters – on identity, social fragmentation, value shift and conflict. Quite simply, there isn't a 99 per cent. In terms of a politically motivated force for particular change there isn't even much more than 30 per cent of any particular outlook or commitment.

This assumption to be speaking on behalf of the majority is part of what is turning people off the modern left – both mainstream and populist. Rather than humbly seeking to win support, movements and parties of the left simply assume that they have the support, and all that is needed is clarity and organisational energy to convert it into votes, protest numbers or whatever is the objective. As elections approach, this supposed support starts to melt away: it happened to Scottish Labour in 2011 as they saw a poll lead spectacularly reversed as the elections approached, and to the Social Democrats in Sweden in 2010, again just a few weeks before the election. Traditional social democratic parties, in both government and in opposition, have failed to create the deep trust necessary to build strong coalitions behind them.

Martin Luther King, Jr once said, 'A riot is the language of the unheard.' His statement is often misunderstood and misquoted. Put in its rightful context, he said:

> Where do we go from here: chaos or community? Living with the daily ugliness of slum life, educational castration and economic exploitation, some ghetto dwellers now and then strike out in spasms of violence and self-defeating riots. A riot is at bottom the language of the unheard ... As long as people are ignored, as long as they are voiceless, as long as they are trampled by the feet of exploitation, there is the danger that they, like little children, will have their emotional outbursts which will break out in violence in the streets.

It is the chaos – whether civil disorder or violence – of new political movements that is so off-putting to potential allies. Ultimately, this is why populism has its limits. The civil rights movement in the US or the Indian independence movement were unique. They had moral purpose and force, mass support, clear objectives, inspirational and poetic leadership. Historically, their time had come. The Tea Party-esque left lacks all these elements. The mainstream left damages itself even by a flirtation with it. These movements have an emotional and energetic pull that traditional politics does not. However, they do not constitute an energy for real change. The question is how to change traditional party institutions so that they are more open and energetic in form without becoming part of the chaos. The answers are in opening up organisation and providing a humbler yet determined leadership.

Politics: Open or Closed?

Civic activism lies deep in our political history. Michael Braddick's *God's Fury, England's Fire* – a new history of the English Civil War – describes this energy in seventeenth-century England. The most surprising aspect is the degree of civic activism. As Braddick puts it:

> English people were encouraged by practice and precept to be active for the public good. Self-government was crucial to the order of local communities and also to the public image of those individuals responsible for it – officeholders cultivated the image of virtue necessary to carry out their duties to the public good.

At times, Braddick's account taps into the spirit of Tocqueville's *Democracy in America*, and one can certainly see the threads of republicanism and civic activism that reached from the Old World to the New, though with the latter losing the hierarchy and gaining social equality in the process (with the notable exception of slavery). Braddick estimates that one in ten English adult men held some sort of public office during their lifetime in the period immediately prior to the Civil War. We have more democracy now, but do we have a more active civic life today? It is difficult to conclude that we do. Parties of the left were a means of translating civic activism into political power after universal suffrage. Much of that civic energy has gone, and power has disappeared with it.

Britain's national democracy has ossified and seems ill-suited to the pluralistic society and culture the British have become. It is ill-adapted to the economic and institutional challenges the country faces. As fast-moving and changing networks proliferate, the country seems unable to respond effectively. The main political parties constitute one type of institutional brittleness. The two main parties secured a combined 65 per cent of the vote in 2010, on a 65 per cent turnout. In 1951, the parties' combined support was 97 per cent, on an 84 per cent turnout. There comes a point when two-party democracy no longer works – and Britain is now either at or very close to that moment. Neither of the two main parties shows any appreciation of the need to change the way democracy is pursued.

Labour itself is now more akin to a guild than a party – and a nepotistic one at that. Diversity is so important. Labour interprets diversity in purely gender or racial terms. Racial and gender diversity are important, but so is a party having access to a range of thought and perspective. The decline of the working class in Parliament has impoverished politics. Without diversity there is only groupthink and an absence of creativity. This is the fate of closed institutions in a more networked political environment. The similarity of experience and narrowness of outlook of the party's leading figures is a consequence of this. It is not about recruiting through new categories of positive discrimination. Rather, the challenge is truly to open up the party to a diverse set of experiences. For all its troubles, the Labour government of the late 1970s had figures from Tony Benn and Peter Shore on the left, through Barbara Castle, Harold Wilson, James Callaghan to Dennis Healey, David Owen and Shirley Williams. This was a real diversity of intellectual and political prowess.

Open and closed institutions cannot coexist for long: one has to win. In *The Master Switch*, Tim Wu's formidable history of information revolutions, the danger of closed institutions being imposed on open politics is clear. Choice, diversity, freedom and self-expression are limited. Wu recounts how, in 1920s America, radio was a cacophony. It was limited by frequency and amplitude in a way that the internet in the broadband age is not, but there are still striking similarities. Local enthusiasts (compare with bloggers, facebookers and tweeters) would broadcast their take on the world, local gossip and critical community information; it was a true people's medium. Alongside that, there were early radio networks – Radio Corporation of America and AT&T's National Broadcasting Service, which merged in 1926 to become what we know today as NBC. Thu, radio of the mid-1920s was a blend of national commercial might and enthusiastic amateurism – much like today's internet. Could the two sit together in perpetuity?

Of course not. The big guy won. It wasn't even a fair fight. The Federal Radio Commission stepped in and, in the interests of clearing the airwaves to enable a higher-quality service, all but killed amateur radio. The 'master switch' was flipped. In Nazi Germany, Goebbels centralised radio with the purpose of harnessing the power of the medium and bringing 'a nation together'. The US did it in the interests of corporate power and customer service. In each case, however, they chose a closed over an open form of information provision and carriage. One must out.

A similar switch has been flipped in political parties. Rather than institutions in which open conversation takes place and creativity is encouraged, they have tended to become ever more machine-like. In Labour's case, this occurred partly as a response to Militant entryism and partly to secure greater electability. But Militant entryism was a quarter of a century ago. Things have moved on, but the 'closed' mentality has remained. It is little wonder that so many younger political activists look elsewhere. This argument is not about left or right. It is about open or closed. The more open and free it is, the greater the outlet for energy and creativity.

One or two European social democratic parties are starting to understand this insight. The French Socialist Party selected their candidate for French president in a primary. Despite the €1 participation fee, somewhere in the region of three million people participated. Five million watched the TV debates. The successful candidate – François Hollande – was the most centrist. The party – members, unions and representatives – still controls the nominations, which is as it should be. But the final say is given to those who have signed a declaration of support of the party and paid their €1. Hollande went on to triumph in the 2012 presidential election.

Primaries locally have proved to be a useful democratic device. Unfortunately, it is the right that has experimented with them in the UK, and not Labour. In Totnes, over 16,000 people voted in a local primary and overwhelmingly supported a local GP, Dr Sarah Wollaston. In a tight Conservative–Liberal Democrat marginal, Wollaston secured a better-than-national-average swing and won. Since her election, she has been an independent voice on the Conservative backbenches, opposing aspects of the Coalition's health reforms from a position of professional expertise. Candidate expenditure could be capped at a low level, as could donations, so the cost objection would not apply. If there was to be an increase in the state funding of parties, it should be spent on advancing democracy through primaries rather than on parties' campaigning funds – voters may be persuaded to accept the former, but not the latter. This is real rather than tick-box diversity. It is open politics.

These local and national primaries bring a greater number of people into party decision-making and conversation. Local community action has also contributed to party re-engagement (and success) in a number of constituencies: Dulwich and West Norwood, Gedling, Oxford East, Birmingham Edgbaston, Dagenham, Bassetlaw and others. This is only the beginning of what needs to be done. Labour's shock defeats in the Scottish elections in 2011 and Bradford West in 2012 show just how it has an organisation fit for another era: one that relies on accumulating blocks of loyal support. Those days are vanishing, however. People now want a real politics – one of issues and engagement – rather than a politics of solely identifying your support and getting out your vote. George Galloway of the Respect party was able, in Bradford West, to engage young activists through social media and deploying an issues-based politics (though one often based around culture and religion). The activists' energy then spread through their neighbourhoods and among their groups of friends. Labour's vote disintegrated and Respect came from nowhere to win the seat. Labour has been warned about what could happen on a wider scale (from all sorts of angles, not simply Respect) – such is the loosening of political and social bonds in a context of networked politics.

Networks of interest and expertise, local and national, are exposed through social media as never before. The party that understands how to link into these and adapt its policy and understanding as a consequence will be one step ahead. This is no easy task: it requires measured risk-taking, a spirit of openness, a willingness to get things wrong, a genuine commitment to engage in open dialogue, and a desire to widen the discussion beyond the elites. It can no longer just be a case of meeting interest group leaders, professional bodies, trade unions or corporate interests. There must be a much wider engagement and conversation. None of the political parties is particularly good at this at present (though some individual politicians are): they still pursue an exclusive conversation. Recall of parliamentarians who are underperforming, and contested selections – through primaries – for sitting MPs are essential in a system where the majority of seats are not marginal.

New democratic institutions open up further possibilities. Elected mayors and police commissioners are two new institutions that could expand the democratic conversation. Almost all the councils with directly elected mayors have shown significant improvements in their local service standards. More direct forms of accountability are good for governance – and with a little imagination, it can be good for open political engagement too. That requires a different party mindset. The setbacks in the referendums for directly elected mayors in major English cities in 2012 should be seen in the context of an anti-politician mood. It is not the end of the line but rather the beginning of a deeper conversation.

As we have seen, Britain has a definitively pluralistic society but a majoritarian politics. Self-determination has to be a core component of this territorial pluralism – something that has been evident but asymmetric since devolution of power to Scotland, Wales, Northern Ireland and London. More open parties, more local democracy, more independent-minded politicians, greater creativity, real diversity, and the cracking open of the political closed shop are imperatives for an open society.

Our democracy is a relic that must be changed fundamentally: we may even be able to learn something from our early-seventeenth-century ancestors about the value of a more participatory civic life. The guild-type party that has emerged from the ideological divisions of the past and the marketing techniques of the mass-media age is ill-suited to the age of open networks and social media. The master switch should be flicked back. The open party will need a different type of leadership. Parties and politicians gain an entry to conversations by being invited. That is exactly what building trust is about

– finding a way into the conversation. It is, yet again, about meeting people on their terms rather than your own.

Leadership

The Nobel-Prize-winning psychologist Daniel Kahneman discussed the nature of leadership and its biases in his extremely important work, *Thinking, Fast and Slow*. The world of biases, error, heuristics (a psychological short cut), reflexive and reflective reasoning, and the relationship between emotion and rationality are inevitably of political interest. Indeed, scientists such as Drew Westen and George Lakoff as well as the political strategist and pollster Frank Luntz have explored how human beings' psychological conditioning has an impact on their political decision-making. These psychological insights are critical to leadership and politics. Leaders must beware of selectivity: fitting the world to their outlook. Kahneman would describe this as a 'confirmation bias': a selective use of evidence. It is a sure-fire way to become irrelevant in the eyes of the public.

The favourite psychologist of the left is the oft-quoted Professor George Lakoff – not least because he is on the liberal left himself, and vocally so. Of particular use has been Lakoff's exploration and research into 'framing': the way in which a proposition is articulated influences the degree to which it will be accepted or rejected. For Lakoff, conservatives in the US did not just win a political battle. They also won a psychological battle, with the prize being the American brain. Through reinforcement, repetition and the manipulation of trauma – 9/11, for example – they skewed neural bondings towards a conservative outlook and ideology: authority, discipline, moral order, individual responsibility and competition. Conservatives won the brain – at an emotive and subconscious level – and so they won America.

The politics of the left tends to be reflective and systemic. There has been something that is reflexive and direct about conservative politics. The left appreciates that we live in complex social, economic and environmental systems. Crime, welfare dependency, national debt, terrorism, despotism, educational failure and the cost of fuel can be articulated within the reflexive, authoritarian conservative frame. But they can also fit into an empathetic, compassionate and systemic leftist frame. This is not the contest of the rational versus the emotional. It is a contest of two different ways of thinking – instinctive and considered – as Kahneman makes clear. Which one wins out is dependent on which can win the battle of the mind – and therefore which of our moral frames, liberal (social democratic) or conservative, wins. So far, so good.

There is a problem, though. If the political conversation was subject to blanket 'priming' – people were to receive nothing but your messages – it might conceivably work. Inconveniently, however, we live in a liberal democracy where there is freedom of the press and of speech. So there is a cacophony of political messages flying around, mixed with even more eye-catching imagery and words of consumer culture. There is no point, in the style of the *Pravda* newspaper in the former Soviet Union, arguing that black is white when it self-evidently is not. There is no scope for 'big brother' political communication – you are in a market place of ideas, policies, personality and messaging. This means that you can get the framing right and win some arguments, but others will win the race to frame at other times. It becomes much more demanding of leaders as a result – it is about more than top-down communication; it's about engaged conversation.

As Ezra Klein has observed in his *Washington Post* blog: 'One of my rules in politics is that whichever side is resorting to framing devices is losing. In 2004, when Democrats became obsessed with George Lakoff, it's because they felt unpopular and were looking for a quick fix.' Quite. Our cognitive processes – a combination of the emotional, reflexive and reflective – are in a swirl that includes our values, identity, morality, needs, attitudes and experiences. As a leader, there is no way of controlling the democratic political conversation, and so it is not even worth trying. You would be marginalised very quickly. 'Framing' is just one political device. The simple fact is that the frame may already have been set by these other factors. If your 'frame' doesn't fit – if it conflicts with the emotional response of what is called the 'affect heuristic' – there is little you can do other than hope that events drift in your direction, so that the underlying instinct moves in your favour. These complications are all beyond the scope of modern political communication to resolve. Political leadership becomes something more humble and subtle, interspersed with moments of conviction and clarity. The 'conviction leader' is often just a presentational device crafted on to something rather more sophisticated.

The left has responded to opposition in four ways: hard realism, soft realism, 'change the conversation', and 'not for turning'. Over-optimsitic 'framers' are to be found in the 'change the conversation' camp. They tend to say that Labour should be talking about jobs and growth rather than deficit reduction or welfare reform, say. But what if that is not a complete response? Then you are ignored. Another 'framing' tactic is to focus on your opposition's weaknesses. What if people are more interested in what you would do? Framing can work in a contested and unsettled political environment. Once a political question is posed, however, leadership must answer it rather than try to change the terms of the debate. Get it wrong and framing means marginalisation – exactly the predicament in which parties of the left currently find themselves. 'Change the conversationalists' are one aspect of the populist left that is proving so ineffective.

This group are joined by the 'not for turning' set to their left and the 'soft realists' to their right. 'Not for turning' proponents are the fringe direct-action groups that have popped up since 2010. It is also becoming the outlook of many hard-line trade unionists. Essentially, it means denying that any fiscal consolidation or public sector cuts are necessary. 'Soft realists' argue that the political reality is that the left and Labour *do* have to say something about the deficit and cuts, but where it proposes fiscal consolidation it should be consistent with an orthodox social democratic argument. So this view supports a large increase in tax for the wealthy, looks to raise tens of billions of pounds through combating tax evasion, and suggests defence budgets and little else in terms of cuts. It is 'realist' in that it acknowledges that the deficit is an issue, but it is less 'realist' when it comes to identifying realistic political means of reducing it.

Hard realism is essentially the position outlined in the *In the Black Labour* paper and variants of it. This approach advocates a clarity of economic approach, specifying the cuts as clearly as possible, and being clear about priorities in a constrained fiscal environment. In other words, it is an approach where fiscal and economic limits and risks are taken into account. Economic and fiscal policy should be flexible and pragmatic, but follow a clear policy of deficit reduction, of which short-term stimulus should be a part, as discussed in Chapter 3. The economic argument comes first and politics second.

Unfortunately, the four positions listed are mutually exclusive. A leader cannot flit between each of them in turn without leaving an almighty political mess. A choice between them has to be made. 'Soft realists' and 'change the conversationalists' can join forces, as can the latter and the 'not for turning' set. But that is it. Hard realism may touch the edges of soft realism but cannot be combined with it – there is a mutual exclusivity.

In tough times, leadership is about hard realism. It should be compassionate. It should be visionary. But it cannot duck reality. This is the choice between populism and leadership. It is the right choice and takes leadership beyond the tactical and even beyond the horizon of the next election. It starts to build a real, immediate and sustainable argument for change.

Passion is not a substitute for strategy and creativity. Leadership brings emotion and strategy together. Hard realism should not be passionless. In fact, there is much in the social, economic and democratic case outlined in the earlier chapters of this book that is worth being passionate about: a vision of long-term political and economic change to rebalance power in favour of those without it. This is an argument for a fundamental yet achievable national change. It takes a long-term view. With honest leadership it can fire activists and attract support.

The populist alternative offers the fool's gold of temporary support that will evaporate as the argument intensifies and credibility hits home. It is not enough for the left to pretend that everyone thinks in the same way as it does. The left must have a case that appeals to a conservative morality as well as a liberal one; to those who want security as well as those who crave social mobility; to people motivated by their identity or personal interest as well as class; and to those committed to their locality as much as those who see themselves as part of a universal global ethic.

Daniel Kahneman cites Isaiah Berlin's parable of the 'hedgehog' and the 'fox' to look at what types of people have the best judgement. The hedgehog has one big idea that it falls back on time and again, whereas the fox adapts to each new situation as it finds it. He cites research by Philip Tetlock, which shows that hedgehogs tend to get more airtime because of the confidence of their singular argument. Hedgehogs have their appeal, but it is ultimately a sectional one – the converted love them. Foxes are more adapted to the modern pluralistic environment – they are more dextrous and engaging, and they respond more rapidly to shifts in the policy environment. The 'Tea Party left' is a hedgehog and will ultimately fail, as it will be unable to adapt to the complex and pluralistic environment in which it finds itself.

Perhaps the best leaders will be able to flit between 'hedgehog' and 'fox-like' behaviour. Whatever the situation that arises, there must be a clear objective. That is what leaders do: even though they can adapt to any situation, they have to return unfailingly to the strategic direction. They must make a case for long-term change. That requires significant interventions in the economy, democracy, engagement with culture, and an understanding of people's basic and varying needs. Kahneman reflects on his life's work and rejects the notion of human irrationality; rather, he sees biases and heuristics, and imperfections in our rational make-up. He puts it like this: 'Although humans are not irrational, they often need help to make more accurate judgements and better decisions, and in some cases policies and institutions can provide that help.' These institutions are designed to help and incentivise people to make better decisions in their own interests. If the left is to have a future it is through such institutions that initiate and secure long-lasting change: to people's working lives, their security, to the services they use, to the way they are able to interact to make a real difference, and to their ability to have their voices heard. The leadership that achieves this requires more than anger, oppositionalism, populism and false promise. It requires a strong blend of hope and realism.

The left will have an energetic future if it can craft a more practical social justice. That is to be found in the space between honesty, humility, passion and leadership. In other words, at precisely the point where the left must lead along a different but careful path – where it deserves to have a future.

CHAPTER 9

Conclusion: We've Been Travelling on Rocky Ground

The economic collapse was a moment of disruption; a critical juncture. It was a moment when all the elements of shift in our economy and society revealed themselves; we are now faced with a choice between change or resuming our previous course. Old habits die hard. No sooner had the initial shock dissipated than both the right and left defaulted back to their historical personality. The right sees neo-liberalism as a resolution to a crisis in neo-liberalism. The social democratic left sees ever greater transfers from the rich to the poor through the tax system in years of growth, and borrowing in years of no growth, as the solutions to all social ills. Neither course resets our national trajectory: one drives us towards another disaster, while the other is unsustainable but is easily reversed – as we have seen. In March 2012, the Chancellor of the Exchequer, George Osborne, announced his Budget for 2012/13. It was a return to neo-liberal type. At its core was a real reduction in pensioner tax allowances in order to fund a reduction in the 50p top rate of tax, based on some extremely premature calculations on the impact of the tax. At the same time, he decided to boost mortgage borrowing with state-subsidised 90 per cent mortgages. *Plus ça change*.

It is quite clear that the Tory vision for the nation means ever greater rewards for those at the top, driving down wages for the lower middle classes (the least well paid are protected to some extent by the minimum wage – one of the left's more permanent changes), stoking up house-price inflation again to get the political gain from the feel-good factor, and overlaying this with a rhetoric of national mission. We have seen it all before and we know how this story ends: in crisis. It is the same low-wage, low-saving, high-debt, volatile, rewards for a few, struggle for the many, feel-good then feel-bad economics that we've seen since the end of the 1970s.

The opportunity for the left, and the Labour Party in particular, is to make a different argument. Instead of playing retail politics – targeting this or that group of voters – and trying to cultivate antipathy towards the government, it could dislodge itself from its recent historical path dependency. This requires a disruptive moment; a break with orthodoxy. The reality is that the deficit will make any additional spending in this decade a tough ask. Demographic change – the ageing society – means that almost half of what the state spends in the next decade will go on the NHS, social care and pensions.

In this environment, the usual political response of tax, borrow and redistribute that has dominated the mainstream left since it turned its back on state socialism in the early 1980s no longer suffices. Politically, the left is desperate to return to business as usual. But it is an option with severe constraints. Other courses of action will need to be considered and pursued. Across Europe, social democratic parties have failed to understand why their message has become muted. The simple fact is that European societies have changed from the social democratic golden years after the desperate tragedy of the two world wars.

Where class solidarity once stood, there is now variety, fragments of 'bubbles' and 'tribes', affinities and antipathies, values and needs that are about people's experiences, hopes and expectations. Institutions such as church, labour, locality, workplace and the traditional family have weakened and taken new forms. Networks of ideas and interest, creativity and destruction, political mobilisation and cultural affinity have assumed new power and provide an even greater threat to our settled ways of life and relationships. The political as well as the economic answers become more challenging as a consequence.

At the same time, the economy has shifted from industry to services, and as a result the institutions that would have protected people in work have disintegrated. Now it is only laws and regulations that stand in the way of poverty pay and frequent misery. The nature of value in a service economy is different from that in an industrial economy. By failing to understand this shift, there is a huge under-investment in what really counts: people. Business and government alike treat such expenditure as a cost rather than as an investment. Rewards are skewed towards shareholder profit, senior executive remuneration and bonuses over wages. Real value is under-appreciated. Low wages for many create instability and volatility, and force households into unsustainable debt and low savings.

The institutional weakness that the UK has faced as a result of not keeping up with economic change makes this problem more acute; it now has an economy with one of the largest proportions of low pay in the Western world, despite the introduction of the minimum wage. Without a fundamental change to the structure and culture of Britain's economic life, this will persist.

At a national level, this means reconsidering the impact of the fiscal, economic and business decisions we make. Every line of government spending should be re-assessed for its economic impact. Much public current expenditure is actually investment. This applies most clearly to investment in people – skills, welfare to work and higher education. Where expenditure is investment it should be treated as such. Capital investment should be safeguarded and prioritised. A national infrastructure bank is an obvious intervention to make: it should invest in public, physical and even human capital. In government accounts, this borrowing should be assessed on a real risk basis so that there is no unnecessary choice between spending and investment. Government bonds themselves need to be separated between those earmarked for investment and those to cover gaps in current expenditure. This would create a clear separation between what in normal times is 'good' and 'bad' debt. Tight fiscal rules will nonetheless be necessary.

Alongside these reforms at a national level there needs to be a re-consideration of the nature of 'productivity' in a service economy. This applies to public as well as private services. We need to better understand value in an economy that is no longer predominantly industrial. Once this has been done, new institutions can be created to ensure that people are getting a decent wage for the actual contribution they make. Work associations would be a primary innovation: they would be local, sectoral and respond to the voice of business as well as workers. They would be backed up by a suite of measures of last resort, should business not respond positively. In time, they could also take responsibility for supplementary welfare and skills provision. This is not a new 'quangocracy'. It is a set of adaptive institutions that will encompass public, business and individual interests – a place for dialogue and for action. Where they become simple ciphers for conflict, they are no longer serving any purpose. Work associations will only work if all stakeholders see value in them, and there will be value only if they have freedom to adapt.

By linking remuneration to real value at low-wage levels, business benefits through having motivated employees, workers benefit from a more stable working life and employers will have a greater incentive to invest in them, and society as a whole benefits through the creation of a more stable, less volatile economy with higher investment. This will also mean that we can divert public expenditure from income transfers such as tax credits either to lower taxes for business and individuals or greater spending on public goods, or a mixture of the two. Where there are competitive imperfections that would lead to an inflationary response to dealing with low wages, robust competition authorities should intervene. They should be doing so in any case in sectors that are able to bamboozle customers through complex or anti-competitive pricing.

These interventions will begin to rebuild the middle class. They will protect people both as consumers and producers. They will drive investment in people – the real source of value in a creative and service economy. By sustaining demand while taking care not to stoke inflation, they will create a more solid base to the economy, both in the regions and nationally. New work associations will give greater support to workers – through advice and guidance as well as wage support – in an economy where the major trade unions have failed to transfer convincingly to the service economy other than in the public sector. These new institutions mean greater, more embedded freedom in the context of a market economy.

Without positive rather than convulsive economic change, the fraught elements of cultural identity anxiety will persist. Along with this come hostility and antagonism. Occasionally, violence will spill over. As a society, surely we cannot just sit back and allow this to happen? As a political movement, the left has a blind spot when it comes to cultural identity. This was demonstrated to Labour in the

Bradford West by-election, when George Galloway of the Respect Party – a party that mines the politics of cultural antagonism in inner-city Islamic communities while claiming to be a party of the socialist left – came from nowhere to win. Labour did not even see it coming, so divorced is it from the reality of the politics of cultural identity, which is morphing continuously.

The left has a problem with the politics of identity. It sees it as a throwback, or simply as a symptom of economic strife. There is no doubt that optimism about one's economic future is an antidote to cultural antagonism, but people's deeply held attachments and anxieties also need to be acknowledged and a response given. These concerns can no longer be left to the extremes of the populist and far right, who want to cultivate fear and hatred, or the racially divisive left. The challenges are faced within communities but also discussed increasingly in the mainstream media and political discourse – and often in an irresponsible way. The left cannot stand aside while others play with fire when it comes to cultural identity.

It is critical that the cultural dimension of politics is not ceded to the right or the extreme left. Labour has tended to treat cultural anxieties as class anxieties. Even then, they have not had many answers, so it has ultimately given half an answer to half of the question. Instead, acknowledge people's concerns and appreciate that immigration can cause stress on public services, and some localised downward pressure on the wages of the least well paid. Rapid social change also creates a sense of anxiety and insecurity. Neither local nor national government has been able to respond with any real degree of success. Where there is sudden demographic change there has to be an equally fast shift of public resources. A house-building programme needs to respond more quickly to needs. Groups that create a sense of common rather than sectional identity – as we saw with the TV programme *The Choir* – need support. Immigration policy should be transparent, clear and closely aligned to economic and social need (e.g. to support public services). The economically damaging and unworkable immigration cap should be dropped. New institutions to support skills development and reward work with decent wages will help to soothe a sense of insecurity.

All of these responses are aimed at confronting the practical, political and cultural challenges presented by social linked to economic change – of which immigration is just one aspect. There is also a national dialogue surrounding cultural issues. This focuses on religion, terrorism, custom, ethnicity, values and institutions. The left tends to shy away from cultural issues until it is too late – by which time the terms of the debate have been set by others. Time should be called on mainstream politicians and media voices who play politics with cultural anxiety. The feeding tube needs to be severed from the mainstream media and populist politics to the corrosive attitudes of those at the extreme edges of politics. Where there is an attempt to 'other' certain groups and generalise in a way that creates fear and suspicion, there cannot be any holding back. This debate cannot be left to those who peddle division.

A particularly forceful form of identity is, of course, the sense of attachment that people tend to feel towards their nation. Again, the comfortable path is to ignore the strength of these attachments. Unfortunately, that is not sensible, as the contours of allegiance are shifting. British people generally have dual nationhood. The Scottish have not only grown a greater sense of national distinctiveness and independence, but they have also managed to craft their sense of nationhood as a pluralistic identity both civically and politically. The English have begun a similar journey, though this is sometimes difficult to discern. To divert Englishness from a potentially antagonistic course will require real statecraft and imagination. This is not an easy task. As the Scots move towards greater autonomy, be it within or outside of the union, to ignore the emerging politicisation of English national identity would be a historic mistake. It is an error that the English left seems remarkably relaxed about. A new commitment to self-determination for the towns, cities, counties, regions and nations of these islands is critical.

In true democratic republican spirit, a new 'Self-Determination Bill' would be sensible. If an area demands certain powers and it has a democratic mandate for making the request, it should be given the power. Only if it fails to be competent should a national intervention be made. Where more powers are demanded locally they should be granted – as a legal right – in return for an agreement on a handful of outcomes for the population that demonstrates the area's ability to meet need. This mechanism could pave the way for an English Parliament. Such a parliament should be pluralistic in nature, to reflect the plural nation of the people it would represent.

National identities that are constructed as ethnically exclusive, especially within the reality of a pluralistic society, are headed for disaster. The full diversity of commitments, needs and sense of belonging must be accommodated within any notion of nationhood that is to resonate and succeed. The creeds of market and asocial individualism drive people apart and set them against one another. The British have been at their best when they have built institutions that empower rather than dominate; liberate rather than restrict; and enable people to develop the capability to pursue their own lives. A new moralism or a rigid egalitarianism fails to accommodate the variety of modern life. Human beings are naturally social and moral, but this does not mean that they flourish when 'virtue' or a numeric equality is legislated for from above, or projected downward with a particular community.

Instead, people need the support of institutions – democratic, civic, public service, and economic – that facilitate their freedom to live their lives in the way they choose without impinging on the freedom of others. These institutions would sit between the state and the market. Where silos of responsibility currently form a blockage to getting appropriate help to people at the right time, instead new networks of institutions would meet their needs. These would be more effective and more efficient.

A band of institutions that combine economic and social purpose will drive our political economy away from neo-liberalism and the limits of mainstream social democracy. At their core, these institutions would invest in the capabilities that give the individual real power within the marketplace. This requires a re-orientation of the state in a way that builds networks of local institutions that invest in innovation, skills and social capital. These institutions must be adaptive and less 'state-like'. They would work on the basis of stakeholder commitment rather than bureaucratic process, and would be local, entrepreneurial and embedded. Welfare, technical education, child care and economic development should be transmuted into a unified system of support to meet local employers' and individuals' needs. Child care and support for parents is desperately needed. So is a breaking down of the barriers between business, welfare systems and education. A new layer of technical education is critical to this, as is a closer relationship between business, further and higher education, and welfare to work systems. New directly elected mayors with greater powers would help to network these institutions as they use their authority and creativity for change.

Finance is critical to the nation's economic destiny. It has become divorced from Britain's real economic needs. High-growth SMEs have rich potential for innovation and job creation. A new co-operative bank set up by the businesses themselves would help to meet their needs – the government could help to finance this initially. Peer-to-peer platforms also have a place: networked finance is a huge opportunity. Large firms themselves can be encouraged to become lenders to firms in their supply chain – they have large cash balances, as noted in an earlier chapter. LEPs should be able to partner with venture capital to boost equity finance to firms with a high growth potential. These local initiatives should concentrate on thickening domestic supply chains. Capital and resources can come together with greater employee ownership to invest in the businesses of the future. All these changes require an enterprising outlook that builds institutions, but also ensures that they can adapt to the market and networks of knowledge, finance and business opportunity. In the long run, this will achieve more than any redistribution-led politics – which are fairly limited in any case in an age of austerity and demographic change. The limits of traditional social democracy have now been exposed.

Beneath all this, a better relationship is needed between individuals and business. New insights about what really motivates human beings have much to contribute by refreshing political and commercial thinking. Britain's commercial *and* social success depend on responding to a new, more balanced understanding of humanity. One essential way of reflecting this shift is to give employees a greater say in the workplace. Significant tax breaks should be given to companies who transfer stock to employee trusts. More co-operative housing or increased child care can help individuals to participate more fully in their neighbourhoods. Mutually owned electricity generation can turn consumers into producers and engage them in the process of energy production. Co-operation increases trust, commitment, value creation and stability. Instead of seeing co-operation as quaint or idealistic, we should instead understand that it appeals to some of our deepest human inclinations. We should have the courage to make it real and take it to a grander scale. Even if certain businesses cannot or do not move towards greater employee ownership, these insights about people are germane: stability, trust and support generate real long-term value for them as businesses, and for their workers and customers.

The agenda here is not structural reform for its own sake. It is centred on the insight that humans have a need to belong that is expressed in different ways. It is not stolid or lacking energy. It is founded on the understanding that creativity and security go together. When institutions work in an inclusive way they generate and safeguard these feelings of belonging. One of the causal factors behind the riots in 2011 was a lack of a sense of belonging and attachment. Pompous lectures about moral character do not address this need. The institutions that have a real impact will be cultivated rather than imposed. They will make sense to people, and will contribute to individuals' ability to reach their goals. There will be resistance, as there always is to something new. So be it, but nevertheless a compelling case should be made.

Essentially, a new political economy is needed in anxious times. Neither neo-liberalism nor orthodox social democracy suffices once account is taken of new insights into the way humans behave and interact. These insights should be augmented with an appreciation of a transmuting, diversifying society, and awareness about the role and balance of networks and institutions. Ideas based on this social understanding of humanity, such as the new fraternalism and policy responses that flow from it, are of great value. They are not enough, though. There needs to be a more disruptive politics if the cause of social justice is to be advanced.

A new political economy and statecraft reaches towards a set of ideas that suggest a different practical course. To get there will require a different type of leadership. The bitter irony is that, in a weak institutional context with networks acquiring greater and increasingly disruptive power, there is one set of institutions that are, if anything, becoming more insular and detached: the Labour Party and the labour movement more widely. Both the party and the movement were stitched into British life in the period after World War II. Those stitches have now been loosened and the seam has split. There is no single outlook or machine that can properly engage with the flows and complexities of modern life. The party and movement need to adopt a more network-like mentality. This means opening out policy, organisation and conversation, and becoming embedded more effectively in the reality of local life.

The disastrous electoral results for the left in Bradford West and in Scotland in 2011 shows that the Labour Party, despite a degree of organised campaigning nous, has lost the art of politics. As social change has meant a severe loosening of party ties, this can have dramatic consequences. It is rather like climate change. The underlying temperature is rising, but where and when extreme weather events will occur as a consequence is very difficult to predict. Labour's machine-mentality will leave it prone to ever more extreme political 'weather events'.

Through the pursuit of leadership, which fixes on long-term change rather than pursuing the short-term tactics of retail and micro politics, a stronger voice from the left can emerge. Short-term politics and the temptation to pitch to certain groups will be audible siren voices. They will drag Labour backwards. Real leadership would detach the movement from its most recent unhappy past. It would re-build and argue for a different long-term future for Britain – a new national purpose.

There is a hard realism to this, but is the left about real change? Or is it just about the toing and froing of the electoral game? Does it seek simply to milk the outrage at the actions of the right without it ultimately leading very far? The answer to these questions will determine whether the left is to fulfil its hope of securing greater social justice. There can be election victories without visionary, practical leadership. It is, in the UK at least, a national market with only two products. Sometimes the right's product will be very faulty, and so people will be tempted by the left's product, even if it is unsatisfactory. But surely the politics of the left need to be something more than the selling of a tatty product in a rigged market?

From the creation of the NHS to the protection of and access to national parks, the rapid expansion of higher education, the creation of the national minimum wage and Sure Start to support families with young children, Labour's fingerprints are on some of our most vital and cherished institutions. The left's enduring achievements have been through the institutions it has planted and cultivated, and which incoming centre-right governments have found difficult to uproot. Conversely, the left has been at its weakest when it has failed to win the argument, and hard-won reforms have failed to flower, because they were planted in poor soil. Now, in an age of austerity, when post-war social democracy has reached its social and economic limits, it is time to return to core principles. The task is to plant an orchard that will bear fruit over many generations. It may take some time to bear fruit: nothing worth doing can be achieved in one lifetime, as Niebuhr reminds us.

At a time of cultural and economic strife, we have to accept our differences but remember that there is far more that unites than divides us. It is worth working together to create a different national story: one of re-birth. Now is the moment that the left can change – indeed, it *must* change. There is scope for real national rejuvenation. In Seamus Heaney's words, 'hope and history can rhyme'. By combining respect for the past, honesty about failure, and a frank look at the present, a different future can be imagined. The alternative is to be a victim of the past and dishonest about what is possible. Avoid this pitfall and greater social justice is within reach; each hand will hold a pen with which to write a new dramatic story of life and freedom. It is here that the left will have a better future: as will the nation.

Bibliography

Acemoglu, D. and Robinson, J. A., *Why Nations Fail: The Origins of Power, Prosperity and Poverty* (Profile Books, 2012).

Alinsky, S., *Rules for Radicals: A Pragmatic Primer for Realistic Radicals* (Vintage, 1989 edn).

Anderson, B., *Imagined Communities: Reflections on the Origins and Spread of Nationalism* (Verso, 2006 edn).

Attlee, C. R., *The Labour Party in Perspective* (Victor Gollancz, 1937).

Baumol, W. J. and Bowen, W. G., *Performing Arts: The Economic Dilemma – a Study of Problems Common to Theater, Opera, Music and Dance* (MIT Press, 1968).

Bishop, M. and Green, M., *The Road from Ruin: A New Capitalism for a Big Society* (A & C Black, 2011).

Blanden, Jo and Machin, Stephen, *Recent Changes in Inter-generational Mobility in Britain*. Centre for Economic Performance (London School of Economics, 2007).

Blond, P., *Red Tory: How the Left and Right Have Broken Britain and How We Can Fix It* (Faber and Faber, 2010).

Bonnett, A., *Left in the Past: Radicalism and the Politics of Nostalgia* (Continuum, 2010).

Braddick, M., *God's Fury, England's Fire: A New History of the English Civil Wars* (Penguin, 2009).

Breedon, T., *Boosting Finance Options for Business (The Breedon Report)* (Department for Business, Innovation and Skills, 2012).

Canovan, M., *Nationhood and Political Theory* (Edward Elgar, 1998).

Clift, B., 'The Jospin Way', *The Political Quarterly*, 72/2 (2001).

Cole, G. D. H., *Guild Socialism: A Plan for Economic Democracy* (Red and Black Publishers, 2009 edn).

Collins, M., *Hate: My Life in the British Far Right* (Biteback Publishing, 2011).

Cooke, G., *Still Partying Like It's 1995* (Institute of Public Policy Research, 2011).

Cooke, G., Lent, A., Painter, A. and Sen, H., *In the Black Labour: Why Fiscal Conservatism and Social Justice Go Hand-in-hand* (Policy Network, 2011).

Cowen, T., *The Great Stagnation: How America Ate All the Low-hanging Fruit of History, Got Sick and Will (Eventually) Feel Better* (Dutton Books, 2011).

Coyle, D., *The Economics of Enough: How to Run the Economy as if the Future Mattered* (Princeton University Press, 2011).

Crosland, A., *A Social Democratic Britain* (Fabian Society, 1970).

——, *The Future of Socialism* (Robinson Publishing, 2006 edn).

Curtice, J., *Thermostat or Weather Vane? Public Reactions to Spending and Redistribution Under New Labour*, British Social Attitudes, 26th Report, 2010.

DeLong, J. B. and Summers, L. H., *Fiscal Policy in a Depressed Economy* (National Bureau of Economic Research (NBER), 2012).

Denning, S., 'Does it really matter that Amazon can't manufacture a Kindle in the US?', *Forbes Magazine*, 20 August 2011.

Drucker, H. M., *Doctrine and Ethos in the Labour Party* (George Allen & Unwin, 1979).

Emmerson, C., Johnson P. and Miller, H., *The IFS Green Budget: February 2012* (The Institute for Fiscal Studies (IFS), 2012).

Fisher, M. L., Krisnan, J. and Netessine, S., *Retail Store Execution: An Empirical Study* (The Wharton School, University of Pennsylvania, 2006).

Florida, R., *The Great Reset* (Collins Business, 2010).

Frum, D., 'Is the white working class coming apart?', *Newsweek*, 6 February 2012. Available at: www.thedailybeast.com.

Gilroy, P., *There Ain't No Black in the Union Jack: The Cultural Politics of Race and Nation* (Routledge, 2002 edn).

Glaeser, E., *Triumph of the City: How Our Greatest Invention Makes Us Richer, Smarter, Greener, Healthier and Happier* (Macmillan, 2011).

Glasman, M., Rutherford, J., Stears, M. and White, S., *The Labour Tradition and the Politics of Paradox: The Oxford–London Seminars 2010–2011* (Lawrence & Wishart, 2011).

Goodwin, M. J., *New British Fascism: Rise of the British National Party* (Routledge, 2011).

Graham, J., Haidt, J. and Nosek, B. A., 'Liberals and Conservatives rely on different sets of moral foundations', *Journal of Personality and Social Psychology* 96/5 (2009).

Haidt, J., *The Righteous Mind: Why Good People Are Divided by Politics and Religion* (Allen Lane, 2012).

Haldane, A., *Rethinking the Financial Network*, speech delivered to the Financial Student Association, Amsterdam, April 2009.

Hall, P. A. and Gingerich, D. W., 'Varieties of capitalism and institutional complementarities in the political economy: an empirical analysis', *British Journal of Political Science*, July (2009).

Haque, U., *The New Capitalist Manifesto: Building a Disruptively Better Business* (Harvard Business Review Press, 2011).

———, *Betterness: Economics for Humans* (Harvard Business Review Press, 2011).

Harford, T., *Adapt: Why Success Always Starts with Failure* (Abacus, 2011).

Hayman, J., *British Voices* (Matador, 2012).

Heffer, S., *Nor Shall My Sword: Reinvention of England* (Phoenix, 2000).

Heilemann, J., 'The lost party', *New York Magazine*, 25 February 2012.

Herman, A., *The Scottish Enlightenment: The Scots' Invention of the Modern World* (Fourth Estate, 2003).

Hidalgo, C. *et al.*, 'The product space conditions the development of nations', *Science*, 27 July 2007.

High Pay Commission, The, *Cheques with Balances: Why Tackling High Pay Is in the Nation's Interest* (2011).

Hobsbawm, E., 'The forward march of Labour halted', *Marxism Today*, September (1978).

———, *Nations and Nationalism Since 1780: Programme, Myth, Reality* (Cambridge University Press, 1992).

IMF (International Monetary Fund), *World Economic Outlook* (IMF, October 2012).

Independent Commission on Banking, *Final Report* (2011).

Inglehart, R. and Norris, P., 'The Four Horsemen of the Apocalypse: Understanding human security', Kennedy School research working paper (Harvard University, 2011).

Inglehart, R. and Welzel, C., *Modernization, Cultural Change, and Democracy: The Human Development Sequence* (Cambridge University Press, 2005).

Jones, O., *Chavs: The Demonization of the Working-Class* (Verso, 2012 edn).

Judt, T., *Ill Fares the Land: A Treatise on our Present Discontents* (Penguin, 2011).

Kahneman, D., *Thinking, Fast and Slow* (Allen Lane, 2011).

Kay, J., *Obliquity: Why Our Goals Are Better Achieved Indirectly* (Profile Books, 2010).

Kruger, D., 'The right dialectic', *Prospect Magazine*, September (2006).

Krugman, P., *Keynes and the Moderns*, talk given at the Cambridge conference commemorating the 75th anniversary of the publication of *The General Theory of Employment, Interest, and Money*, 2011.

Kumar, K., *The Making of English National Identity* (Cambridge University Press, 2003).

Lakoff, G., *The Political Mind* (Viking, 2008).

Lampel, J., Bhalla, A. and Pushkar, J., *Model Growth: Do Employee-Owned Businesses Deliver Sustainable Performance?* EOA Report (CASS Business School, London 2010).

Lodge, G. and Wyn Jones, R., *The Dog That Finally Barked: England as an Emerging Political Community* (Institute for Public Policy Research, 2012).

Lothian, T. and Unger, R. M., 'Crisis, slump, superstition and recovery: thinking and acting beyond vulgar Keynesianism', Columbia Law and Economics Working Paper No. 394, 1 March 2011.

Lowles, N. and Painter, A., The *Fear and Hope* report: The New Politics of Identity (Searchlight Educational Trust, 2011).

Luntz, F., *Words That Work: It's Not What You Say, It's What People Hear* (Hyperion, 2008).

Madrick, J., *The Case for Big Government* (Princeton University Press, 2009).

Marquand, D., *Britain Since 1918: The Strange Career of British Democracy* (Phoenix, 2009).

Mazzucato, Mariana, *et al.*, *Financing Innovation and Growth: Reforming a Dysfunctional System* (European Commission, Finance, Innovation and Growth, 2012).

Milbank, J., *The Politics of Paradox*. Talk given at Telos conference, 2009.

Minsky, H. P., 'The financial instability hypothesis', The Jerome Levy Economics Institute Working Paper No. 74, May 1992.

Mintzberg, H., *How Productivity Killed American Enterprise*. Available at: www.mintzberg.org, 2007.

Mirrlees Review, *Tax by Design* (Institute for Fiscal Studies, 2011).

Mulheirn, I., *Osborne's Choice: Combining Credibility and Growth* (Social Market Foundation, 2012).

Murray, C., *Coming Apart: The State of White America, 1960–2010* (Crown Forum, 2012).

———, 'The new American divide', *Wall Street Journal*, 21 January 2012.

Natcen, *British Social Attitudes, 29th Report* (Natcen, 2012).

Nesta, *The Vital 6 Per Cent: How High-growth Innovative Businesses Generate Prosperity and Jobs* (Nesta, 2009).

Niebuhr, R., *The Irony of American History* (University of Chicago Press, 2008 edn).

Norman, J., *The Big Society: The Anatomy of the New Politics* (Buckingham Press, 2010).

Oakeshott, M., *Rationalism in Politics and Other Essays* (Liberty Fund Inc., 1991 edn).

OECD (Organisation for Economic Co-operation and Development), *A Family Affair: Inter-generational Mobility Across OECD Countries* (OECD, 2010).

———, *Towards an OECD Skills Strategy* (OECD, 2011).

Olson, M. Jr., 'Big bills left on the sidewalk: Why some nations are rich, others poor', *Journal of Economic Perspectives* 10/2 (Spring 1996).

Ormerod, P., *Positive Linking: How Networks Can Revolutionize the World* (Faber and Faber, 2012).

Orwell, G., *Orwell's England: The Road to Wigan Pier in the Context of Essays, Reviews, Letters and Poems* (Penguin Classics, 2001).

Ostrom, E., *Governing the Commons: The Evolution of Institutions for Collective Action* (Cambridge University Press, 1990).

Painter, A. and Wardle, B. (eds), *Viral Politics: Communicating in the New Media* (Politico's Publishing Ltd, 2001).

Pettit, P., *Republicanism: A Theory of Freedom and Government* (Oxford University Press, 1999).

Plunkett, J., *The Missing Million: The Potential for Female Employment to Raise Living Standards in Low-to-Middle Income Britain* (Resolution Foundation, 2011).

——, *Growth Without Gain? The Faltering Living Standards of People on Low-to-Middle Incomes* (Resolution Foundation, 2011).

Polanyi, K., *The Great Transformation: The Political and Economic Origins of Our Time* (Beacon Press, 2002 edn).

Porter, M. E. and Kramer, M. R., 'Creating shared value', *Harvard Business Review*, January 2011.

Putnam, R. D., *Bowling Alone: The Collapse and Revival of American Community* (Simon & Schuster, 2001).

——, 'E pluribus unum: diversity and community in the twenty-first century. The 2006 Johan Skytte Prize lecture', *Scandinavian Political Studies* 30/2 (2007).

Rajan, R., *Fault Lines: How Hidden Fractures Still Threaten the World Economy* (Princeton University Press, 2010).

Reinhart, C. M. and Rogoff, K., *The Time Is Different: Eight Centuries of Financial Folly* (Princeton University Press, 2009).

Rifkin, J., *The Age of Access: The New Culture of Hypercapitalism, Where All of Life Is a Paid-for Experience* (Jeremy P. Tarcher, 2000).

Rose, C., *What Makes People Tick: The Three Hidden Worlds of Settlers, Prospectors and Pioneers* (Matador, 2011).

Ruhs, M., *The Labour Market Effects of Immigration* (Oxford Migration Observatory, Oxford University, 2012).

Sachs, J., *The Price of Civilization: Economics and Ethics After the Fall* (Bodley Head, 2011).

Saggar, S. and Sommerville, W., *Building a British Model of Integration in an Era of Immigration: Policy Lessons for Government* (Migration Policy Institute, 2012).

Scruton, R., *England: An Elegy* (Chatto & Windus, 2000).

Sen, A., *Identity and Violence: The Illusion of Destiny* (Penguin, 2007).

——, *The Idea of Justice* (Penguin, 2010).

Sennett, R., *Together: The Rituals, Pleasures and Politics of Co-operation* (Allen Lane, 2012).

Shiller, R., *The Sub-prime Solution: How Today's Global Financial Crisis Happened and What To Do About It* (Princeton University Press, 2008).

Shirky, C., *Cognitive Surplus: Creativity and Generosity in a Connected Age* (Allen Lane, 2010).

Skidelsky, R., *Keynes: The Return of the Master* (Penguin, 2010).

Smith, A. and Bozier, L. (eds), *Labour's Business: Why Enterprise Must Be at the Heart of Labour Politics in the Twenty-first Century* (Labour's Business, 2011).

Storm, S. and Naastepad, C. W. M., 'The productivity and investment effects of wage-led growth', *International Journal of Labour Research* 2/2 (2011).

Strong, R., *Visions of England* (Bodley Head, 2011).

Sullivan, A., 'How Obama's long game will outsmart his critics', *Newsweek*, 16 January 2012.

Tawney, R. H., *Equality* (Harper Collins, 1965 edn).

———, *The Acquisitive Society* (2010 edn). Available at: www.gutenberg.net.

Thompson, E. P., *The Making of the English Working Class* (Penguin, 2002 edn).

Tocqueville, A. de, *Democracy in America: And Two Essays on America* (Penguin Classics, 2003 edn).

Ton, Zeynep, 'Why good jobs are good for retailers', *Harvard Business Review*, January–February (2012).

Van Reenen, J., *Industrial Policy Works for Small Firms*, February 2012. Available at: www.voxeu.org.

Verseck, K., 'A revised portrait of Hungary's right-wing extremists', *Der Spiegel* (online), 3 February 2012.

Waal, F. de, *The Age of Empathy: Nature's Lessons for a Kinder Society* (Souvenir Press, 2010).

Weber, M., *Economy and Society* (University of California Press, 1992 edn).

Westen, D., *The Political Brain: The Role of Emotion in Deciding the Fate of the Nation* (PublicAffairs Books, 2007).

White, S. and Leighton, D. (eds), *Building a Citizen Society: The Emerging Politics of Republican Democracy* (Lawrence & Wishart, 2008).

Wilkinson, R. and Pickett, K., *The Spirit Level: Why Greater Equality Makes Societies Stronger* (Bloomsbury Publishing, 2009).

Wilson, D. S. and Wilson, E. O., 'Evolution "for the Good of the Group"', *American Scientist* 96/5 (2008).

Wu, T., *The Master Switch: The Rise and Fall of Information Empires* (Knopf Publishing, 2010).

Young, M., *Small Man, Big World: A Discussion of Socialist Democracy* (The Labour Party, 1949).

Zick, A., Küpper, B. and Hövermann, A., *Intolerance, Prejudice and Discrimination: A European Report* (Friedrich Ebert Stiftung, 2011).

Index